STUDIES ON WEALTH IN THI

BULLETIN OF THE INSTITUTE OF CLASSICAL STUDIES SUPPLEMENT 133

DIRECTOR & EDITOR: GREG WOOLF

PUBLICATIONS & WEB MANAGER: ELIZABETH POTTER

STUDIES ON WEALTH IN THE ANCIENT WORLD

EDITED BY
ERRIETTA M. A. BISSA
AND
FEDERICO SANTANGELO

INSTITUTE OF CLASSICAL STUDIES

SCHOOL OF ADVANCED STUDY
UNIVERSITY OF LONDON

2016

ISBN 978-1-905670-62-8

Designed and typeset at the Institute of Classical Studies, University of London, by Sarah Mayhew Hinder.

Printed byLightning Source UK Ltd

TABLE OF CONTENTS

Acknowledgements   vii

Errietta M. A. Bissa
& Federico Santangelo   Introduction   1

Benjamin Keim   Non-material but not Immaterial: Demosthenes'
                             Reassessment of the Wealth of Athens   7

John Davies   Aristonikos and the Fishmongers   21

Errietta M. A. Bissa   Wealth and Monopoly in the *polis*   33

Jean Andreau   *Agellus* entre la pauvreté et la richesse   43

Filippo Carlà   Middle Classes in Late Antiquity: an Economic
                             Perspective   53

Leonardo Gregoratti   Legendary and Real Wealth in the Arsacid
                             Kingdom   83

Jeremy Paterson   'The Eye of the Needle'. The Morality of Wealth in
                             the Ancient World   93

Index locorum   105

Index   115

ACKNOWLEDGEMENTS

Most of the papers in this volume originate from a colloquium that was held at Gregynog Hall, Tregynon, Powys, Wales, on 21 and 22 May 2009.

We are grateful to the then Department of Classics of the University of Wales, Lampeter (now School of Classics, University of Wales: Trinity St David), the Universities in Wales Institute for Classics and Ancient History (UWICAH), and the University of Wales Gregynog Staff Colloquia Fund for their generous financial support to the conference.

We should also like to thank the contributors to this volume for their commitment to the project, and the colleagues who have generously offered counsel and guidance at various stages in the preparation of this book: Makis Aperghis, Clara Berrendonner, Henning Börm, Mirko Canevaro, Angelo Giavatto, Cam Grey, Stephen Lambert, Giulio Marchisio, Guido Schepens, and Catherine Steel. John Dillon and Melissa Beattie offered invaluable support in the final stages of the production of the manuscript. We are especially grateful to John North and the *BICS Supplements* referees for giving this project favourable consideration and for offering invaluable advice on matters large and small, and to Greg Woolf and Elizabeth Potter for seeing the book through production.

ACKNOWLEDGMENTS

INTRODUCTION

ERRIETTA M. A. BISSA & FEDERICO SANTANGELO

Wealth has seen better days. Any discussion of the topic – whether of its ancient or modern incarnations – in the mid-2010s can hardly be undertaken without a pressing awareness of the problems that it presents us with here and now. There is a wide, and broadly justified, perception that the economic turmoil through which the West has been struggling in the last few years was chiefly caused by profound distortions and deficiencies in the circuit of wealth creation and management. Thomas Piketty's major study on the distribution of wealth in the twentieth and early twenty-first centuries is the impressive (and controversial) outcome of more than a decade of research on large datasets for a number of countries, chiefly tax records.[1] That a work of such complexity and ambition has readily become a global bestseller is as much as the result of its ability to offer strong explanatory models as of the wide urge to reflect on the foundations of the inequality of wealth distribution, on the consequences that this has for the very survival of the capitalistic system, and on the fundamental relationship between wealth and power. *Habent sua fata libelli.*

The impact on the 'real economy' of a crisis that had its roots in the financial markets and the subsequent government strategies that have concentrated on securing the stability of financial institutions have suddenly presented Western public opinions with a bleak picture of the limits of wealth creation and of the major shortcomings of wealth distribution. At the same time, a number of societies at different ends of the planet are facing the challenges that intensive wealth creation and unequal wealth distribution present. Yet, as the work of Jeffrey Sachs has powerfully argued, wealth remains an unequalled opportunity: the study of the strategies that may lead to the end of global poverty must be accompanied by an attempt to chart the avenues along which global sustainable development can be pursued and achieved.[2] These two pursuits are very much part of the same story: in this model, it is wealth creation, the free development of entrepreneurial initiative, which has to be supported by sustained political and economic investments, and by a sensible blend of enlightened self-interest and a deeper human need, which can eventually lead to driving poverty 'out of history'. It is unsurprising to see that Adam Smith is repeatedly quoted in Sachs' work, while Piketty is much more interested in engaging with the oeuvre of David Ricardo.

Ostensibly, the studies collected in this volume look in very different directions: they are all devoted to aspects of wealth in Greek and Roman antiquity. Some facets of this pervasive topic have received major treatments in recent years: most notably, Peter Brown's

---

[1] T. Piketty, *Le capital au XXI siècle* (Paris 2013); English trans., *Capital in the Twenty-First Century* (Cambridge, Mass. and London 2014).

[2] J. D. Sachs, *The end of poverty. How we can make it happen in our lifetime* (London 2005); *id.*, *Common wealth. Economics for a crowded planet* (London 2008).

studies of wealth and the rise of Christianity in Late Antiquity and Brent Shaw's discussion of agriculture and wealth in Roman North Africa.[3] A comprehensive treatment, however, remains a desideratum; poverty has comparatively received better attention, at least at the Roman end of the spectrum.[4] This is, in a way, not surprising in this day and age. The papers in this collection do not set out to provide a full overview of a subject that is probably inexhaustible, nor of all the factors that make it a worthy object of investigation. However, they hope to offer some distinctive contributions to the study of three issues: the sources and maintenance of wealth; the implications for differently organised societies of the division between wealthy and impoverished individuals and groups; and the moral implications of that division.

Taken individually, the papers included in this volume set out to make original contributions to the understanding of specific aspects of wealth in the Greek and Roman worlds, whether individual, collective, or state-owned. Some address general methodological issues and engage with developments of the modern scholarly debate in sociology and economic theory; in others the focus is on specific historical problems and clusters of evidence, but may still yield lessons of more general import. They cover a diverse range of topics and evidence, and span a broad chronological range. In different ways, they all revolve around the relationship between wealth and power, and the tensions and contradictions that it entails. Some deal with the mechanics of wealth creation and distribution in specific historical contexts; others tend to focus on how wealth, or indeed some forms of wealth, were conceptualized and represented. Crossovers between these two areas of investigation are inevitable, and indeed desirable. Readers will be exposed to a variety of different methodological approaches. There will be some engagement with methodological and theoretical issues, as well as instances of close linguistic and literary analysis, and discussions of aspects of material culture. Links between individual papers may be identified, of course, as well as instructive differences in the approaches used and the evidence examined. We are leaving them for the readers to pursue and develop. The volume is arranged chronologically, focussing firstly on the Greek world, before moving on to Roman and late antique themes. What follows is merely an overview of the main themes that the contributions to this volume explore.

Wealth, just like poverty, must be approached through the filters and hurdles of definitions. These are as acute in the modern world as they are in the study of ancient societies. Even the most perceptive analysts will sometimes fall prey to sweeping generalizations. Sachs gives an assessment of pre-industrial societies that any informed student of the ancient world will reject outright: 'two hundred years ago ... [j]ust about everybody was poor, with the exception of a very small minority of rulers and large land-owners'.[5] Several papers in this volume go some way to disproving that facile generalization.[6] Drawing attention to the diversity of the economic and social positions that are attested in the ancient world is

[3] P. Brown, *Through the eye of a needle. Wealth, the fall of Rome, and the making of Christianity in the West 350-550 AD* (Princeton 2012) and *The Ransom of the Soul. Afterlife and Wealth in Early Western Christianity* (Cambridge, Mass. 2015); B. Shaw, *Bringing in the sheaves: economy and metaphor in the Roman world* (Toronto 2013).

[4] *Poverty in the Roman world*, eds M. Atkins and R. Osborne (Cambridge 2006). *Cf.* also L. Cecchet, *Poverty in Athenian Public Discourse. From the End of the Peloponnesian War to the Rise of Macedonia* (Stuttgart 2015).

[5] Sachs, *The end of poverty* (n.2, above) 26.

[6] *Cf.* the comments by I. Morris, R. P. Saller and W. Scheidel, 'Introduction', in *The Cambridge Economic History of the Greco-Roman world*, eds I. Morris, R. P. Saller and W. Scheidel (Cambridge 2007) 1-11, at 11.

not so much a way of joining the primitivists-modernists debate that has long occupied the historians of the ancient economy, as it is to convey a measure of complexity.

Definitions, of course, also require caution. Contemporary politics, again, provides useful instances. What do we mean, for example, by middle class? Plenty of examples of how problematic this concept is may be drawn from recent and ongoing political developments in the West. Some of the papers in this volume set out to provide working definitions that take into account criteria pertaining to economic status and to social position. Nonetheless, for all the pitfalls that it presents us with, wealth is arguably a less problematic concept than poverty; its social and ideological construction has received comparatively less attention. The word itself, however, has a complexity that 'poverty' lacks: it refers to the status of being wealthy, of course, and also to the sources of the wealth, its creation, its consolidation, and its distribution. Wealth is also, perhaps intrinsically, a symptom and a factor of inequality.

Discussions of inequality invariably tend to concentrate on the extremes of the scale: the very rich and the very poor. Governments, public bodies, think tanks, and international councils concentrate on ameliorating or even eradicating poverty. At the same time, the position of the extremely rich is under constant scrutiny in our time – their standing in society, their spending choices, even their tax arrangements. They are the subject of study, gossip (media-presented or otherwise) and, more often than not, suspicion. The morality of the means of wealth creation, and any means of preserving wealth (including tax-avoidance), are a matter of common debate. Morality and legality can coincide, but often do not, and it is the morality of wealth creation that often catches the public eye more than its legality. A central contention of Piketty's study is that one of the fundamental challenges that faces capitalism in the early twenty-first century is that of devising new forms of democratic control over capital: a wider availability of economic information and knowledge is the necessary condition for that process to unfold.[7]

Even as much modern discussion, public and academic, concentrates on the consumption and creation of wealth, the very nature of wealth itself is under intense consideration. In spite of the discussions and importance of material wealth in modern society, social discourse has expanded wealth to encompass more than money or income. Leisure has become a measure of social, rather than economic, wealth. Its connection to wealth is of course no news to students of the ancient world. Yet, just as economists sometimes have difficulties conceptualizing non-material wealth as impactful on both economy and society, ancient economic historians have often viewed wealth in purely economic terms. Benjamin Keim's paper opens up avenues in discussing the nature of wealth, and its conceptualization, in the ancient world in correlation with modern theoretical departures in this area: in doing so, it chooses fourth-century BC Athens as its vantage point.

Keim's study is also concerned with other kinds of constructions, albeit not necessarily less treacherous ones. A large body of literary evidence clearly shows that the definition of what wealth was in the ancient world included non-material terms. A number of immaterial features were considered to be a fundamental part of wealth, which invites us to look beyond the traditional 'balance sheet' approach that underpinned most of the scholarship on the Athenian 'political' economy, from August Böckh to Moses Finley. Drawing attention to the immaterial facets of wealth also means exploring the values underpinning the institutions that, in the New Institutional Economy paradigm, enable the functioning of the economy. Demosthenes is a central source, and his originality is not undermined by the fact that some of his themes are already voiced, for instance, by Thucydides' Pericles.

---

[7] Piketty, *Capital* (n.1, above) 569-70.

Rather than voicing concerns about the dangers that wealth presents the community with, he stresses that wealth must be underpinned by a set of laws and patterns of behaviour that may secure its continuity across the generations. There is no tension, in Demosthenes' assessment, between the pursuit of wealth and the practice of virtue; it is, on the contrary, a distinctive feature of what being Athenian is about. At the same time, the wealth of the *polis* is incomplete without a strong non-material dimension that impinges on a set of values and behaviours. The picture that may be gleaned from the Athenian evidence, then, is one in which wealth is good, provided it is not confined to the material domain. Wealth must also be supported by intelligent economic choices: as Keim stresses, recognising the intrinsic rationality of economic dynamics does not in itself entail adding yet another footnote to the dispute between primitivists and modernists.

Like oratory, comedy offers invaluable evidence for wider social and political attitudes to wealth in classical Athens. John Davies' paper starts with the close discussion of two fragments of Alexis, quoted by Athenaeus, in which there is a reference to a law put forward by the Athenian politician Aristonikos in the 330s or 320s BC, setting restrictions on the variation of the prices at which fishmongers could sell their goods at different times of the day. Far from being a narrow matter for learned enquiry or a technical aspect of Athens' legislative history, this issue has important historical implications; exchange is an invaluable viewpoint on the dynamics of wealth creation and distribution. The debate on the control over transactions within the fresh fish market reflects wider concerns on the process that leads to the accumulation of wealth, but is also affected by the concerns over the distorting effects that wealthy consumers may have on market dynamics. Davies argues that different standpoints must be explored: that of the buyer, which is reflected in Alexis' fragments, as well as that of the vendor, which emerges in a small but significant cluster of texts, among which a passage of Theophrastus' *Characters* (6.9) stands out. A strategy of price modification that led to changes in the hours preceding the closure of market was a practice that addressed one of the pressures under which the fishmongers found themselves, and which Davies proposes to read through the lenses of what modern economists call 'yield management'. It is important to add another level to the discussion: the standpoint of the public community, and the widely held view on what 'the just price' (τῆς ἀξίας: a concept that Alexis explicitly invokes) may have amounted to. In turn, contemporary references to (and debates on) the just price require linking up the fragmentary evidence of the comic poets with more familiar material, notably the discussion of exchange in the first book of Aristotle's *Politics*. The law proposed by Aristonikos engaged with discontent surrounding the supply of a crucial commodity, and with the emergence of wider concerns about the limits of profitability in fourth-century BC Athens.

Errietta Bissa's study of monopolies in the archaic and classical *polis* takes the focus beyond Athens, and addresses an aspect of the use of state wealth that requires further analysis. It draws attention to the overlap and potential tension between the economic choices of private individuals and those of states by concentrating on two main areas: on the one hand, it stresses the significance of a fundamental force in the distribution of wealth and, on the other, it pursues the recent drive towards exploring specific institutional choices and concentrating on specific regional contexts. Bissa's earlier work stressed the importance of basing research on ancient economic processes on the study of specific commodities.[8] The majority of attested monopolies are specifically related to individual valuable commodities

---

[8] E. M. A. Bissa, *Governmental intervention in foreign trade in Archaic and Classical Greece* (Leiden and Boston 2009).

and have no demonstrable links with emergency situations. The received wisdom on the topic has so far concentrated on the evidence of the pseudo-Aristotelian tract *Oeconomica*; Bissa advocates the importance of casting the net somewhat more widely, and of approaching monopolies in classical Greece as major devices of wealth creation.[9] New insights may be drawn from the exploration of typological complexity.

It is by now a commonplace – and one that is broadly speaking accurate – to argue that most of the wealth in the ancient world was derived from land, and notably from agriculture. Unsurprisingly, then, its representation takes a range of different, sometimes very creative forms. In his chapter Jean Andreau explores the occurrences of the word *agellus* – that symptom of 'spurious modesty', as Finley put it.[10] On the face of it, one would expect this diminutive of *ager* to refer to small plots of land, more or less interchangeably with a word like *fundus*. That is not the case: *agellus* is not used in the technical literature, and it may not be strictly applied to a specific type of land. One the one hand it may also serve the depiction of indigence and dignified poverty; on the other, it may also apply to the land possessed by wealthy individuals such as Pliny the Younger.

Of course, one should not ask too much of any representation of wealth. It will always be far from exhaustive. As Andreau notes, the complex pattern of usages of *agellus* does not shed light on the unpropertied and on those who do not have land property, but are involved in other economic activities. This draws attention to a problem that is central to Filippo Carlà's exploration of middle classes in Late Antiquity. Carlà takes issue with the alleged increasing polarization between *honestiores* and *humiliores* that some literary and legal sources convey and sets out to give depth to the cohort of people of middling means. He points out that it is essential to define the middle class as constituted of people with varying occupations (from farmers to tradesmen, artisans, and doctors), rather than concentrating on one category, that of the groups involved in trade and urban production, as E. Mayer has recently done in his important volume on middle classes in the Roman Empire.[11] Carlà's discussion is framed around economic categories, and argues that rank and class did not overlap in Late Antiquity. Middle classes did exist in Late Antiquity and played a conspicuous role in the economic process; a question is raised of why they played such a modest role in the intellectual discourse on society, as opposed to the late Classical and early Hellenistic periods. The literary evidence, of course, has its limitations: the appearance of a title like *laudabilis* in the epigraphical evidence, however, would suggest that there was public recognition of individuals that were deemed to belong in a middle rank.

The representation of wealth can also cloud – whether intentionally or not – the actual quality of the issues at stake. Leonardo Gregoratti probes the historical value of the well-attested Roman views on the wealth of the Arsacid kingdom and concludes that there was a failure on the Romans' part in understanding the complexity and versatility of the Parthian state. King Vologaeses (AD 51-77/80) played a central role in the creation of what may be termed the 'structural wealth' of the kingdom, in which there was a close integration of urbanization, logistical support provided by the cities to trade and goods circulation, and a considerable role of state officials. The stereotype of Eastern luxury, merely geared up to

[9] On contemporary monopolies and the 'moral hierarchy of wealth' *cf.* Piketty, *Capital* (n.1, above) 445-46.

[10] M. I. Finley, *The ancient economy* (London 1985²) 36.

[11] E. Mayer, *The ancient middle classes: urban life and aesthetics in the Roman Empire, 100 BCE-250 CE* (Cambridge, Mass. and London 2012), esp. 2-21 on matters of definition. *Cf.* the important reservations of H. Mouritsen in *Bryn Mawr Classical Review* 2012.09.40. On the intrinsic limits of the notions of lower, middle, and upper classes, see the sobering remarks of Piketty, *Capital* (n.1, above) 250-52.

display and ostentation, fails to do justice to this historical reality and to convey any sense of its depth and complexity.

In the final contribution to this volume, Jeremy Paterson explores the development of a moral discourse on wealth in Late Antiquity, which he introduces with a point of considerable historical significance: along with the tradition of euergetism, which has some intrinsic limitations, there was another one that advocated the responsibility of a state to help the poor and improve their material condition. The radical statements on poverty that may be encountered in the Christian sources are therefore not emerging in a vacuum; and there is evidence for Christian responses to the approach of Jesus to wealth and its morality that sought to downplay its significance. The work of Clement of Alexandria is a striking example of that effort. In turn, wealth turned into a problem for the Church as it became more successful: a problem that remains open to this day. This should be no surprise. As Paterson points out, developing an insight of John Stuart Mill, poverty and wealth are intrinsic components of the human condition. Precisely for that reason, they are constantly the subject of debate, tension, and negotiation. It is to this process and its historical understanding that this book sets out to contribute.

University of Wales: Trinity St David
& Newcastle University

NON-MATERIAL BUT NOT IMMATERIAL: DEMOSTHENES' REASSESSMENT OF THE WEALTH OF ATHENS

BENJAMIN KEIM[1]

ἀπὸ δὲ οἴας τε ἐπιτηδεύσεως ἤλθομεν ἐπ' αὐτὰ καὶ μεθ' οἴας πολιτείας καὶ τρόπων ἐξ οἴων μεγάλα ἐγένετο, ταῦτα δηλώσας πρῶτον εἶμι καὶ ἐπὶ τὸν τῶνδε ἔπαινον

But by what institutions we arrived at this, by what form of government and by what means we have advanced the state to this greatness, when I shall have laid open this, I shall then descend to these men's praises.

Thucydides 2.36.4 (trans. Hobbes)

I

The following remarks, aimed at encouraging ancient historians to engage more actively with diverse modern debates over the nature of wealth, have been written against the backdrop of a worldwide economic crisis. Here, by examining Demosthenes' early speech *Against Timocrates*, I argue that both these modern debates and this ancient oratory warrant our reassessment of the wealth of Athens and our recognition of the range of non-material resources, from honor to institutions, that have been overlooked by earlier studies. Although Demosthenes offers no advice on the Eurozone, nor Pierre Bourdieu on the workings of the Second Athenian League, engaging these ancient and modern sources in conversation may nonetheless enhance our understanding of classical Athens.

In his ground-breaking study of Athenian public finance August Böckh devoted considerable attention to subjects such as 'The Sources of Wealth in Attica,' 'The Distribution of the National Wealth,' and 'Approximate Determination of the National Wealth of Attica'.[2] Although many of his conjectures have been superseded,[3] a range of similar questions and concepts continue to circumscribe modern discussions of Athenian wealth. Both specialist studies and broader summaries focus on the material components

[1] I would like to express my great appreciation to Errietta Bissa and Federico Santangelo for their efforts in organizing the 2009 Gregynog Classics Colloquium and for their invitation to contribute to the present volume. Subsequent versions of this chapter were read by Dr Jed Atkins, Professor Paul Cartledge, Professor J. E. Lendon, Professor Robin Osborne, Dr James Watson, and Professor Hans van Wees, who invited me to present some of these thoughts at the 2010 ESSH Conference in Ghent. These readers' remarks, as well as those by the editors and by Dr Mirko Canevaro on the penultimate version, gave me much to think about and resulted in numerous improvements; all remaining infelicities are my own.

[2] A. Böckh, *Die Staatshaushaltung der Athener* (Berlin 1817); English trans., *The public economy of Athens*, trans. G. C. Lewis (London 1842²).

[3] See *e.g.* J. K. Davies, *Wealth and the power of wealth in Classical Athens* (New York 1981) 35-36.

of Athenian wealth, their discussions centering on questions such as: How and from where were Athenian civic revenues derived? How was wealth distributed within the Athenian community? What assets – land, livestock, slaves, *ergastēria*, and so on – might comprise an individual's wealth? What investment strategies were employed by richer Athenians, and how were these strategies affected by risk, legislation, and social norms? How were the wealth of the Athenians and the wealth of Athens related? With the exception of discussions about liturgies,[4] where the exchange of material and non-material resources is readily apparent, there remains a staunch focus in modern scholarship on the material nature of Athenian wealth,[5] civic as well as personal.[6]

Some responsibility for this emphasis must be given to the ancient sources. When Aeschylus, for example, has Atossa wondering whether the wealth (*ploutos*) of Athens was sufficient to trouble Xerxes' campaign, her councillors' response was swift and sure: the Athenians, they said, possessed 'a fountain of silver, a treasury in their soil' (*Pers.* 237-38). Later, as they awaited the arrival of another enemy campaign, Pericles encouraged his fellow citizens by recounting the substantial *chrēmata*, in monetary and non-monetary form, that lay ready at hand for the defense of Athens (Thuc. 2.13.2-7). At the most basic level, Aristotle defined the constituent parts of *ploutos* as 'abundance of money and land, possession of tracts distinguished by number and size and beauty, and also possession of implements and slaves and cattle distinguished by number and beauty' (*Rhet.* 1361a12-15). Throughout the ancient sources there is often a strong material aspect to discussions of *ploutos*, *chrēmata*, and the related vocabulary of wealth.

Nor should the critical importance of material resources for Athenian interests be denied. The availability of economic capital conditions the opportunities available to an individual or a community: without the discoveries of the Laurion mines, there would not have been such an expansion of the Athenian navy, and perhaps no victory at Salamis, no hegemony or money-spinning empire; without empire, perhaps no jury-pay and flourishing of radical democracy, no elaborate civic improvements on the scale witnessed in those heady days of the fifth century. Yet ancient authors regularly acknowledge more than these merely material aspects of wealth. Socrates, conversing with Critobulus at the beginning of Xenophon's *Oeconomicus*, draws out the necessity of possessing appropriate knowledge, without which *chrēmata* cannot be profitable (*ōphelounta*, 1.1.7-16). In his speech *On the Chersonnese* Demosthenes asserts that the *ploutos* of a *polis* consists of 'allies, trust, and goodwill' (Dem. 8.66). These and many other contemporary passages suggest that the

---

[4] On liturgies in classical Athens see *e.g.* Davies, *Wealth and the power of wealth* (n.3, above); P. J. Wilson, *The Athenian institution of the* khoregia (Cambridge 2000) 172-84; L. Kallet, 'Wealth, Power, and Prestige: Athens at Home and Abroad', in *The Parthenon*, ed. J. Neils (Cambridge 2005) 48-49.

[5] One earlier exception to these staunchly materialist considerations is H. C. Montgomery, *The way to Chaeronea. Foreign policy, decision making and political influence in Demosthenes' speeches* (Bergen 1983), which acknowledges both *timē* and *argurion* as components of Athens' wealth. For an additional, related discussion of the interplay of 'honor' and 'profit' in Athenian trade policy, see D. T. Engen, *Honor and profit: Athenian trade policy and the economy and society of Greece, 415-307 B.C.E.* (Ann Arbor 2010).

[6] It should be noted that there are some resources that may be held by both individual and community, and others (especially more complex non-material goods, such as the Athenian legal system discussed below) that, although they benefit both community and individuals, may only be ascribed to the wealth of the community.

wealth of ancient Athens ought to be thought about more holistically, with ample regard for non-material, as well as material, components.

In other words, the 'balance sheet' approach encountered from Böckh to Finley and beyond must be replaced by a broader model of wealth.[7] To say this is not to discount the many excellent assessments which have been, and continue to be, carried out about the material resources available at Athens. Since access to such resources does shape actions of individuals and communities, our ability to discern, for example, the approximate monetary and non-monetary economic capital available to the Athenians during the Peloponnesian War is important. Such assessments have often been limited, however, by their tendency to focus both on material resources and on one particular time period. Rather than using Pericles' aforementioned assessment of Athenian *chrēmata* as our model, we would be better off considering the words of the Ephebic Oath, with which young citizens swore that they would 'not hand on the fatherland (*patris*) lessened'.[8] Within this Oath we encounter the intergenerational ebb and flow of Athenian wealth; the resonance of the *patris*, at once inclusive of *chrēmata*, *timē*, and many other forms of capital; and the overriding importance of maintaining the Athenian way of life.

II

Before we turn to focus on Demosthenes, a few introductory words might be said about the ongoing debates that have guided the evolving scholarly and institutional views on wealth. Well before the current economic crisis began, the World Bank and its peer institutions had been moving away from the traditional bottom-line assessments of national wealth in favor of assessments that emphasize both development and sustainability.[9] Such estimates encourage multi-generational (rather than short-term) perspectives[10] and stress the attainment of non-material goals – especially human freedom(s) – rather than GDP benchmarks.[11] Although there remains considerable debate over the most effective ways to describe national wealth, assessments regularly contain separate categories for natural, physical, human, and social capital.[12] This emphasis on the non-material is acknowledged by the authors of the World Bank study *Where is the Wealth of Nations?*, who argue that 'the preponderant form of wealth is intangible capital . . . which includes raw labor, human capital, social capital, and other factors such as the quality of institutions.'[13] Thus, while the categories and nomenclature vary somewhat between studies, the emerging consensus

---

[7] Consider the remark made, in his classic article on Athenian imperialism, by M. I. Finley, 'The fifth-century Athenian Empire: a balance sheet', in *Imperialism in the Ancient World*, ed. P. D. A. Garsney and C. R. Whittaker (Cambridge 1978) 103-26, 306-10, at 121 = *Economy and society in ancient Greece* (New York 1981) 41-61, at 57: 'In what follows, I shall remain within my narrow framework, restricting "benefits", "profits" to their material sense, excluding the "benefits" (not unimportant) arising from glory, prestige, the sheer pleasure of power.'.

[8] P. J. Rhodes and R. G. Osborne, *Greek Historical Inscriptions, 404-323 B.C.* (Oxford 2003) 88.9-11. I am indebted to Professor P. J. Rhodes for his remarks on the relevance of the Oath for this discussion.

[9] J. Dixon and K. Hamilton, 'Expanding the measure of wealth', *Finance and Development* (1996) 15-18, at 15.

[10] As with the Ephebic Oath, discussed above.

[11] A. Sen, *Development as freedom* (Oxford 1999) 14.

[12] P. Kotler *et al. The marketing of nations: a strategic approach to building national wealth* (New York 1997) 22. These developments are reflected within the arguments of dozens of articles, written in recent decades, which discuss the importance of 'X and the wealth of nations', where 'X' is any of a number of diverse material and non-material resources.

[13] World Bank, *Where is the wealth of nations? Measuring capital for the 21st century* (Washington DC 2006) 3-4, emphasis added.

from the sciences – whether social or 'dismal' – is that there is more to wealth than simply the material.

Underlying this revolution in the understanding of national wealth are a series of scholarly influences, at turns complementary and contrasting, two of which are mentioned above and deserve further discussion here on account of their potential utility for ancient historians. First, drawing on the theories of Bourdieu and Godelier, there is the analysis of the many 'forms of capital' we encounter throughout our daily experiences.[14] 'Bourdieu's reformulation of Marx's concept of capital ... consists of two original observations. First, many different forms of capital exist, from material (physical, economic) to non-material (cultural, symbolic, social). Second, with varying degrees of difficulty, it is possible to convert one form of capital into another.'.[15] Like Marx, 'Bourdieu ... defined capital broadly as "accumulated, human labor"';[16] unlike Marx, however, he focused on the individual, on the micro-sociological and micro-economic. Two additional notes, derived from a later writing, may be added to this summary of 'Bourdieuconomics': the primacy of financial capital amongst other forms, and the importance of time, over which 'labor' and 'capital' are accrued.[17] Although historians of ancient Greece have almost exclusively applied Bourdieu's theories to (aristocratic) individuals, these principles may be readily extended to the *polis* level.[18]

Second, there have been waves of discussions, especially within New Institutional Economics, about the value of institutions and of rule sets (comprised of diverse formal laws, agreements, and customs) as means of increasing order and wealth by decreasing inefficiencies and conflicts (violent or otherwise).[19] Especially interesting in this regard is the recent work of Avner Greif, who envisions his research as part of the 'sociological turn' in institutional economics.[20] Although there has been considerable hostility between the disciplines (and their subsidiaries),[21] he wants to bring the respective contributions of

[14] P. Bourdieu, *Le sens pratique* (Paris 1980); English trans., *The logic of practice*, trans. R. Nice (Cambridge 1990); *id.*, *Les structures sociales de l'économie* (Paris 2000); English trans., *The social structures of the economy*, trans. C. Turner (Cambridge 2005); and especially *id.*, 'Ökonomisches Kapital, kulturelles Kapital, soziales Kapital', in *Soziale Ungleichheiten*, ed. R. Kreckel (Göttingen 1983) 183-98; English trans., 'The forms of capital', in *Handbook of Theory and Research for the Sociology of Education*, ed. J. G. Richardson (London 1986) 249-58. Although Bourdieu was far from the only scholar to engage with Marx's thought in this way (*e.g.* M. Godelier, *L'idéel et le matériel: pensée, économies, societies* [Paris 1984]; English trans., *The mental and the material: thought economy and society*, trans. M. Thom [London 1986]), his work has been the most influential across academia. Although it has been suggested that the plethora of (often overlapping or occasionally contradictory) categories of 'capital' introduced in the wake of Bourdieu is itself indicative of methodological weaknesses, I would acknowledge this concern without wishing to abandon the concept's heuristic power.

[15] G. L. H. Svendsen and G. T. Svendsen, 'On the wealth of nations: Bourdieuconomics and social capital', *Theory and Society* 32 (2003) 607-31.

[16] Svendsen and Svendsen, 'On the wealth of nations' (n.15, above) 608.

[17] See Bourdieu, 'The forms of capital' (n.14, above). The importance of this latter point has already been touched on with the Ephebic Oath above, and will be revisited within the discussion of Dem. 24.176-86 below.

[18] Hammer, 'Bourdieu, ideology, and the ancient world', *American Journal of Semiotics* 22 (2006) 87-108 surveys the impact Bourdieu's thought has had on classicists' and ancient historians' research.

[19] On NIE see E. Brousseau and J.-M. Glachant, *New Institutional Economics: a guidebook* (Cambridge 2008); on the importance of rule sets see T. P. M. Barnett, *The Pentagon's new map: war and peace in the twenty-first century* (New York 2004), and, with regard to ancient Greece, P. Low, *Interstate relations in classical Greece* (Cambridge 2007).

[20] A. Greif, *Institutions and the path to the modern economy* (Cambridge 2006) xv.

[21] For an alternate view on NIE and economic sociology see V. Nee and N. Swedberg, 'Economic sociology and New Institutional Economics', in *The handbook of New Institutional Economics*, eds C. Ménard and M. M.

the sociological and economic views of institutions together. Greif's lengthy discussion of institutions, building on the fundamental work of Nobel laureates Douglass C. North and Oliver Williamson, leads to their definition as a 'system of social factors generating a regularity of behaviour,' that is, a man-made, non-physical factor.[22] Such institutions, in their diverse forms, bear in many ways on the wealth and interests of a community.

Although Greif's work focuses on the medieval and early modern world, an increasing number of studies applying aspects of NIE to the ancient world have appeared in recent years. Most of these consider Roman-era economies,[23] although a few focus on Greece[24] or on Athens.[25] The recent *Cambridge Economic History of the Greco-Roman World* contains a chapter on 'Law and Economic Institutions', where it is argued that 'an analysis of the complex relationship between legal institutions and the economy can help us to understand better the basic relationships that characterized the economy of the Greco-Roman World'.[26]

The most extensive contribution written on classical Athens from this kind of institutional perspective is Josiah Ober's *Democracy and Knowledge*.[27] Although there is no extended discussion of NIE in the text, Ober engages on several occasions with North, Williamson, and Greif. Ober argues that Athens was able to out-compete her competitors (and thereby become the 'pre-eminent *polis*') because her ability to aggregate knowledge led to better use of resources and exploiting opportunities; all of this was the result of democracy[28] and the democratic advantage of a specifically Athenian type.[29] Although Ober here is not directly interested in Athenian wealth or the Athenian economy (save as metrics by which the impact of the democracy might be measured) his remarks on incentivization are of some importance,[30] and are especially relevant given Demosthenes' belief that the greatness or weaknesses of Athens was directly tied to those laws which prescribe *timē* or

Shirley (Heidelberg 2005) 789-818, as well as (with a focus on ancient Greece) I. Morris and J.G. Manning, 'The economic sociology of the ancient Mediterranean', in *The handbook of economic sociology*, eds N. J. Smelser and R. Swedberg (Princeton 2005²) 131-59.

[22] Greif, *Institutions* (n.20, above) 29-57. F. Boldizzoni, *The poverty of Clio: resurrecting economic history* (Princeton 2011) 56-60 offers a methodological critique.

[23] See *e.g.* the contributions to I. Morris and B. R. Weingast, 'Symposium on institutions, economics, and the ancient Mediterranean world', *Journal of Institutional and Theoretical Economics* 160 (2004) 702-85.

[24] I. Morris, 'Economic growth in Ancient Greece', *Journal of Institutional and Theoretical Economics* 160 (2004) 709-42.

[25] E. E. Cohen, 'Unintended consequences? The economic effect of Athenian tax laws', in *Symposion 2001*, eds R. W. Wallace and M. Gagarin (Vienna 2005) 159-73, who notes that his is the first attempt to bring these theories to bear on Athens.

[26] B. W. Frier and D. P. Kehoe, 'Law and economic institutions', in *The Cambridge economic history of the Greco-Roman world*, eds W. Scheidel, I. Morris, and R. Saller (Cambridge 2007) 113-43, at 113. Note, at the end of that first paragraph, the authors' interest in the impact of the law(s) on *e.g.* the distribution of wealth. The idea that the system might contribute (as an 'exogenous factor') to the wealth of the community appears plausible within their model, but is not something they explore.

[27] J. Ober, *Democracy and knowledge: innovation and learning in Classical Athens* (Princeton 2008). C. Mann, Review of Ober, *Democracy and knowledge, Gnomon* 82 (2009) 334-39 examines some of the difficulties with Ober's interpretation. Ober has subsequently argued for increasingly widespread Hellenic prosperity during the Archaic and Classical periods, first in 'Wealthy Hellas', *Transactions of the American Philological Association* 140 (2010) 241-86 and now in *The rise and fall of Classical Greece* (Princeton 2015). I outline my concerns with this overly materialist model of 'the efflorescence that was Greece' in B. Keim, Review of Ober, *The rise and fall of Classical Greece, Classical Review* 66 (2016).

[28] Ober, *Democracy and knowledge* (n.27, above) 17.

[29] Ober, *Democracy and knowledge* (n.27, above) 40.

[30] Ober, *Democracy and knowledge* (n.27, above) 119-24.

timōria (24.215, discussed below). Ober acknowledges that both non-material and material incentives were used, explicitly and implicitly, to encourage volunteerism and participation, but does not elaborate on what, exactly, such non-material 'honor' or 'social capital' might entail, or how it might work. Demosthenes' remarks here offer the opportunity to develop Ober's thoughts and add more Athenian *realia* to his model.

Although concerns might be raised about the distance between, say, Demosthenes' Athens and the developing economies overseen by the World Bank, these concerns are answerable and do not undermine the value that these modern developments might have for students of ancient Greece. Yes, there are some differences between the ancient and modern which warrant caution (even where a 'development' emphasis works rather nicely with regards to the fourth-century Athenian economy) and there is much, especially on the microeconomic scale, that cannot be applied to our fragmentary sources.[31] Nevertheless these diverse, overlapping and contesting concepts remain 'good to think with', and are a means of breaking us out of our rather fossilized (if sometimes indubitably ancient) categories.[32]

III

The trial for which Demosthenes composed *Against Timocrates* was merely one encounter in an ongoing quarrel between prominent Athenians.[33] Three years earlier (355/54 BC) Androtion had been charged with a *graphē paranomōn*: the proximate cause was his decree crowning the previous year's Councillors (of whom he was one) despite their failure to supply the requisite triremes, but the ultimate cause was his enmity with his fellow Athenians Euctemon and Diodorus. Despite Diodorus' delivery of *Against Androtion* their prosecution was unsuccessful, and shortly thereafter (*c.* 354) Androtion and two others were dispatched as ambassadors to Mausolus of Caria. *En route* the envoys overtook a ship from Naucratis and, on the grounds that it was an enemy vessel, seized 9.5T worth of cargo. When an Athenian commission subsequently inquired about the cargo, the ambassadors admitted that the property was in their possession and said, since any additional penalties were beyond their ability to repay, they would simply return the goods. Now (early 353/52) Timocrates, an associate of Androtion, introduced legislation that would postpone debtors' imprisonment until the ninth *prytany*, if they could offer sureties. He was immediately met with another prosecution by Euctemon and Diodorus.[34]

Once more enlisted by Diodorus, Demosthenes seized the opportunity provided by this *graphē* to compose an elaborate consideration of the Athenian legal system, its workings,

[31] Leaving aside a few relevant sections in the Attic Orators and *IG*, we cannot acquire the microeconomic information from the Agora that one studying shopkeepers in Warsaw might. On what we are able to learn, see E. M. Harris, 'Workshop, marketplace and household: The nature of technical specialization in classical Athens and its influence on economy and society', in *Money, labour, and land: approaches to the economies of ancient Greece*, eds P. A. Cartledge *et al.* (London 2002) 67-99.

[32] To cite Low, *Interstate relations* (n.19, above) 32, these modern developments provide 'an extremely valuable set of tools with which to think about ancient [wealth], and a range of important new questions to put to, often very familiar, material.'

[33] On the events surrounding these trials see R. Sealey, *Demosthenes and his time: a study in defeat* (Oxford 1993) 118-28; E. Badian, 'The road to prominence', in *Demosthenes: statesman and orator*, ed. I. Worthington (London 2000) 9-44, at 20-24; D. M. MacDowell, *Demosthenes the orator* (Oxford 2009) 167-96.

[34] Sealey, *Demosthenes* (n.33, above) 119 argues rightly that Timocrates' legislation may have been intended as a permanent measure. The earlier debate over whether this legislation was met with a *graphē paranomōn* (S. Usher, *Greek oratory: tradition and originality* [Oxford 1999] 201; Badian, 'The road to prominence'

and its value for the *polis*.[35] The themes of money and law run throughout the speech: such extraordinary sums of money were always of interest to the *polis*, especially in the penurious days after the demise of the Second Athenian League, while Demosthenes' pronounced interest in legal matters encouraged him to elaborate at great length about the institutional importance of Athenian *nomos*.[36] The nascent statesman demonstrates throughout his knowledge of Athenian institutions, desire for Athenian interests, and care for the place and role of Athens in the world. Here I will focus first on his remarks about the importance and value of the institution of Athenian *nomos*, and then, by turning to one densely-argued passage, elaborate on his relation of *ploutos, timē,* and the *paradeigmata* inherited by the Athenians.

I begin at the very end of the speech, with a curious passage that encourages us to recognize both the economic value and the institutional importance of *nomos* at Athens (24.212-4). Demosthenes describes an occasion on which Solon was prosecuting another citizen for promulgating an unprofitable law (*nomon ... epitēdeion*).[37] As the lawgiver reached the end of his case, he coaxed the dikasts into acknowledging that the law prescribing death for the debasement of coinage was 'just and good', and then argued that debasing the laws of the city was an even worse transgression. This, he explained, was due to their respective uses: while coinage (*argurion*) was the currency (*nomisma*) of individuals, laws (*nomoi*) were the *nomisma* of the *polis*. The former might, as necessity demanded, be officially degraded without repercussion, but no city with debased laws had ever escaped the consequences. Others have already discussed the material aspects of this analogy;[38] what is most important here is that 'the conceptual link between *nomisma* and *nomos* remained a generally perceived one'.[39] The presence of such wordplay indicates that contemporaries might recognize not only the economic effect of laws, but also the possibility of the laws themselves having value. As to why *poleis* (such as contemporary Athens) might endure the debasement of

[n.33, above] 23 n.40) or a *graphē nomon mē epitēdeion theinai* (M. H. Hansen, 'Solonian democracy in fourth-century Athens', *Classica et Mediaevalia* 40 [1989] 71-99, at 44; Sealey, *Demosthenes* [n.33, above] 128; H. Yunis, *A new creed: fundamental religious beliefs in the Athenian polis and Euripidean drama* [Göttingen 1988] 365 n. 18; L. Kurke, *Coins, bodies, games, and gold: the politics of meaning in archaic Greece* [Princeton 1999] 317) should be resolved in favor of the latter.

[35] W. Jaeger, *Demosthenes* (Cambridge 1938) 42-67 (cited by A. Moreno, *Feeding the democracy: the Athenian grain supply in the fifth and fourth centuries BC* [Oxford 2007] 252) argues that Demosthenes' earliest public speeches (20, 22, 24) were a concerted attack on the older generation of Athenian politicians. The Budé commentary by O. Navarre and P. Orsini, *Démosthène: Plaidoyers politiques, tome I* (Paris 1954) remains a useful introduction to *Against Timocrates*, with more recent discussions including Usher, *Greek oratory* (n.34, above) 201-204; J. Roisman, *The rhetoric of conspiracy in ancient Athens* (Berkeley 2006) 103-14; Moreno, *Feeding the democracy* (see above) 272-79, and MacDowell, *Demosthenes* (n.33, above) 181-96. Although the verdict remains unknown, the subsequent publication of the speech (*e.g.* Badian, 'The road to prominence' [n.33, above] 24) might have been occasioned for multiple reasons, including advertisement of Demosthenes' prowess and threat of his opposition. For arguments against such ideas about publication, see J. Trevett, 'Did Demosthenes publish his deliberative speeches?', *Hermes* 124 (1996) 425-41 and MacDowell, *Demosthenes* (n.33, above) 7-9.

[36] J. de Romilly, *La loi dans la pensée grecque* (Paris 1971) 153 notes Demosthenes' keen interest in Athenian law. On the breadth and meaning of Demosthenes' thoughts on *nomos* in *Against Timocrates* see below, as well as the discussion in V. Wohl, *Law's cosmos: juridical discourse in Athenian forensic oratory* (Cambridge 2010) 292-300.

[37] The similarities between this fictitious Solonian prosecution and its Demosthenic frame would not, I think, have been missed by the dikasts. On the ideological importance of Solon within fourth-century Athenian democracy see Hansen, 'Solonian democracy' (n.34, above).

[38] Kurke, *Coins, bodies, games, and gold* (n.34, above) 317-18; S. von Reden, 'Demos' *Phialē* and the Rhetoric of Money in Fourth-Century Athens', in *Money, labour, and land: approaches to the economies of ancient Greece,* ed. P. A. Cartledge (London 2002) 52-66, at 54-55.

[39] von Reden, 'Demos' *Phialē*' (n.38, above) 54.

their coinage, but not their laws, we ought, I think, to return to Demosthenes' remark just before the Solon anecdote, that 'all *sophoi* view *nomoi* as *tropoi* of the city' (24.210). To debase currency was, as Athenian history demonstrated, embarrassing but survivable; to debase the *nomoi*, and thereby herald the debasement of *polis* and *politēs*, was to destroy the very foundations of the community.

Although the prosecutors of this *graphē nomon mē epitēdeion theinai* focus on the negative effects that the acceptance of Timocrates' legislation would bring about, there are several positive (albeit rather abstract) statements about the benefits which accrue for Athens on account of her *nomoi*. On two occasions *nomoi* are described as the cause (*aitios*) of every good thing (*agathōn*) for Athens, among which are specified her characteristic freedom (*eleutheria*), democratic governance, and even preservation (24.5, 155-6).[40] Besides these domestic goods, the *nomoi* are the means through which the *polis* has become august (*semnē*) and renowned (*lampra*) beyond her borders (24.95). These latter remarks reveal the presence of an external audience, both for Demosthenes' speech and, especially, for Athens' actions generally. The orator strives to remind his Athenian listeners of the successes and recognition they have garnered on account of their *nomos*, successes wrought by *nomos* indirectly as well as directly. Twice Demosthenes refers to the *philotimia*, the love of honor that the Athenian *nomos* fostered: the first occasion refers to successes indirectly achieved by *nomos*, with the plural *philotimias* referring, in a martial passage, to the ambitions for individual honor that are engendered by the law and that drive the public services that underwrite military victories (24.91); on the second, more direct, occasion, the Athenians are rightly filled with honor (*philotimeisthe humeis*) when 'many of the Hellenes have often voted to use your laws (*nomois ... humeterois*)' (24.210).[41] Thus Demosthenes encourages his fellow-citizens to guard these laws keenly, lest they lose this *philotimia* and tarnish the *doxa* of the city (24.210). Here, amidst discussion of the positive aspects of the law, we see the Athenian and the Hellenic, the *nomos* and the *nomoi* interwoven: decisions made at Athens would affect many, in many different ways.

The damages wrought by bad legislation are described in some detail. After laying out why Timocrates' *nomos* is 'unacceptable and disadvantageous' (24.68-90), Demosthenes details the military and domestic effects in turn. The first section tackles the damages to the *politeia* and the affairs of the *polis*, including the loss of 'many *philotimiai*' (24.91-5). The Athenian military was funded and filled as a result of numerous decrees and laws requiring various sorts of participation both financially and physically (24.92). Since Timocrates' law would allow individuals to defer paying their civic obligations until the ninth *prytany*, the Athenian military would, if everyone were to take advantage of this loophole, be summarily disabled. Unable to attack, an impotent Athens would simultaneously be exposed to disrepute and to attack by others.

The second section surveys the impact that the impoverishment of the *dioikēsis* (including both *hiera* and *hosia* monies)[42] would have on the workings of the Athenian democracy (24.96). If all of those responsible for supporting the treasury were to withhold their payments until the ninth *prytany*, the *polis* would not have any monies and would

---

[40] The passage of laws in democratic Athens was done, Demosthenes says, by convincing those who will be using them that there will be benefits accordingly (24.76): see *infra*.

[41] On the meaning(s) of *philotimia* D. Whitehead, 'Competitive outlay and community profit: φιλοτιμία in democratic Athens', *Classica et Mediaevalia* 34 (1983) 55-74 remains essential.

[42] On *hiera* and *hosia* see A. Maffi, 'τὰ ἱερὰ καὶ τὰ ὅσια: Contributo allo studio della terminologia giuridicosacrale greca', in *Symposion 1977*, eds J. Modrzejewski and D. Liebs (Cologne 1982) 33-53 and W. R. Connor, '"Sacred" and "secular": ἱερὰ καὶ ὅσια and the classical Athenian concept of the State', *Ancient Society* 19 (1988) 161-88.

be unable to render payment for public service – a characteristic and expanding feature of Athenian life over the previous century. Because civic income from taxes (*telōn*) was inadequate, Demosthenes reports, a law 'as good as was ever proposed' required those holding *hiera* and *hosia* monies to submit them to the Bouleuterion lest they be punished. In this way funds were recovered for 'the expenses of the Assembly, religious services, the Council, and the cavalry' and so on (24.96-7). With increasing fervor Demosthenes runs through the ramifications: without subsidies for the Assembly, Council, and *dikasteria* those citizen-bodies will be unable to meet, everything will be thrown into disorder, and, without its institutions, even democratic governance itself is at stake (24.99, 101). It is for this reason, the ultimate outcome of his legislation, that Timocrates ought, says Demosthenes, to be punished and renowned as a negative *paradeigma*, an example of exactly how an Athenian ought not to act.

Thus Demosthenes argues that Timocrates' legislation encourages a variety of catastrophic outcomes for his fellow Athenians, in both practical and symbolic ways. Given such effects, the stakes are considerable. Demosthenes has described an environment in which *nomos* – good *nomos*, properly instituted and understood, or bad *nomos*, wrongly adopted – carries tremendous importance. Now, in order to understand fully the case made for the nature and value of Athenian *nomos*, we need to look, briefly, at the inner workings of the *nomos*, at what is said by Demosthenes about the individual *nomoi* and their management at Athens.

First, he declares that there are two basic types (*eidē*) of laws: one concerns social relations between members of the community, the other concerns the duties owed to the community. Each has its own distinct character: the former ought to be distinguished by 'clemency and humanity', the latter ought to be firm and harsh (24.192-3). Second, he discusses on several occasions the characteristics which contribute to a good law: it must be the same for everyone (24.17); it ought to be drawn up simply and intelligibly, without ambiguities; the actions which it requires must be possible; and there must not be any concession (*rhastōnē*) for anyone who has been convicted of acting unjustly (24.69).[43] Third, although Demosthenes uses a universal perspective regularly throughout the speech, he clearly identifies Athenian *nomoi* as being democratic: such laws are repeatedly described with regard to their effect on the *plēthos, hoi polloi*, and *dēmos* (24.68-9, 192).

This democratic aspect also frames Demosthenes' systemic history of the Athenian *nomos* as well. The democratic roots of this system run, anachronistically but ideologically, back to Draco and Solon (24.211). Despite this conservatism[44] he realizes that the law will need to change and evolve, and the procedures for augmenting or changing the laws are similarly democratic. Indeed, Demosthenes concludes his remarks on procedure by noting that the only just and good guardian (*phulakē*) of Athens' *nomos* is the people (*hoi polloi*, 24.37). Although various safeguards had been established, bribery and connections might undermine justice; but so long as the people angrily defend the system and act to preserve their own interests, the laws, critical to the *polis* and *politai*, will be maintained. Although the people need individuals to act as individuals, their ultimate protection is their corporate body.

Although Demosthenes readily admits that there are problems with the way *nomos* was being used in contemporary Athens, he argues in this and other contemporary addresses that the ways adopted by Athens are the best for Athens, and ought to be maintained and

[43] See the related discussion on 'Codification' in Ober, *Democracy and knowledge* (n.27, above) 211-63.

[44] See also his famous anecdote about Locrian procedure, 24.139-41.

improved, but not replaced. The present case reveals two complementary threats to the system: first, Timocrates' legislation was perceived as a threat to the *nomos* which was the foundation of Athenian strength; second, there was the worry that contemporary Athenians were effectively abandoning the successful ways (*paradeigmata*, see below) of their ancestors and were, in their docility, running grave risks by letting Timocrates and other *rhetores* manipulate legislation for their own personal ends.

Despite these errors, however, there is no doubt that the ways of Athens were the best ways for Athens. In the slightly earlier *Against Leptines*, Demosthenes does supply a more robust critique and comparison of Athenian laws and those of other *poleis*, notably Sparta and Thebes (20.105-111; *cf.* 20.15-6).[45] He frames these remarks as a preemptive response against arguments supporting the abolition of *ateleia* ('tax-exemption') on the grounds that neither of the other leading *poleis* bestowed such rewards. Demosthenes assures the audience that he knows very well that the three *poleis* are separated by their institutions ('we use neither the same laws nor customs nor *politeia*') and, after a charitable (if error-strewn) assessment of Sparta and a highly-critical vision of Thebes, he arrives at the conclusion that the other *poleis*' practices, if not always commendable, are understandable given their constitutions, but offer nothing for Athens. And, after all, Athens ought to stand by the ways which had earlier brought her success. For Athenian ways are thought best for Athens, and, what is more, thought best for others as well. Athens was the *paradeigma* for others (24.210, *cf.* 21.48-50, Thuc. 2.40). The Athenian *nomos* emerges, as described by Demosthenes, as superior to others, and as profoundly democratic as the *politeia* it upholds (24.59).

Let us conclude this section by returning to the very end of the speech, after the episode with Solon, as Demosthenes reminds the Athenians that they ought to be especially angry with those 'who destroy the laws through which the *polis* is great (*megistē*) or small (*mikra*)' (24.215). These laws, we learn, are those laws that prescribe *timē* and *timōria*, 'that avenge you against evil-doers, and bestow certain honors on the well-behaved'. These, in other words, are the laws which incentivize (or disincentivize) certain behaviours. If all were to behave accordingly, believing that reward or punishment would be delivered accordingly, then Demosthenes believes nothing could keep Athens from greatness.[46]

Why is this so? Because their material resources – as Demosthenes elaborates – far surpass those of other *poleis*: her number of triremes, hoplites, and cavalry are unmatched; her revenues, fortifications, and harbors are notable; yet these possessions, these resources are only profitable so long as their *politeia* conforms to these laws (24.216). The institution of *nomos* – and the individual *nomoi* – are the requisite guides for behavior and action. Without them confusion (*tarachē*) is the result.

Resources are made profitable because these *nomoi* facilitate understanding, they guide actions and ensure the interests of the *polis*. These *nomoi* make clear the *tropoi* of the city. They were enacted (24.76) by citizens who felt they would be advantageous; they are prescriptions of how Athenians are to act, of the beliefs of the city, visible to citizens, residents, and foreigners alike. How these *nomoi* and systemic *nomos* are perceived is of the utmost importance, with regards to inter-*polis* affairs as well as domestically. *Nomoi* are the

---

[45] See now C. Kremmydas, *Commentary on Demosthenes* Against Leptines (Oxford 2012) *ad loc.*

[46] On Athens' offering of incentives see C. W. Hedrick Jr., 'Democracy and the Athenian epigraphical habit', *Hesperia* 68 (1999) 387-439.

enacted resolutions of the *dēmos* which govern their lives together, both among themselves and with regards to their civic obligations.[47]

In these closing remarks Demosthenes admits that the material resources available at Athens were far beyond those available elsewhere. The crucial components of the Athenian success, however, were their *nomoi*, their *tropoi*, their way of managing and using their diverse resources in the interests of the *polis*. They and their forefathers have enjoyed success and have now inherited the pattern for that success, the laws and ways of life were the foundation on which Athens might extend her wealth and her interests.

IV

These same themes of honor, wealth, and the Athenian way of life are examined within a tightly-argued passage, originally composed for Demosthenes' *Against Androtion*, which criticizes the defendants' actions with regard to the Acropolis treasuries (24.176-86 ~ 22.69-78). On some occasion before the initial trial Androtion introduced a decree proposing the restoration of the *pompeia*; once this decree had been passed, he arranged to have himself elected to carry out the restoration, and chose Timocrates as an assistant (24.176-77, *cf. IG* 2².216-17). Such endeavors were undertaken regularly during the fourth century, despite the orator's rhetorical claims to the contrary, and Androtion has been variously connected with the reorganizations of 377/76, 368/67, and 355/54.[48] Leaving aside the inevitable accusations of thievery and general depravity (24.177, 181), there remain a series of interrelated remarks, bursting with symbolism and resonant with many implications, on the forms of Athenian wealth.

At the center of Demosthenes' criticisms are the many crowns which, along with other dedications, were melted down under Androtion's supervision and recast as a variety of ritual vessels (*pompeia*). The orator assumes that the dikasts were well-acquainted with these dedications and reviewed them regularly; whether or not this was the case, they would have been aware of their existence and importance.[49] The transformation wrought by Androtion destroyed both the crowns and their inscriptions, and the orator is eager to draw specific lessons from each in turn.

The crowns were adorned with *kala kai zēlōta epigrammata*, whereas the *pompeia* were simply inscribed with Androtion's name. Six of the lost inscriptions are specifically mentioned by Demosthenes, a selection chosen both for its variety and typicality.[50] The dedicators range from the collective 'Allies' to individual *poleis* to Athenian leaders such as Conon and Chabrias; the honorands are the *dēmos* and their patron goddess; the reasons mentioned for the dedication range from the more abstract ('for courage and justice') to the more concrete ('for freeing the Euboeans'). What emerges from these examples is an exalted vision of Athens: an Athens that is successful in battle, that is in communion with the gods, that is honored by other *poleis* which are delighted to be her allies. These

---

[47] On civic obligations at Athens see P. Liddel, *Civic obligation and individual liberty in ancient Athens* (Oxford 2007).

[48] D. Harris, *The treasures of the Parthenon and Erechtheion* (Oxford 1995) 32-33 summarizes the relevant bibliography.

[49] J. M. Hurwit, *The Athenian acropolis: history, mythology and archaeology from the Neolithic era to the present* (Cambridge 1999) 54-63 discusses access to the Acropolis and surveys the treasuries' dedications.

[50] Compare the various *euergetai* celebrated at Dem. 20.29-87.

dedications attest networks of relationships connecting the Athenian *polis* and *politai* with each other and with others.[51]

The selected dedications are more than descriptive, however, they are prescriptive. They attest examples of how Athenians ought to behave, of how leaders ought to serve the *polis* (and not their own interests, as the contemporary *rhetores* are said to do), and of how the *polis* ought to be perceived by others. Recall Demosthenes' earlier remarks about Athenian *nomoi* making the *polis* august and renowned (*semnē, lampra*, 24.95). These inscriptions evoke a vision of Athens as a strong, able, virtuous *polis* filled with brave and successful *politai*.

The critical distinction drawn between the two sets of inscriptions concerns their ability to inspire worthy action. Whereas the crown inscriptions 'contained much ambition and honor' for the Athenians, the new inscriptions, which are nothing more than bureaucratic records, cannot bear, attest, or promise honor equal to their predecessors (*philotimian isēn*).[52] This disturbance within the Athenian economy of honor is reiterated within Demosthenes' formulation of the defendants' crimes (24.182): they have 'robbed the Goddess of her crowns', have 'removed from the *polis* the eager rivalry that arose from the achievements which the crowns, while extant, commemorated', and have wronged the donors by depriving them of their recognition. By erasing these inscriptions Androtion has simultaneously erased both the record and the memory of these deeds; by destroying their crowns he has removed indications that the Athenians were honored by others, and why they were honored, and how they might be further honored, as well as the encouragement to younger Athenians to act in such a way.

Similarly damaging was the conversion of the crowns into ritual vessels and bullion.[53] Here attention is drawn to Androtion's perceived ignorance: he is so uncouth[54] *(skaios)* that he does not realize the symbolic resonances of these crowns, and their importance for the interests of the *polis*.

> He does not realize that crowns are a mark of valor (*aretēs sēmeion*), while bowls and such things are a sign of wealth (*ploutos*). Every crown, no matter how small, embodies as much *philotimia* as a large one; chalices and censers, if their number exceeds the normal amount, rub off on their owners a certain reputation for wealth (*ploutos*). But if a man takes pride in trifles, far from gaining honor (*timē*) through them he also appears lacking in taste. By destroying the objects that gave you your fame (*doxa*), he has cheapened the objects that constituted your wealth (*ploutos*) and made them unworthy of you. (24.183)

There are two economies here: one is entirely material, the other uses material means to evidence non-material achievements and possessions. Demosthenes does not deny the importance of material wealth, merely that trouble ensues when it is improperly viewed or valued. Whether to an individual or a *polis*, bullion and silver-plate are valuable in a

---

[51] Such notices would have been especially poignant for an Athenian audience in the wake of the Social War, with Athens bereft of treasure and allies.

[52] On the *philotimia* contained by Athenian memorials see R. Thomas, *Oral tradition and the written record in Classical Athens* (Cambridge 1989) 50-51.

[53] Demosthenes ridicules these vessels by using a variety of diminutives, a point worth bearing in mind given the continued symbolic value of even the smallest crown.

[54] Here and throughout the discussion of this passage I draw on E. M. Harris, *Demosthenes: Speeches 20-22* (Austin 2008), who translates the corresponding passage of *Against Androtion* (22.75).

quantitative sense: the more one has, the greater one's *ploutos*. But if one tries to transcend this sense, one is clearly caught out. On the other hand, argues Demosthenes, even the smallest crown bears with it indication of merit, engagement in that other economy, recognition (of the sort that has supposedly eluded Androtion) that there is more to life than the acquisition of money. There is an audience (who will dub the haughty *plousios* 'vulgar') and this is, in several senses, the problem with Androtion's actions: by destroying the crowns, the 'items of *doxa*', Androtion has effectively removed Athens from this economy, and left it entirely within the monetary economy. Given the effects of the Social War, the abandonment of 'economies of honor' and the acknowledgement of ties to others outside the community were particularly unwise.

Related to this ignorance was Androtion's ignorance about the historic mindset of the Athenian *dēmos*. These two Demosthenic chapters bring my arguments about the wealth of Athens together: the Athenian *politeia*, broadly construed, was the underlying cause behind their success, with its appropriate (relative) valuation of money and non-material resources, and a clear inter-generational accumulation and transferal of a variety of capital – material and non-material, everything from legal systems and regulations to infrastructure such as boat-sheds – to their descendants. At the root of this was their sublimation of money into *philotimia*. They used their money, even when they had the most in the world (they did not rest on their laurels), on *philotimia* and the pursuit of glory. It is worth noting what Demosthenes says about this: first, they achieved this greatness not by taxing themselves, but by spending money, incurring danger, and instituting a new order. Their enemies were defeated, there was *homonoia* within the *polis*, and bad men were excluded from civic life (24.185). As a result, the ongoing *dēmos* inherits 'deathless possessions': the memory of their *erga* and the beauty of their memorials, as well as the infrastructure of those memorials and more – the Parthenon, Propylaia, stoas, docks (24.184). Demosthenes contrasts the outcomes of the two systems: unlike these enduring memorials and infrastructure, the bullion-plate will endure only until it is melted down, again, on a polypragmatic whim.

It was with this mindset, Demosthenes argues, with *philotimia* valued more than *chrēmata*, with *aretē* sought through *ploutos*, that the Athenian *dēmos* reached its height. Although he does not mention *nomos* explicitly, the sentiments expressed here are the same as those expressed throughout the speech. The strength and interests of Athens are dependent on her citizens' adherence to the traditional workings of the *nomos*, and the appropriate incentivization (of both citizen and non-citizen) of actions in the *polis*' interests. The *polis* has been rendered poorer by the loss of these crowns and their functions, with their inscriptions and their memorial indications of past ways and deeds.

V

I have focused here on one early speech by Demosthenes, chosen as a means of introducing and examining the ramifications that our conceptions about the wealth of Athens have for our broader understanding of Athens and the Athenian experience. *Against Timocrates* encourages us to consider both neo-institutionalist and Bourdieuian approaches as means of expanding the measure of Athenian wealth: the former, through Demosthenes' discussion of Athenian *nomos* and the status (and success) that, in diverse ways, it accords the *polis*; the latter, as we turn to assess the complementary currencies of money and honor, and the interwoven economies which these crowns and vessels represent. Both the law and honor of Athens are shown to be non-material resources which are integral to the wealth of Athens.

There are a number of ways forward from this stage, some of which involve building on the foundations already established by others. First, further research ought to be done on the vocabulary of wealth, especially *ploutos*, and its evolution, as it comes to be used increasingly in the fourth century with both material and non-material components.[55] Second, Davies' recent study on the export of Athenian expertise encourages further consideration both of the development of this knowledge within Athens, and the recognition of its benefits and adaptation of its ways within other classical and Hellenistic *poleis*.[56] Assessing the overseas adaptation of the Athenian *nomos* as described by Demosthenes above (24.210) would also be worthwhile. Third, looking more carefully at the fourth century, there is reason for continued reappraisal of the ongoing debates over the ancient economy. The case for 'rationalism' in mid-fourth-century Athens has carried the day, yet this is not a 'modernist' over 'primitivist' triumph, rather another call for the realization of the complexities of these realities.[57] Combining aspects from each side of the old debate, one can be rational about honor, and honors, and further explanation needs to be made of the ways in which Athens, both in her imperial pomp and later renaissance, managed these economies.

What must be stressed, in conclusion, is that this is not a case of shoehorning modern concepts into ancient brogues, but of unpacking what is already there.[58] Consider again Atossa's queries of her councillors (Aesch. *Pers.* 231-45). Besides asking about its *ploutos*, she asks about Athens' location, standing among the Greeks, manpower, weaponry, and governance. If not associated with *ploutos*, each of these (as well as Athens' past successes) are recognizable as different forms of capital, and might easily be conceived as components of a whole – which is just what she does, recognizing, as the Messenger runs nearby, the meaning of these answers. *Ploutos*, understood materially, was a central aspect of Athens' wealth and success but was by no means entirely responsible. Although we overlook this with our modern blinkers, Thucydides and his Pericles had reached this same conclusion as well: while the *chrēmata* of Athens were important, even more critical, for the interests, success, and wealth of Athens, were the *politeia* and *tropoi* through which these successes were engendered (Thuc. 2.13, 36.4). This central lesson would be taught once again by Demosthenes, here in *Against Timocrates*, that when we assess the wealth of a community, the non-material is far from immaterial.

Pomona College

---

[55] Besides Dem. 8.66, quoted above, there is a series of other passages in the Demosthenic and Isocratean *corpora* which ascribe non-material components to *ploutos*. Usages in the more traditional, material sense continue as well.

[56] J. K. Davies, 'Athenian fiscal expertise and its influence', *Mediterraneo Antico* 7 (2004) 491-512.

[57] See *e.g.* E. M. Burke, 'The economy of Athens in the Classical era: some adjustments to the primitivist model', *Transactions of the American Philological Association* 122 (1992) 199-226 and P. Christesen, 'Economic rationalism in fourth-century BCE Athens', *Greece & Rome* 50 (2003) 31-56.

[58] By this I am not suggesting, in the spirit of, *e.g.*, S. T. Lowry, *The archaeology of economic ideas* (Durham, N.C. 1987) and *id.*, *Pre-classical economic thought: from the Greeks to the Scottish Enlightenment* (Boston 1987), that Demosthenes or his Athenian contemporaries had developed a formal economic framework remotely similar to modern frameworks such as those of Bourdieu, the Neo-Institutionalists, or their respective influences. Moreover, taking heed of the arguments of Boldizzoni, *Poverty of Clio* (n.22, above) 6, I would encourage the pursuit 'of a different paradigm of historical research that is not subject to economic theory but contributes towards renewing it.'.

ARISTONIKOS AND THE FISHMONGERS[1]

JOHN DAVIES

Aristophanes was far from being the only Athens-based writer of comedies whose plays provide not just political historians, but also social and economic historians with much invaluable information. Even Menandros, for all his tendency to confine himself to inter-personal relationships, has been very productively called in aid,[2] while there remain whole volumes of fragments of the hundreds of other lost plays that Athenian and other audiences saw in the course of the three centuries during which Greek comedy was an active literary genre. Indeed, such is the size of the corpus that much of it has still to be fully exploited by historians,[3] but justice has been done for some at least of the major poets, and those who know their way round the fragments of the plays of Alexis will have decoded my title with ease. It alludes to two fragments[4] of his *Lebēs*, which are quoted by Athenaios 6.226a-c and run as follows:

κἀν τῷ Λέβητι δέ φησιν ὁ αὐτὸς ποιητής:

οὐ γέγονε κρείττων νομοθέτης τοῦ πλουσίου
Ἀριστονίκου ... ... τίθησι γὰρ νυνὶ νόμον,
τῶν ἰχθυοπωλῶν ὅστις ἂν πωλῶν τινι
ἰχθὺν ὑποτιμήσας ἀποδῶτ' ἐλάττονος
ἧς εἶπε τιμῆς, εἰς τὸ δεσμωτήριον
εὐθὺς ἀπάγεσθαι τοῦτον, ἵνα δεδοικότες
τῆς ἀξίας ἀγαπῶσιν, ἢ τῆς ἑσπέρας
σαπροὺς ἅπαντας ἀποφέρωσιν οἴκαδε.
κἀνταῦθα καὶ γραῦς καὶ γέρων καὶ παιδίον
πέμπτης ἅπαντες ἀγοράσουσι κατὰ τρόπον. (F130)

[1] This paper appears in two languages: in English, in the present volume, and in Greek, in a volume edited by Katerina Panagopoulou, Ανταλλαγές – Συναλλαγές στην αρχαιότητα. In both volumes, as a paper directly concerned with the practice of exchange and therefore more directly related to the common theme, it replaces the paper that was originally submitted. I am therefore very grateful to all editors for their kindness and generosity in allowing me to make the substitution. I also thank Jamie Box, Nicky Davies, Dominique Demougin, Edward Harris, David Lewis, Robin Osborne, and Christopher Tuplin for helpful interventions and references.

[2] As by S. Lape, *Reproducing Athens. Menander's comedy, democratic culture, and the Hellenistic city* (Princeton and Oxford 2004), with the many relevant references in her bibliography.

[3] Old Comedy is the best served period, as for example by the papers in the section 'Social themes' in *The Rivals of Aristophanes. Studies in Athenian Old Comedy*, eds D. Harvey and J. Wilkins (London 2000).

[4] Reference numbers for all fragments cited from the comic poets are those of the Kassel-Austin edition.

καὶ προελθὼν δέ φησιν·
οὐ γέγονε μετὰ Σόλωνα κρείττων οὐδὲ εἷς
Ἀριστονίκου νομοθέτης· τὰ τ' ἄλλα γὰρ
νενομοθέτηκε πολλὰ καὶ παντοῖα δὴ,
νυνί τε καινὸν εἰσφέρει νόμον τινὰ
χρυσοῦν, τὸ μὴ πωλεῖν καθημένους ἔτι
τοὺς ἰχθυοπώλας, διὰ τέλους δ' ἑστηκότας:
εἶτ' εἰς νέωτά φησι γράψειν κρεμαμένους,
καὶ θᾶττον ἀποπέμψουσι τοὺς ὠνουμένους
ἀπὸ μηχανῆς πωλοῦντες ὥσπερ οἱ θεοί. (F131)

I subjoin, but with some amendments, Douglas Olson's translation from the Loeb C.L., vol. 3.

The same poet says in *The Cauldron* (fr. 130):

There's never been a better legislator than rich
Aristonikos. He's now proposing a law
that any fishmonger who is selling someone a fish
and then lowers the price, and sells it for less
than the price he specified, is to be taken off
to the prison immediately, so that in alarm
they are content to sell[5] for a just price, or else
take all their fish home in the evening rotten.
Then every old woman, old man, or slave
who's sent for fish will buy what he's supposed to. (F130)

And further on he says (fr. 131):
After Solon, there's never been a better legislator
Than Aristonicus. He's passed
All kinds of other laws,
And now he's proposing a wonderful new
One, that fish-sellers are no longer allowed to sit down
When they conduct their business, but have to stand continuously.
Then next year, he says, he'll draft one requiring them to hang in midair:
They'll send their customers away faster,
If they're selling from a crane, like the gods!

The second excerpt clearly inhabits the realm of fantasy, but the first one reads more realistically, as if illustrating a reaction to the practices of market-based exchange. In consequence it has not lacked recent commentators, who are inclined to take it seriously and therefore compare it with other known examples of laws that regulate the prices of fresh fish.[6] However, I venture to revisit it in this brief paper, animated by the sense that there is

---

[5] W. G. Arnott, *Alexis: the fragments. A Commentary* (Cambridge 1996) 379-80 expresses acute unease with the verb ἀγαπῶσιν in the transmitted text and proposes ἀποδῶσιν *vel sim.* instead. However, the implication of ἀγαπῶσιν, that the fishmongers should not be greedy, fits the political logic of the passage (see below). The two other textual cruces in the two quotations do not affect the material point of this paper, and may be left on one side.

[6] *Imprimis* J. N. Davidson, 'Fish, sex, and revolution in Athens', *Classical Quarterly* 43 (1993) 53-66, at 56; Arnott, *Alexis* (n.5, above) 363-64 and 377-78; J. N. Davidson, *Courtesans and fishcakes. The consuming passions of*

still something more to say in respect of both the commercial and the legislative registers of the passage.

First, its context in Athenaios' text. At the start of Book VI his banqueters have reached the fish course, the provision of which is described as lavish (224b-c). Its arrival characteristically prompts a torrent of citations from Athenaios' card-index, almost all taken from Attic comedy and all concerned with fishmongers. In sequence they are: Antiphanes' *Neaniskoi*, F164 (224c-d): Amphis' *Planos*, F30 (224d-e): Alexis' *Apeglaukomenos*, F16 (224f-225a); Diphilos' *Polupragmōn*, F67 (225a-b); Xenarchos' *Porphura*, F7 (225c-d); Antiphanes' *Moikhoi*, F159 (225e), and his *Philothēbaios*, F217 (225f); Alexis' *Pulaia*, F204 (226a); the excerpts from Alexis' *Lebēs* cited above; Antiphanes' *Misoponēros*, F157 (226d-e); Diphilos' *Emporos*, F32 (226e-f); Alexis' *Hellēnis*, F76 (226f-227a); Arkhippos' *Ikhthues*, F23 (227a); Alexis' *Epiklēros*, part of F78 (227b); Anaxandrides' *Odusseus*, F34 (227b-d); Alexis' *Epiklēros* again, F78 (227d-e); Diphilos' *Emporos* again, F31 (227e-228b); Sophilos' *Androklēs*, F2 (228b-c); and finally a prose author, Lunkeus of Samos, F20 Dalby[7] (228c). The conversation then turns to silver vessels, a topic which I have discussed elsewhere,[8] and the reader can recover from the onslaught.

Elsewhere, especially in Books VII and VIII, Athenaios' interest in fish is that of a connoisseur, but here the tone of the texts that he cites is vitriolic. Various motifs include: the high prices charged *(passim)*, unscrupulous exploitation of the difference between the Attic and the Aiginetan coin standards (Diphilos' *Polupragmōn*), manipulation of prices (Alexis' *Lebēs*), evasion of law (Xenarchos' *Porphura*), and selling decayed goods (Antiphanes' *Moikhoi* and *Philothēbaios*). The men themselves are characterized as arrogant (Alexis' *Apeglaukomenos*), slaves (Diphilos' *Polupragmōn*), murderers (Amphis' *Planos*), men who elide their words *(ibid.)*, and in one case explicitly foreign (Hermaios the Egyptian in Arkhippos' *Ikhthues*). However, the fishmongers are not the only target,[9] for both here (in Diphilos' *Emporos*) and elsewhere some purchasers themselves become the target.

One could without difficulty add other passages from the comedians in the same vein,[10] whether directed against the vendors or against the influence exerted by gourmets (the *opsophagoi*) in pushing up prices. That very fact helps to render unattractive any explanation of the passages that is couched wholly in terms of a specific crisis or shortage.[11]

Classical Athens (London 1997) 189-190; N. R. E. Fisher, 'Symposiasts, fish-eaters and flatterers: social mobility and moral concerns in Old Comedy', in *The Rivals of Aristophanes* (n.3, above), 355-96, at 368-69; A. Bresson, *La cité marchande* (Bordeaux 2000) 177. The text is not discussed by L. Migeotte, 'Le contrôle des prix dans les cités grecques', in *Économie antique. Prix et formation des prix dans les économies antiques*, eds J. Andreau, P. Briant and R. Descat (St Bertrand-de-Comminges 1997) 33-52.

[7] *Ap.* Athen. 7.313-314; text also in A. Dalby, 'Lynceus and the anecdotists', in *Athenaeus and his world. Reading Greek culture in the Roman Empire*, eds D. Braund and J. Wilkins (Exeter 2000), 372-94 and 580-81, at 389.

[8] J. K. Davies, 'The Phokian hierosylia at Delphi: quantities and consequences', in *Corolla Cosmo Rodewald*, ed. N. Sekunda (Gdansk 2007) 75-96.

[9] I know no evidence that any group concerned formed a cult-group of their own.

[10] *E.g.* Aristophanes' *Nesoi*, F402, Kratinos' *Trophōnios*, F236, Antiphanes' *Plousioi*, F188, and *Timōn*, F204; possibly also Ar. *Wasps* 788-791, but it is not clear (as D. M. MacDowell, notes *ad loc.*) whether in the latter passage the act of giving three mullet-scales instead of obols as change for a drachma was committed by the fishmonger or by Lusistratos as the intermediary in the transaction.

[11] As argued by Arnott, *Alexis* (n.5, above) 364: but he himself had noted elsewhere (Arnott, *Alexis*, 64) how the theme of high prices had already become a comic *topos*, for which much evidence is assembled by Davidson, 'Fish, sex, and revolution in Athens' (n.6, above), and A. Marchiori, 'Between ichthyophagists and Syrians. Features of fish-eating in Athenaeus' *Deipnosophistae* Books Seven and Eight', in *Athenaeus and his world* (n.7, above) 327-38 with 573-76.

True, as will be set out in detail below, the allusion to Aristonikos as an active politician dates Alexis' *Lebēs* in the 330s or 320s, in a period during which a prolonged grain-famine caused widespread disruption, but fish is no substitute for grain, and in any case allusions to the fishmongers' behaviour in other plays such as those by Arkhippos, Antiphanes, and Anaxandrides must belong in an earlier generation, while those in the plays of Kratinos and Aristophanes are of an earlier generation still. It is therefore better to use these passages as symptoms of a structural feature of the Athenian market for fish, not of a cyclical or spasmodic feature, and to try to understand what is going on.

Within that market, it is essential to distinguish between the sub-market for fresh fish and that for salted fish (τάριχος).[12] The former was fluid and volatile, for reasons explained below, but the latter perhaps rather less so.[13] That was because the time-scale of production from sea to market for τάριχος was much longer in time and distance, with supplies known to emanate from long distances,[14] with substantial costs being incurred for transportation in consequence, and with production requiring space (for the pickling containers) and the purchase of other commodities (principally salt). The unit of supply will therefore have been the consignment, *i.e.* part[15] (or even all) of a ship's cargo, so that the supply-chain will have comprised a small number of large units, not (as with fresh fish) a large number of small units. The activity was therefore evidently much more capital-intensive than the market for fresh fish,[16] an inference which may help to explain why the one fishmonger at Athens[17] who is known to have become wealthy, Khairephilos of (later) Paiania, was a

---

[12] Since salt-fish are referred to in Khionides' *Ptochoi*, F 5, it has to be assumed that early fifth-century audiences were already familiar with the product: an inference which itself has implications for the growth of trading patterns (see n.14, below).

[13] Though even for salt-fish the comedians can caricature both glut (Nikostratos' *Antullos*, F 5 *ap*. Athen. III 118e) and scarcity (Diphilos' *Emporos*, F 32).

[14] Thus Nikostratos (F 5) mentions Byzantion and Cadiz in the same sentence, and Eupolis (F 199) likewise Phrygia and Cadiz, while Pollux (6.48) has picked up Egypt as another place of production. That Kratinos (F 44) and Hermippos (F 63, line 5) both cite the Black Sea or the Hellespont as *the* area of origin on its own is a further reminder that the Athenian obsession with creating and retaining a secure route to and from the Hellespont was not just a matter of safeguarding the corn-supply. Consistently enough, the salt-fish that formed part of the cargo at issue in Dem. 35 is said to have been loaded at Pantikapaion in the Crimea (35.32 and 34). However, such evidence is impossible to reconcile with the figures cited by T. W. Gallant, *A fisherman's tale: an analysis of the potential productivity of fishing in the ancient world* (Ghent 1985) 34-35 for catches from the Sea of Marmara and the Black Sea for 1922-58 'which would barely be capable of supplying local needs, let alone furnish the raw material for an "export industry"': one can only assume that over-fishing and (more recently) pollution have created a very different level of availability from that current in the fifth century BCE. Gallant's portrayal is also challenged in more detail by T. Bekker-Nielsen, 'Fish in the ancient economy', in K. Ascani *et al.* (eds), *Ancient history matters. Studies presented to Jens Erik Skydsgaard on his seventieth birthday* (Rome 2002), 29-37.

[15] Thus explicitly in Dem. 35.34.

[16] The logistics of the industry need extended description on their own, which is impracticable here. The brief sketch in D. Bohlen, *Die Bedeutung der Fischerei für die antike Wirtschaft* (Diss. Hamburg 1937) 21-22 may be supplemented by Gallant, *A fisherman's tale* (n.14, above) 36-37 and 42-43; B. Lowe, 'Between colonies and emporia. Iberian hinterlands and the exchange of salted fish in eastern Spain', in *Hellenistic economies*, eds Z. H. Archibald, J. K. Davies, V. Gabrielsen, and G. J. Oliver (London and New York 2001) 175-200, and C. Carusi, *Il sale nel mondo greco (VI a.C.-III d.C.). Luoghi di produzione, circolazione commerciale, regimi di sfruttamento nel contesto del Mediterraneo antico* (Bari 2008) 25-28.

[17] The qualification 'at Athens' implicitly alludes to Korinthos, where imports of Punic *amphorae* imply a role for the city as another partner in the exchange-network for the commodity (Y. Maniatis *et al.*, 'Punic amphorae found at Corinth, Greece: an investigation of their origin and technology', *Journal of Field Archaeology* 11 [1984] 205-22).

salt-fish seller.[18] It is therefore appropriate that salt-fish had a separate market[19] and that the manumission documents of the 320s distinguish fish-seller (ἰχθυοπώλης)[20] from salt-fish seller (ταριχοπώλης).[21]

That distinction once made, exposition can now return to the fresh-fish market on its own. Diagnosis of it must of course start from the texts, and by using them to the full Davidson has painted a stark and persuasive portrait not so much of the dietary importance of fish as of their central role in patterns of conspicuous consumption and of social and political symbolism.[22] However, the texts will not suffice on their own, especially for a quest which focuses on economic rather than socio-political aspects, and in any case they are only concerned to excoriate the fishmongers' behaviour, not to explain it. That is because the voice enunciated by the poets is uniformly that of the none-too-wealthy consumer, for whom, as is generally recognized, the protein provided by fish was an essential element of diet. In consequence, and in the heavily urbanized context of Athenai-Peiraieus where much of its population was dependent on market provision by the later fifth century, that voice reflected resentment against the impact of an essential but intrinsically volatile market wherein fish supplies were often scarce. As always, therefore, since each commodity generates a different pattern of production, distribution, and consumption, one must ask what the structure of supply and demand for this particular good or service was: was the basic conflict of interest simply bipartite (between vendors and consumers), or did it become tripartite, containing two (or more) sorts of purchasers with opposed interests, or did it become more complex still? After all, the possibility of complex models is well exemplified by the interests in play in the Athenian market for grain, with a plurality of interested parties and with 'the community' intervening in various ways,[23] and it would not be difficult to construct a comparably complex model for the market for timber.

In the market for fish, then, we hear the consumer, but not the vendor, who remains mute. Yet he absolutely needs to be heard on his own terms if we are not to succumb to a seriously distorted model, a need which is all the more urgent because the variables are complex. The paragraphs that follow therefore attempt to provide that vendor's voice, not indeed directly but by tracing the chain of procurement and payment that supplied the market in such a way as to reveal the pressures and opportunities that prevailed within that chain. Some are obvious: others are not.

First and foremost, as illustrated above all by the comic poets[24] but also by Athenaios' Books VII and VIII, by a limited corpus of epigraphic evidence,[25] and by our knowledge of

[18] References in J. K. Davies, *Athenian propertied families, 600-300 BC* (Oxford 1971) 566-68, no. 15187 and *PAA* 18.975 710. That Nikostratos F 5 characterises one salt-fish seller as *kalos kagathos* should not mislead.

[19] 'At the gates' (Ar. *Hippeis* 1247).

[20] E. A. Meyer, *Metics and the Athenian Phialai-inscriptions. A study in Athenian epigraphy and law* (Stuttgart 2010) 120, no.10, line 87. *Pace* Meyer, I employ the traditional vocabulary for these documents.

[21] Meyer, *Metics* (n.20, above), 83-104, nos.2-9, lines a.510 and b.35; no.20, line 87.

[22] Davidson, 'Fish, sex, and revolution in Athens' (n.6, above); more briefly in Davidson, *Courtesans and fishcakes* (n.6, above) 226-27.

[23] R. J. Seager, 'Lysias against the corn-dealers', *Historia* 15 (1966) 172-84; A. Moreno, *Feeding the democracy. The Athenian grain supply in the fifth and fourth centuries BC* (Oxford 2007); G. J. Oliver, *War, food, and politics in early Hellenistic Athens* (Oxford 2007).

[24] Above all in Arkhippos' *Ikhthues*, with J. Wilkins, 'Athenaeus and the *Fishes* of Archippus', in *The Rivals of Aristophanes* (n.3, above) 523-35 and 592-93.

[25] Notably *SEG* 50.188 *etc.* with Bresson, *Cité marchande* (n.6, above) 151-82.

various lost foodie handbooks,[26] fresh fish was not in fact a single commodity but a wide range of species, of very diverse levels of desirability and availability. Secondly, the size and quality of the catch available to each vendor will have varied daily.[27] Thirdly, though 'producer' (*i.e.* the person who caught the fish), 'shipper' (the person who brought the commodity to the quayside), and retail vendor may sometimes have been the same person, in the mode that is still viable and visible on many a Mediterranean quayside even nowadays, we have clear evidence that the vendor might be at the end of a chain of middle-men. This evidence comprises the final section of Theophrastos' sixth Character, the ἀπονενοημένος.[28] Among his quiver-full of shady activities is his disposition

οὐκ ἀποδοκιμάζειν δὲ οὐδ'ἅμα πολλῶν ἀγοραίων στρατηγεῖν καὶ εὐθὺς τούτοις δανείζειν καὶ τῆς δραχμῆς τόκον τρία ἡμιωβόλια τῆς ἡμέρας πράττεσθαι. καὶ ἐφοδεύειν τὰ μαγειρεῖα, τὰ ἰχθυοπώλια, τὰ ταριχοπώλια, καὶ τοὺς τόκους <τοὺς> ἀπὸ τοῦ ἐμπολήματος εἰς τὴν γνάθον ἐκλέγειν. (*Char.* 6.9).

not to be unwilling to be the Mr Big behind many market-traders at the same time and to lend them money on the spot and to exact three half-obols per drakhma per day as interest: nor to go round the cookshops, the fishmongers' booths, the salt-fish booths, and to collect in his jaw the interest-payments from the takings.

On this evidence the fishmongers (and others) borrowed funds from him with which to buy fish from suppliers (whether the fishermen themselves or shore-porters who brought the catch up the road to the Athenian Agora is indeterminable), and paid him 25% interest on the loan at the end of the trading day. We have no means of determining how common the practice was, but the widespread use in Athenian sources of the word *obolostatēs* ('small-scale money-lender'), together with the evidence of comparable practices in more recent urban markets assembled by Millett,[29] strongly suggests that it may have been normal, reflecting a trading structure wherein the vendors lacked sufficient capital of their own to buy stock in. The usurious rate of 25% per day, foreshadowing the worst practices of today's pay-day lenders, presumably reflects the level of profits that the fishmongers (and other retailers) might expect to make on a normal day, but it also reflects the risks that the lender was taking with an unsecurable loan that was being rolled over from day to day. (For possible sources of the capital see the Additional Note on p.32 below).

A fourth pressure also lies in the background. On the assumption that many if not most market traders were non-citizens,[30] each man was liable to pay either (if of free or freedman status) the *metoikion* (12 dr. per year)[31] plus the *xenikon telos*[32] (levied at

[26] *E.g.* the Τέχνη ὀψωνητική (*The art of buying seafood*) of Lunkeus of Samos (fragments *ap.* Dalby, 'Lynceus' [n.7, above] 388-89); the Ἡδυπάθεια (*Life of luxury*) of Arkhestratos of Gela, and Dorion's Περὶ ἰχθύων (*About fish*).

[27] Different levels of variability are identified by Gallant, *A fisherman's tale* (n.14, above) and Gallant, *Risk and survival in ancient Greece* (Stanford 1991) 120-21.

[28] A near-untranslatable term, as P. Millett, *Lending and borrowing in ancient Athens* (Cambridge 1991) 179 documents: Edmonds' version 'wilfully disreputable' in the Loeb L.C.L. is as good as any.

[29] Millett, *Lending and borrowing* (n.28, above) 179-88.

[30] *E.g.* the fishmonger Hermaios the Egyptian in Arkhippos' *Ikhthues*, F23 *ap.* Athen. 6.227a.

[31] Harp. *s.v.* μετοίκιον.

[32] Dem. 57. 34, with the comments of A. Böckh, *Die Staatshaushaltung der Athener*, I³-II³ (Berlin 1886 [1967]) I³, 403-404.

an unknown rate) for trading in the Agora, or (if a slave) an *apophora*[33] to his owner. A fifth was that opportunities for vending were in any case limited by festivals or by the occupation of the City Agora for other purposes (though presumably the many deme-agorai[34] would have been available as alternative venues). A sixth, clearly visible even in the excerpts quoted by Athenaios, was the direct conflict of interest among purchasers. This is portrayed by the poets as being between the general population on the one hand and the wealthy, the gourmets, the ostentatious spenders, and the politically ambitious on the other: there was no one unified market, but at least two (and maybe more) which overlapped and conflicted. The final constraint, and the most fundamental of all, was of course the very limited life-span of fresh fish as a merchantable good: one may envisage a half-life of at most twelve hours without ice or refrigeration at the height of an Athenian summer.

These pressures combined to place fishmongers under significant and continuous stress. Rational profit-maximizing behaviour on their part was therefore essential. It will have comprised (a) reducing to a minimum the lapse of time from net to market, (b) maintaining the freshness of the fish – or at least the appearance of freshness – as long as possible, (c) keeping prices high for as long as possible, (d) prioritising the satisfaction of high-cost demand from gourmets for as long as possible, but also (e) modifying prices at appropriate moments in order to ensure that all fish were sold before the *Agora* was closed to traders. Each component needs some comment and illustration.

Component (a) cannot be illustrated directly, but is placed in a wider context by Diphilos F67,[35] which portrays a fishmonger who replies to the question 'How much for the sea-bass?' by answering

> 'Ten obols', without specifying the currency.
> Then if you pay him the money,
> He charges you on the Aeginetan standard, and if he has
> To give change, he offers Attic coins!
> Either way, he makes money on the deal.
>
> (trans. S.D. Olson, Loeb C.L.)

This does not merely illustrate sharp practice in manipulating currency-exchange, but also suggests what we should in any case expect, that the market for fresh fish was not just being supplied by catches from the coastal waters of Attika[36] but also from the Saronic Gulf and perhaps even further afield, and not just by residents of Attika but also by traders from (say) Aigina or Korinthos who used currency on the heavier Aiginetan standard as a common currency. For component (b) one can turn to Antiphanes' *Moikhoi,* F159, or to the

---

[33] References assembled in Böckh, *Staatshaushaltung* (n.32, above), I³ 91 note *a*.

[34] Details in 'Introduction', in *The ancient Greek economy: markets, households and city states*, eds E. M. Harris, D. M. Lewis, and M. Woolmer (Cambridge 2016) 1-37, esp. 7-19.

[35] From his *Polupragmōn, ap.* Athen. VI.225b.

[36] *E.g.* the mullets of Aixone praised in Kratinos' *Trophōnios*, F236 *ap.* Athen. VII. 325e, with Hesukhios *s.v.* Αἰξωνίδα τρίγλην [A 2015].

passage listed above from Xenarchos' *Porphura*, where the speaker describes a fight staged by a fishmonger whose fish were drying out:

> Punches were thrown; and he pretended to have received
> A good shot, and fell down and was lying among his fish,
> Apparently unconscious. Someone shouted
> 'Water! Water!', and another man in the business
> Picked up a pitcher and poured just a little
> On him – and all the rest over the fish!
> You would have said they'd just been caught.[37]

Components (c) and (d) are fully documented in Davidson 1993 and Marchiori 2000[38] and need no further illustration. Component (e), however, deserves closer consideration, for the proposed law attributed to Aristonikos in Alexis' F130 was clearly attempting to make the practice illegal. For the fishmongers, of course, it was both rational and essential, for it perfectly exemplifies the practice of what has come to be known since 1985 as 'yield management'. A useful current definition is that it is:

> ... a variable pricing strategy, based on understanding, anticipating and influencing consumer behaviour in order to maximise revenue or profits from a fixed, perishable resource (such as airline seats or hotel room reservations or advertising inventory). ... This process can result in price discrimination, where a firm charges customers consuming otherwise identical goods or services a different price for doing so ... There are three essential conditions for yield management to be applicable:
>
> • That there is a fixed amount of resources available for sale.
> • That the resources sold are perishable (there is a time limit to selling the resources, after which they cease to be of value).
> • That different customers are willing to pay a different price for using the same amount of resources.
>
> Yield management is of especially high relevance in cases where the constant costs are relatively high compared to the variable costs. The less variable cost there is, the more the additional revenue earners will contribute to the overall profit. ... [39]

It is gratifying to find in our texts a practice which shows all three 'essential conditions' and for which the constant costs (of time taken in fishing, transporting, and selling; of maintaining a boat; of renting a pitch in the *Agora*; of borrowing working capital) will have been considerable. True, it will be futile to attempt to apply the mathematical models which have been developed, for we plainly cannot credit the fishmongers with anything more than a practical knowledge of their markets, driven by experience. That does not preclude us

---

[37] Xenarchos F7 *ap.* Athen. VI. 225d, trans. S. D. Olson, slightly modified. *Cf.* also Aristophanes' *Nēsoi*, F402 (mackerel two days old).

[38] Note especially her melodramatic (and fully referenced) list of aspects of the behaviour of fish-lovers (Marchiori, 'Between ichthyophagists and Syrians' [n.11, above] 330), especially their tendency to buy up the market (no.3 of Marchiori's catalogue).

[39] Wikipedia *s.v.* 'Yield management' (accessed 7 June 2014): brief sketch in much the same terms also in P. Kotler *et al.*, *Marketing management* (Harlow 2012²) 677-78.

from attempting to represent their strategy in terms of a standard indifference curve.[40] If, as is clear from the texts cited by Athenaios and others, the basic tension was between quality and quantity, it can be well enough represented thus:

Quality

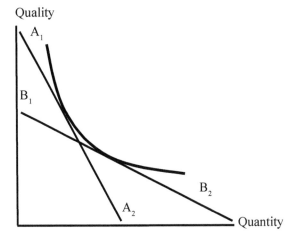

Quantity

In the figure, line A_1-A_2 represents the pricing strategy appropriate for the gourmet clientele, while line B_1-B_2 represents that appropriate for the generality of the population, including the poor. One may also envisage line A_1-A_2 as representing the pricing strategy that was appropriate in the early stages of trading each morning, and B_1-B_2 as that which was more appropriate later on, when the need to dispose of stock took priority.

One may take one further step towards re-creating the experience and attitudes of the fishmongers. Scrappy and unreliable though reports in our texts of actual prices are, even if the obviously exaggerated prices are left out of account they do paint a picture wherein the cost of fresh fish was no negligible portion of a day's wage. Such prices had to accommodate risk, scarcity, and volatility as well as profit-seeking: it is wholly understandable that the fishmongers had to maximise their profits by charging whatever the market would bear as it fluctuated from hour to hour.

This is therefore the moment where a third voice, that of the collective community, also needs to be heard. For us Aristonikos is its *persona*, and he is now himself well enough attested[41] for a tentative picture of his position and priorities to emerge, against which the activity credited to him in Alexis' F130 and 131 can be assessed. Since there is no serious doubt about attributions, the evidence can be presented as a narrative. His father was almost certainly the Aristoteles of Marathon (*PAA* 3.174 985) who is known as the proposer of the 'charter' of the second Athenian alliance in March 377 (RO 22.7) and of a second related decree (RO 22.91), being then appointed to a three-man embassy which was to go to Thebes (RO 22.76). Aristonikos himself first appears forty years later in 335/4, responsible – via an unparalleled joint proposal with Lukourgos of Boutadai – for a decree despatching a naval expedition against pirates (*IG* 2^2.1623.276-285), and responsible *c.* 335-330 on behalf of the panel of *nomothetai* (law commissioners) for a law specifying how the income from an area called the Nea was to be used to finance the Lesser Panathenaia (RO 81 = *IG* 2^3.447). He is then lost to sight until an unknown person commissioned a speech from Deinarchos

---

[40] Such a curve represents, for any given individual, the balance of preference between two goods.

[41] *PAA* 3.174 070, with 3.173 950: M. H. Hansen, *The Athenian Ecclesia*, II (Copenhagen 1989) 37.

with which to prosecute him 'about the monies from Harpalos',[42] probably in spring 323, but he is recorded a year later as having himself 'denounced' a warship,[43] interestingly called *Aristonikē*: the precise background of the action within the context of the Lamian War is indecipherable. Yet by the autumn of that year (322), evidently as one of the leaders of Athens' bid to regain her independence, he had fled to Aigina to escape a death penalty voted through by the Assembly: in vain, for he was hunted down and killed in revenge by the Makedonians.[44]

That he is also the Aristonikos of Alexis' *Lebēs* has been generally accepted since Lewis's first publication[45] of what is now *IG* 2³.447, even though no evidence yet supports Alexis' description 'wealthy' (*plousios*) for him (but there is no other obvious alternative candidate). On that basis, his intervention calls for an explanation. The key plainly lies in the ascribed motive, 'so that in alarm they are content to sell for a just price'. It is unfortunate that the acceptability of the text of the line has been impugned (see note 2 above), but no matter whether ἀγαπῶσιν in the transmitted text is emended or not, the critical words τῆς ἀξίας (*sc.* τιμῆς) unmistakably reflect some idea of 'a just price'. Once translated thus, the phrase has both echoes and pre-echoes, unfortunately not explored by Arnott 1996, which need to be identified. Admittedly, this is not the place to explore its mediaeval and later resonances,[46] illuminating though they also are for the overall topic of the present volume, but rather to consider why a seasoned politician (as we may fairly view Aristonikos) should seek to apply it to the fish trade.

Three possible answers offer themselves. The first, as noted above, lay in the register of straightforward practicality: the idea behind the phrase could have been adopted in order to respond to what may have been a period of scarcity in the 320s by applying to another life-or-death commodity, fish, the model of the heavily regulated grain trade that was familiar to all inhabitants of Attika. A second possible answer stemmed from political populism, in that it might give the appearance of curbing the conspicous consumption of the gourmets and the politically unsound, at least marginally. The initiative would thereby allow Aristonikos to identify himself with all those who shared the attitudes that are reflected by the comic poets and were no doubt also shared by all those who for whatever reason felt themselves to be the victims of the tactics practised by the traders in the fish market.

A third possible answer, however, would bring in a fourth voice. The idea could have been adopted, at least in part, in order to apply in a previously unregulated area of exchange the set of analyses of, and attitudes towards, exchange that runs through much of Book 1 of Aristotle's *Politics*. This is obviously not to claim Aristonikos as a previously unrecognized pupil of Aristotle, for in the light of his prominent activity in the mid-330s he is very unlikely to have been born after 370, but at most to canvass the possibility that he was indirectly open to ideas that emanated from what was becoming the Lukeion after 335. Two comments are however appropriate. The first is to recall the long-standing observation[47]

---

[42] Known only from the list in Dion. Hal. *Dein.* 10.654.

[43] *IG* 2².1631.169-70 and 1632.189-90, with A. R. W. Harrison, *The law of Athens: procedure* (Oxford 1971) 218-21 for the *phasis*-procedure.

[44] Plut. *Dem.* 28.4; Arrian, *FGrHist* 156 F 9.13-14; Loukian, 58 (*Dem. Enkomion*) 31.

[45] D. M. Lewis, 'Law on the Lesser Panathenaia', *Hesperia* 28 (1959) 239-47 with Pl. 43, at 241.

[46] Detailed exposition in R. de Roover, 'The concept of the just price: theory and economic policy', *Journal of Economic History* 18 (1958) 418-34, with comments by J. A. Raftis and D. Herlihy in the same volume, 435-38.

[47] W. L. Newman, *The Politics of Aristotle*, I-IV (Oxford 1887-1902) II, 196-98, also reporting (though rejecting) a suggestion that 1. 11 had a different authorship.

that the set is not internally consistent. One the one hand, sections 1. 8-10, 1256a1-1258b4, make a clear distinction between household management (*oikonomia*) and the art of gaining resources (*khrēmatistikē*). The most explicit and pertinent passage states:

Διὸ κατὰ φύσιν ἐστὶν ἡ χρηματιστικὴ πᾶσιν ἀπὸ τῶν καρπῶν καὶ τῶν ζῴων. διπλῆς δ᾽οὔσης αὐτῆς, ὥσπερ εἴπομεν, καὶ τῆς μὲν καπηλικῆς τῆς δ᾽ οἰκονομικῆς, καὶ ταύτης μὲν ἀναγκαίας καὶ ἐπαινουμένης, τῆς δὲ μεταβλητικῆς ψεγομένης δικαίως (οὐ γὰρ κατὰ φύσιν ἀλλ᾽ ἀπ᾽ ἀλλήλων ἐστίν), εὐλογώτατα μισεῖται ἡ ὀβολοστατικὴ διὰ τὸ ἀπ᾽ αὐτοῦ τοῦ νομίσματος εἶναι τὴν κτῆσιν καὶ οὐκ ἐφ᾽ ὅπερ ἐπορίσθη.

Hence the art of gaining resources (*khrēmatistikē*) in accordance with nature is in all cases from crops and animals. Since it is then of two kinds, as we have said – that concerned with household management (*oikonomikē*) being necessary and praiseworthy, while that concerned with trading (*kapēlikē*) is a method of exchange (*metablētikē*) which is rightly viewed with disapproval, since it [*i.e.* the gain which it brings] is not in accordance with nature but is at the expense of others – petty usury (*obolostatikē*) is very reasonably loathed, because the gain comes from the currency itself, not for the purpose for which it was provided (1258a38-b4).

On the other hand, section 1. 11, especially 1258b12-33, makes a tripartite division of *khrēmatistikē*, takes a far more equable view of the activities which it encompasses, and comes close (at 1258b23-25) to recognising the trade-off between security and profitability. Neither version, moreover, broaches the issue of price-fluctuation which Aristonikos' proposed law sought to address.

Yet there is one respect in which Aristotle's discussion is pertinent. The passage at 1258a38-b4 just cited runs together two separate activities, trading and petty usury, both in terms of the attitude adopted towards them (which Aristotle takes for granted as being one of moral disapproval) and in terms of the reasoning behind that attitude. In the light of the structural role played in at least some retailing activities by Theophrastos' ἀπονενοημένος as quoted above, Aristotle's amalgamation is understandable, but is economically illiterate in its failure to isolate and to acknowledge either of the two distinct but mutually supportive elements of utility that are provided respectively (1) by the provision of working capital on the part of the ἀπονενοημένος (indeed this is explicitly excluded) and (2) by the time and effort expended by the fishmonger in manning his stall (for a price) in a convenient central place.

The contrast is fundamental. On the one hand, in order to satisfy what had become a substantial and steady demand for a specific commodity, the men and women who got a living from one or other of the various stages of bringing fish from sea to market had devised a practical system of a chain of exchanges, using whatever symbolic means of establishing value were available, which achieved the objective of satisfying the demand. Comparable systems had been developed by all those who were in the businesses of providing other commodities and services, whether tangible or intangible, cheap or costly, brought from a long distance[48] or from close at hand. The 'market', both physically and theoretically, had become a reality of everyday exchanges. On the other hand, by their use

---

[48] The supply of aromatics, explored in J. K. Davies, 'Towards a general model of long-distance trade: aromatics as a case-study', in *The ancient Greek economy: markets, households and city states*, (n.34, above) 299-315, is an extreme case.

of a brutally pejorative terminology – ἀπονενοημένος ('wilfully disreputable'), ψεγομένης ('viewed with disapproval'), μισεῖται ('loathed') – Theophrastos and Aristotle between them were delegitimating the very activities on which they and their fellow inhabitants of Attika depended: and they were presumably not alone in harboring such views.

In this way what began as a curiosity-driven exploration of two fragments of Alexis has turned into a study of a relationship between attitude and reality within Athenian society wherein it is hard not to diagnose a severe cognitive dissonance. The difficulty is to locate it. It does not coincide with the boundary between citizen and non-citizen – far from it – , still less with that between slave and free. Nor does it coincide with the fuzzy and permeable boundary between the leisure class and the poor, for if my work of fifty years ago proved anything,[49] it was that many of the leisure class were active and energetic participants both in estate- and household-based gainful activity[50] and in this or that component of a chain of commodity provision such as grain or silver bullion: such men had as little inhibition as a fishmonger about maximising profits.[51] Far more plausibly, we should follow the lead of the comic poets themselves and locate the dissonance within the generality of the population itself, obliged against its will to negotiate with the providers of an essential commodity who held the better cards if they played them properly. One can well understand that such a situation combined well enough with the two other considerations sketched above to offer a politician of the 320s a solid basis of action. All the same, we have no idea whether the proposed law was ever enacted, and the record of such laws across the spectrum of the Greek states is very limited.[52] It looks as if for the most part realism prevailed over irritation.

Additional Note:

Theophrastos' text does not specify whether the *aponenoēmenos* was lending his own capital or was acting as agent (for a cut of the profits, naturally) for a lender whose investment captial he was managing. If the latter, one may perhaps look towards the practice of lending 'by 200s and 300s' which Demosthenes reports of his father in the 370s (Dem. 27.11). Sums of such a size might reasonably serve to provide a fishmonger with the float that allowed him to buy in a day's stock.

University of Liverpool

---

[49] Davies, *Athenian propertied families* (n.18, above); id., *Wealth and the power of wealth in Classical Athens* (New York 1981).

[50] The key words are *auxēsis* ('increase', a *leitmotif* of the later pages of Xenophon's *Oikonomikos*) and *kerdos* ('profit'). Other, complementary, pressures to maximize disposable income are explored by R. J. Osborne, 'Pride and prejudice, sense and subsistence: exchange and society in the Greek city', in *City and country in the ancient world*, eds J. Rich and A. Wallace-Hadrill (London and New York 1991) 119-45.

[51] A range of case-studies that illustrate the point is assembled in P. Cartledge *et al.*, *Money, labour, and land. Approaches to the economies of ancient Greece* (London and New York 2002).

[52] Migeotte, 'Contrôle des prix' (n.6, above); Bresson, *Cité marchande* (n.6, above) 151-82.

WEALTH AND MONOPOLY
IN THE CLASSICAL GREEK *POLIS*

ERRIETTA M. A. BISSA

Any reflection on wealth involves some engagement with how it is distributed and controlled, and on the aspects of those processes that are dysfunctional or controversial. Monopolies – whether imposed and managed by the state, or created by the ingenuity and ruthlessness of individual market players – are a distinctive form of wealth concentration, which has a set of very significant consequences on wider economic dynamics, and has often polarised the debate: they are a threat to the very existence of a stable and effective market for some, a necessary compensation force for others. It is not surprising, therefore, that the role of monopolies in the archaic and classical Greek world has received considerable attention over the last century of scholarship on the ancient economy.[1] Old modernism was quick to find monopolies, even where they did not exist, such as, for example, in Sutherland's argument on an Aeginetan monopoly of grain and coin in Egypt in the archaic period.[2] That kind of inquiry into the Greek economy has now been laid to rest, mainly due to Finley's powerful riposte to Sutherland.[3] Yet, the debate on the ancient economy is strikingly prone to strong overcompensations when a scholarly consensus comes to an end: the debate on monopolies is no exception, and is in fact an instructive case in point. Once the Heichelheim/ Sutherland paradigm came to a crisis, scholarship went to the opposite extreme, as Finley in his seminal statement in *The ancient economy* showed clearly: 'All ancient states retained at least regalia rights over mineral resources. Beyond that, monopolies in the Greek city-states were rare emergency measures'.[4]

Indeed, for the study of the economy in the classical Greek world, monopolies have essentially become absent from the scholarly debate. That is not true, of course, for the study of the Hellenistic economies, or indeed of the Roman one, where it is accepted that both kings and emperors employed a range of monopolies.[5] Even there, however, an important

[1] F. Heichelheim, 'Monopole', *RE* 16 147-99; A. Andreades, 'De l'origine des monopoles ptolémaiques', *Mélanges Maspero* 2 (1935-1937) 289-95; C. H. V. Sutherland, 'Corn and Coin: A note on Greek commercial monopolies', *American Journal of Philology* 64 (1943) 129-47; M. I. Finley, 'Classical Greece', in *Deuxième Conférence internationale d'Histoire Économique* (Paris 1965) 11-35; V. Gabrielsen, 'Profitable Partnerships: Monopolies, Traders, Kings and Cities', in *The economies of Hellenistic societies, third to first centuries BCE*, eds Z. H. Archibald, J. K. Davies and V. Gabrielsen (Oxford 2011) 216-50.

[2] Sutherland, 'Corn and Coin' (n.1, above) 129-47.

[3] Finley, 'Classical Greece' (n.1, above) 21.

[4] M. I. Finley, *The ancient economy* (London 1985²) 165.

[5] See Gabrielsen, 'Profitable Partnerships' (n.1, above) on Hellenistic monopolies outside Egypt.

proviso was inserted: Finley, and many scholars after him, saw only fiscal motives in the institution of monopolies.[6]

In the simplest of terms, the current orthodoxy on monopolies in the classical Greek world rests on two assumptions: firstly, that monopolies were rare and emergency measures and, secondly, that the motives and aims for instituting monopolies were strictly fiscal.

The purpose of this paper is to concentrate on the available evidence for monopolies in the classical Greek world under three specific inquiries:

1.   Were monopolies rare emergency measures?
2.   Did they have only fiscal motives?
3.   Are there differences in the usage of monopolies between different polities in the Greek world?

Before continuing to examine the evidence on monopolies in the Greek world, it is essential to make some notes regarding monopolies and their understanding in both the ancient and the modern world. Scholarship suffers from an incomplete definition of monopoly. In modern economics, it is still a lamentable fact that there is no clear and specific definition of monopoly, as different theoretical standpoints have coined their own definitions of the term.[7] Modern works have concentrated on the monopoly of firms (or businesses), but some theorists, particularly of the Austrian school of economics, have specifically defined monopoly as an arrangement created by the state.[8] For the Greeks, as Aristotle pointed out,[9] monopoly was understood in its wider definition of 'an enterprise that is the only seller of a good or service',[10] including when the 'seller' is the state itself.

Further, and most importantly, monopolies are considered an inefficient method of dealing with resource allocation, as they essentially eliminate competition and hence do not allow the market to create the best deal for the consumer.[11] The nationalization of industries, which is the commonest type of state monopoly in the modern world, is considered to be adverse to a healthy (*i.e.* capitalist) economy and a free (*i.e.* competition-driven) market. At the same time, it is generally accepted that the ownership of some resources, such as oil, belongs to the state as part of the sovereign rights over nationally held territory. This corresponds with the situation in the Greek world, where 'special products' were considered to be under the ownership of the state. Whether this ownership translates into monopoly depends upon whether a state has control of the production of the resource – usually through a state-owned company – or allows control to be exercised by a number of private companies under specific legal terms and conditions. There are definite similarities with the Greek world, where there is evidence of leasing of such 'state' resources to private concerns, such as the leases of the Laurion mines in classical Athens.

For the purposes of this paper, cases where the state retains sovereign rights but lets the production and marketing of a resource to competitive private enterprise are not considered

---

[6] Finley, *Ancient economy* (n.4, above) 165.

[7] M. Rothbard, *Man, economy, and state with power and market* (Auburn 2009) 1143.

[8] Rothbard, *Man, economy, and state* (n.7, above) 661-71.

[9] Arist. *Pol.* 1259a, 18-23.

[10] G. J. Stigler, 'Monopoly', in *The Concise Encyclopedia of Economics*, ed. D. R. Henderson, Liberty Fund, Inc. Library of Economics and Liberty (2008), available online from http://www.econlib.org/library/Enc/Monopoly. html; accessed 8 September 2014.

[11] Rothbard, *Man, economy, and state* (n.7, above) 629-754.

monopolies. On the other hand, if a state takes over a resource when it has already been in private hands and within a competitive environment, that is considered an institution of a monopolistic arrangement.[12]

Before examining the evidence for state monopolies, it is necessary to discuss what the evidence on 'single-firm' monopolies in the Greek world is, and how these were perceived by the Greeks themselves. The most important piece of evidence for the Greeks' understanding of monopoly comes from Aristotle's *Politics* and is the obvious basis of the modern orthodoxy on the matter. Aristotle is clear on the use of monopolies by both states and individuals:

> Thales then is reported to have thus displayed his wisdom, but as a matter of fact this device of taking an opportunity to secure a monopoly is a universal principle of business; hence even some states have recourse to this plan as a method of raising revenue when short of funds: they introduce a monopoly of marketable goods.[13]

Aristotle makes a clear and unproblematic distinction between monopolies instituted by the state and monopolies, or near-monopolies, achieved by individual businessmen. Indeed, both of the examples given in the *Politics* are those of individual businessmen. The first is the familiar story of Thales of Miletos, one of the Seven Sages and a pre-Socratic philosopher, who endeavoured to achieve a monopoly over olive-presses in his native Miletos and nearby Chios. Thales was successful, although his apparent motive, according to Aristotle, was not to acquire profit, but rather to prove that philosophy enabled one to be successful in other walks of life.[14] The second is that of a nameless individual in Sicily in the first half of the fourth century, who achieved a monopoly over iron on the island, or at least the area around Syracuse. His motive was merely to generate profit.[15]

The second example is considerably more interesting than the first one in relation to the Greeks' view of monopoly, and particularly the state's view of individual businessmen achieving monopoly. The state, *i.e.* the tyrant Dionysios,[16] quickly stopped that monopoly of iron and exiled the businessman because, in the words of Aristotle, 'he was inventing means of profit detrimental to the tyrant's own affairs'.[17] Aristotle portrays monopoly as something that any private businessman strives to achieve and as a measure that a state in

---

[12] On such sheltered monopoly arrangements, see Gabrielsen 'Profitable Partnerships' (n.1, above) at 221, 225.

[13] Arist. *Pol.* 1259a, 18-23 (trans. Rackham): Θαλῆς μὲν οὖν λέγεται τοῦτον τὸν τρόπον ἐπίδειξιν ποιήσασθαι τῆς σοφίας· ἔστι δ', ὥσπερ εἴπομεν, καθόλου τὸ τοιοῦτον χρηματιστικόν, ἐάν τις δύνηται μονοπωλίαν αὑτῷ κατασκευάζειν. διὸ καὶ τῶν πόλεων ἔνιαι τοῦτον ποιοῦνται τὸν πόρον, ὅταν ἀπορῶσι χρημάτων· μονοπωλίαν γὰρ τῶν ὠνίων ποιοῦσιν.

[14] Arist. *Pol.* 1259a, 16-18. *Cf.* Cic. *Div.* 1.111, with D. Wardle, *Cicero: On Divination. Book I* (Oxford 2006) 376-78.

[15] Arist. *Pol.* 1259a, 23-31.

[16] Whether it is Dionysios I or II is uncertain: P. L. P. Simpson, *A Philosophical Commentary on the Politics of Aristotle* (London 1998) 62.

[17] Arist. *Pol.* 1259a, 30-31 (trans. Rackham): ὡς πόρους εὑρίσκοντα τοῖς αὑτοῦ πράγμασιν ἀσυμφόρους.

trouble can use to get more revenue. At the same time, however, he also makes clear that the state did not approve of the institution of private monopolies.

Aristotle's subsequent remarks in the *Politics* clearly place monopolies within the greater discussion of wealth, for both states and individuals, in the classical world:

> Yet really this device is the same as the discovery of Thales, for both men alike contrived to secure themselves a monopoly. An acquaintance with these devices is also serviceable for statesmen, for many states need financial aid and modes of revenue like those described, just as a household may, but in greater degree; hence some statesmen even devote their political activity exclusively to finance.[18]

Therefore, for Aristotle monopolies are an essential goal of all who engage in business, or in the acquisition of wealth, including states. Interestingly, in this passage monopolies and other devices for securing revenue are not exclusively connected with times of need, but more widely with the generation of revenue for states, individuals, and households. Questions arise about the financial and moral position of monopolies, state and otherwise, in classical Greek thought. Both of Aristotle's examples of private monopolies are classic examples of the modern fears of monopolistic arrangements, as they constrict choice and competition, and generate wealth for individuals while increasing prices for the public, hence in modern economic thought reducing the aggregate economic welfare of the society in question. A tyranny is not the best representative of the Greek states, but there is evidence to suggest that monopolistic arrangements put in place by individuals were not allowed in other polities and constitutions. Athens had clearly instituted anti-cartel laws regarding the sale of grain.[19] At the same time, states do institute favoured-status arrangements both with other states and with traders, whether operating individually or in groups.[20]

Most of the surviving examples of monopolies are instituted by states, rather than individuals. This relates to both the nature of our sources (particularly the pseudo-Aristotelian *Oeconomica*) and the apparent fact that Greek states did not approve of private monopolistic arrangements.[21]

These monopolies may be listed as follows:

1.   Due to financial problems, Byzantion institutes a monopoly over the fisheries and the trade in salt. This is a case of legislative intervention and there is no

---

[18] Arist. *Pol.* 1259a, 31-36 (trans. Rackham): τὸ μέντοι ὅραμα Θάλεω καὶ τοῦτο ταὐτόν ἐστιν·ἀμφότεροι γὰρ ἑαυτοῖς ἐτέχνασαν γενέσθαι μονοπωλίαν. Χρήσιμον δὲ γνωρίζειν ταῦτα καὶ τοῖς πολιτικοῖς. Πολλαῖς γὰρ πόλεσι δεῖ χρηματισμοῦ καὶ τοιούτων πόρων, ὥσπερ οἰκία, μᾶλλον δέ· διόπερ τινὲς καὶ πολιτεύονται τῶν πολιτευομένων ταῦτα μόνον.

[19] Lys. 22.5-6; D. M. McDowell, *The law in classical Athens* (London 1978) 157; R. Seager, 'Lysias against the Corndealers', *Historia* 15 (1966) 172-84; T. Figueira, '*Sitopolai* and *sitophylakes* in Lysias' *Against the Graindealers*: governmental intervention in the Athenian economy', *Phoenix* 40 (1986) 149-71.

[20] On grants of *ateleia* to traders as a favoured-status institution and its relationship to monopoly, see Gabrielsen 'Profitable Partnerships' (n.1, above) 235-40. On the Spartokids of the Bosporan Kingdom instituting 'favoured-nation' status for some of their grain-trading partners, such as Athens and Mytilene, see E. M. A. Bissa, *Governmental intervention in foreign trade in Archaic and Classical Greece* (Leiden and Boston 2009) 160-63.

[21] The *Oeconomica* is widely regarded as a work of the Peripatos and generally dated to the last quarter of the fourth century BCE: B. A. van Groningen and A. Wartelle, *Aristote. Économique* (Paris 1968) 42-44; K. Brodersen, *77 Tricks zur Steigerung der Staatseinnahmen: Oikonomika* II (Stuttgart 2006) 12-15.

mention of it being a temporary measure ([Aristotle] *Oeconomica* 1346b, 19-26);

2.   Due to financial problems, Byzantion gives monopoly of coinage exchange to one bank. This is a case of legislation and there is no mention of it being a temporary measure ([Aristotle] *Oeconomica* 1346b, 19-26);

3.   Due to financial problems, Herakleia (Pontike) buys up all produce from the market and monopolizes its sale to the troops. This case applies only to the market for the specific troop deployment ([Aristotle] *Oeconomica* 1347b, 3-15);

4.   Due to famine and financial problems, Klazomenai buys up all stores of oil and uses it as security to buy grain. This case is a one-off emergency measure ([Aristotle] *Oeconomica* 1348b, 17-22);

5.   Due to financial problems, Selymbria buys up all stores of grain at a fixed price and gives right to export to any trader. This appears to be a one-off emergency measure, since the original legislation that forbade the export of grain seems to have been retained ([Aristotle] *Oeconomica* 1348b, 33-36);

6.   Kleomenes of Egypt buys up all grain from producers and sells it at a fixed price. This is a case of a monopoly institution taking advantage of the adverse conditions of the 320s famine ([Aristotle] *Oeconomica* 1352b, 14-20 and Demosthenes 56);

7.   Pythocles proposes that the Athenian state institutes a monopoly of lead. There is no indication that this proposal was ever enacted ([Aristotle] *Oeconomica* 1353a, 15-18);

8.   Perdikkas of Macedon gives exclusive rights to the import of oars to Athens. This is a case of a permanent measure in a bilateral agreement; however, it probably lasted only until Perdikkas' subsequent change of policy towards Athens (*IG* 1³.89);

9.   Athens imposes a monopoly of import of *miltos* on the *poleis* of Keos. This appears to have been a permanent measure (*IG* 2².1128);

10.   Macedon employs a royal monopoly on the production and export of timber. This appears to have been a permanent measure (Andocides 2.11);[22]

11.   Cyprus employs a royal monopoly on the production, and possibly export, of timber. This appears to be a permanent measure (Theophrastos, *Historia Plantarum* 5.8.1.11-13);

12.   Philip II of Macedon institutes a royal monopoly over the gold from the Pangaion region. This appears to be a permanent measure (Diodoros 16.8.6-7);[23]

13.   Cyrene institutes a royal monopoly over silphium (Aristotle, *Fragmenta Varia* 8.44.528).

Before considering these monopolies further, it is necessary to note a preliminary division among them. Some of the instances of monopoly discussed above conform to the Aristotelian statement regarding monopolizing marketable goods in case of emergency, such as those of Herakleia, Selymbria, and Klazomenai. The vast majority, however,

---

[22] For the monopoly arrangement, see Bissa, *Governmental intervention* (n.20, above) 112-13.

[23] For the direct (*i.e.* state) exploitation of the Pangaion mines by Philip II, see Bissa, *Governmental intervention* (n.20, above) 37-38.

consists of monopolies of specific commodities, which all fall under the category of 'special products of the country' (πρόσοδος ἡ ἀπὸ τῶν ἰδίων ἐν τῇ χώρᾳ γινομένη) in the breakdown of state revenues given by the pseudo-Aristotelian *Oeconomica*.[24] In this respect, Finley's statement regarding monopolistic and regalia rights needs to be amended to include all 'special products', such as timber and silphium, rather than merely metals and minerals, depending on the specific circumstances of any individual *polis* or polity. The case of the Byzantine saltpans and fisheries shows that 'special products' could be under private control (and indeed *de facto* ownership) until the state decided to declare its ownership of them.[25] Pythocles' proposal to bring lead under state control at Athens does also indicate that products could be redefined as 'special', and, thus, be deemed of direct interest to a state.

There are therefore three main categories of monopolies instituted by states in the classical period:

A.   temporary measures instituted because of emergency conditions;
B.   permanent measures instituted because of emergency conditions;
C.   permanent measures not connected to an emergency.

The monopolies of Byzantion, Herakleia, Klazomenai, Selymbria, and possibly that of Kleomenes of Egypt fall under categories A and B, while the rest of the monopolies come under category C.

There is a clear distinction to be made between the examples of monopoly provided by the sources. The pseudo-Aristotelian *Oeconomica* provides all the cases of Types A and B, in other words the monopolies connected to emergencies, mainly of a fiscal nature. Indeed the vast majority of examples given in the second book of the *Oeconomica* are related to emergencies. There are two explanations for this phenomenon: either the majority of measures taken by Greek *poleis* were due to emergencies, or the author of the *Oeconomica* preferred examples of measures to shore up the finances of a state in case of emergency. The answer is of course given by the author himself earlier in the same work:

> Having spoken thus of administrations and their various departments, we have further proceeded to collect such instances as we deemed noteworthy of the means adopted by certain statesmen in times past for the replenishment of the treasury, and also of their skill in administration. These anecdotes <which follow> seemed to us by no means lacking in utility; being capable from time to time of application by others to the business they themselves have in hand.[26]

It is clear from the introduction to these case studies that the author of the *Oeconomica* intended these as examples of what statesmen of the past did in cases of emergency, and/

---

[24] [Arist.] *Oeconomica* 1346a, 6-9 and 1345b, 33-35.

[25] C. Carusi, 'Régimes d'exploitation et fiscalité du sel dans le monde grec et romain', in *Las salinas y la sal de interior en la historia. Economía, medio ambiente y sociedad*, I, ed. N. Morère Molinero (Madrid 2007) 325-42, at 331 points out that salt was a 'marchandise vraiment stratégique' at Byzantion, because of the importance that fishing, curing fish, and transhipping of cured products from the Black Sea had to the economy of the city; see also *ead.*, *Il sale nel mondo greco (VI a.C.-III d.C.). Luoghi di produzione, circolazione commerciale, regimi di sfruttamento nel contesto del Mediterraneo antico* (Bari 2008) 77-79, 178-80, 199, 251.

[26] [Arist.] *Oeconomica* 1346a, 25-31 (trans. Armstrong): Τὰ μὲν οὖν περὶ τὰς οἰκονομίας τε καὶ τὰ μέρη τὰ τούτων εἰρήκαμεν· ὅσα δέ τινες τῶν πρότερον πεπράγασιν εἰς πόρον χρημάτων, εἴ <τε> τεχνικῶς τι διῴκησαν, ἃ

or insufficient funds. After all, monopoly cases aside, most of the examples, particularly of tyrannical money-grabbing, involve an element of deception and had no potential of being utilized more than once. Thus, it is unsurprising that the examples provided in cases of monopoly institutions are connected with emergencies, and many of them are only temporary.

So, in regards to the first question posed in this paper – whether monopolies were rare and emergency measures in the classical Greek *polis* – the answer is more dependent upon the accidents of survival than appears to be the case at first glance. Monopolies were not common as far as can be deduced from the evidence; yet, they were not rare either: a number of examples are attested, even if one excludes those mentioned in the *Oeconomica*. Secondly, not all known monopolies were instituted in response to emergencies; on the contrary, all monopolies known from sources other than the *Oeconomica* were permanent measures that appear not to have been connected to any discernible emergency.

The second question posed had to do with the motivation and aims that inform the creation of monopolies in the classical Greek *polis*. Once again, the answer is more complicated than appears at first sight. Of the monopolies that were related to emergencies, all appear to conform to the rule provided by the orthodoxy. Thus they appear to have had the express aim of providing fiscal relief to the state.

The monopolies of type C (permanent and not connected to an emergency), however, appear to have been motivated by more than merely fiscal considerations. Some certainly addressed mainly fiscal concerns, such as Pythokles' suggestion to the Athenian assembly. Similarly, Kleomenes' monopoly on Egyptian grain, if it belongs to category C rather than B, appears to have had almost exclusively fiscal motives. The same is true of the Byzantine imposition of monopolies, which is explicitly connected to fiscal problems.[27]

Others, however, appear to have been driven by other factors, in addition to increasing the revenues of the state. Thus, Perdikkas' monopoly arrangements with Athens regarding oars certainly had political, rather than fiscal, motives. Similarly, Athens' imposition of a monopoly on Kean *miltos* had motives other than fiscal. The exact usage of *miltos* has been debated in modern scholarship,[28] but if there was some military usage, possibly in the navy, then the motives and aims of Athens were not primarily fiscal. If it did not, however, it is still possible that the Athenian motives were mainly political: in other words the imposition of monopoly is an Athenian effort to dominate the *poleis* of Keos. The Macedonian and Cypriot timber monopolies were certainly motivated by more than fiscal concerns, since timber was a husbandable commodity; at least Theophrastos makes that point clearly for the Cypriot situation.[29] The kings of Macedon probably had a similar policy, since they retained their monopoly of production, even when they gave up rights to their monopolies of export, as they did with oars for Athens and timber in general for the Chalcidian League.

In the Finleyan view of Greek economy, monopolies are part of the set of tools to which the state may resort in order to 'encourage enterprise', along with patents, charters,

---

ὑπελαμβάνομεν ἀξιόλογα αὐτῶν εἶναι, συναγηόχαμεν. Οὐδὲ γὰρ ταύτην τὴν ἱστορίαν ἀχρεῖον ὑπολαμβάνομεν εἶναι. Ἔστι γὰρ ὅτε τούτων ἐφαρμόσει τι οἷς ἂν αὐτὸς πραγματεύῃ.

[27] [Arist.] *Oeconomica* 1346b, 14. See Carusi, *Il sale nel mondo greco* (n.25, above) 197-98.

[28] See *e.g.* E. Photos-Jones, A. Cottier, A. J. Hall and L. G. Mendoni, 'Kean miltos: The well-known iron oxides of antiquity', *The Annual of the British School at Athens* 92 (1997) 359-71, at 359; C. M. Reed, *Maritime traders in the ancient Greek world* (Cambridge 2003) 46-47; T. Katsaros, 'The redness of Ulysses' ships', in *Science and technology in Homeric epics*, ed. S. A. Paipetis (Dordrecht 2008) 385-89.

[29] Theophr. *Hist. Plant.* 5.8.1.

and subsidies.[30] Yet, a comparative approach may offer instructive suggestions: in the modern world, monopolies are used for other purposes, such as building safeguards against overexploitation, defending against market saturation, and providing revenues for states. The same is true of patents, charters and subsidies. In the simplest of terms, like modern monopolies, the monopolies instituted and imposed by classical Greek states were put in place for a variety of reasons, not all of them relating to increasing revenues in times of emergency, although that probably was a consideration then as it is now.

Therefore, the answer to the second question posed at the outset of the present discussion – whether monopolies have only fiscal aims – is dependent on the monopoly, the polity, and the situation in which the monopoly was instituted.

The third question posed in this paper was whether the apparent usage of monopolies changed according to type of polity. In the first instance, there appears to have been a clear difference between kingdoms and *poleis*. Kingdoms, such as Macedon and the Cypriot kings, had a greater tendency to institute monopolies, both of production and export, than their contemporary *poleis*. In this respect, the Greek kingdoms appear to have followed a policy system that was similar to that of the Eastern monarchies, such as those of the kings of Lydia and Assyria, as well as the Persian kings.[31] The pro-monopoly policy of the oriental and Greek kingdoms was probably later translated into the extensive use of monopolies by the Hellenistic kings.

However, a closer look at the evidence shows that some *poleis,* such as Athens, had both the capability and the political will to institute, or consider instituting, monopolies in the classical period, or at least the fourth century. Different explanations may be invoked for Athens' budding tendencies towards monopoly. They may have been a product of the influence that the use of monopolies by other polities in the Greek world in the same period had at Athens, or merely a consequence of empire on Athenian views and actions. The cases of Keos and Perdikkas' oars are strong indications of the latter possibility. It is important to note that these monopolistic arrangements on the part of Athens are imposed upon other polities: thus they are beneficial to both the Athenian public purse and private enterprise in Athens, as the supply of a commodity is secured in the medium-long term, effectively avoiding competition in the regional markets.

Even more interestingly, it appears that in some cases of emergency-generated monopolies the monopoly is rendered permanent rather than temporary, probably as a long-term measure to increase state revenue. In the same vein, the fact that monopolies belonging to category C are exclusively monopolies of 'special products' shows that, in spite of Aristotle's assertion on the usage of monopolies by states in emergencies, permanent monopolies were restricted to products that were rare or had a definite market outside the *polis*.

A clear difference between kingdoms and *poleis* is of course that kingdoms appear to have been willing to create all-inclusive monopolies without opening up any part of the process to private enterprise, such as the Cypriot monopoly on timber or Philip's monopoly of both the exploitation and usage of Pangaion gold. This would normally conform more closely to

---

[30] Finley, *Ancient economy* (n.4, above) 165.

[31] Lydia: Hdt. 1.69. Persia: Hdt. 6.119 (naptha fields Susiana); G. Posener, *La première domination perse en Égypte* (Cairo 1936) 179-80; G. Goyon, *Nouvelles inscriptions rupestres du Wadi Hammamat* (Paris 1957) 1-9, 128-30 (Waddi Hammurat stone quarries). Persepolis Tablet 52: G. G. Cameron, *Persepolis treasury tablets* (Chicago 1948) 166 (Niriz iron mines). Assyria (Sargon II): *The Correspondence of Sargon II, Part I State Archives of Assyria Vol. I*, ed. S. Parpola (Helsinki 1987) no. 98; *The Correspondence of Sargon II, Part II State Archives of Assyria Vol. V*, eds G. B. Lanfranchi and S. Parpola (Helsinki 1990) 166 (timber at Urartu and Subria). See Bissa, *Governmental intervention* (n.20, above) 45-47.

the modern notion of a nationalized industry. Monopolies in *poleis*, on the contrary, go hand in hand with private enterprise, mainly through the inclusion of private entrepreneurs in the state's monopoly arrangements by direct or bid-based leasing. This is true of the leasing out of coinage exchange in Byzantion and the use of private ships for Kean *miltos*.

This tendency of the *polis* to allow private enterprise a pivotal role in its monopoly operations agrees with the tendency of *poleis* to crack down immediately on the creation of private monopolies or cartels, as can be seen by Dionysios' reaction to the private iron monopoly mentioned in Aristotle[32] and Athens' own anti-cartel laws regarding the sale of grain.[33] The dislike of the classical *polis* for private monopoly can be mirrored in the indignant fury of the private traders towards the institution of monopolies by other polities, as seen in the Athenian reaction towards Kleomenes' institution of a monopoly of grain in Egypt.[34] To be sure, there is an element of hypocrisy, as Gabrielsen rightly notes, in such reaction to monopolies, as states and communities are sensitive to monopolies that disadvantage them, while being perfectly happy to accept monopolies that put them in a favourable position.[35] However, the choice of a *polis* to assign a role in state monopoly to a private enterprise does not only show the positive effects that the institution of a monopoly could have for its citizens. It also provides relief from important practical problems. Thus, the *polis*, with its minimal and, in many cases, annually changing bureaucracy, avoided the problem of having to institute and sustain a state enterprise for its own monopoly concerns.

This brings to the fore the question of efficiency. In modern economics monopolies are considered inefficient; crucially, they are deemed inefficient in regards to the consumer, rather than the monopolist.[36] The issue of the apparent inefficiency of monopolistic arrangements when it comes to providing goods to the market with a clear understanding of consumer welfare (one of the mainstays of the modern position regarding the flaws of monopolies)[37] was understood by the Greeks, as can be seen by the accusations against the grain-dealers in Lysias, particularly in relation to the price of grain, under a supposed publicly beneficial temporary monopoly/cartel arrangement.[38] On the other hand, when it comes to state-controlled monopolies there appears to be no question of the efficiency of the mechanism. This can best be explained by two contributing factors. Firstly, the state is the monopolist and hence the creation of profit for the *polis* is to be considered of greater importance than consumer welfare on an individual basis. Secondly, and more importantly, most of the monopolies in categories B and C above relate to commodities whose main consumer base resides outside the *polis*. There is no reason to argue that the *polis* is interested in the welfare of consumers beyond its own borders. Even in cases when the monopolistic

---

[32] Arist. *Pol.* 1259a, 28-31.

[33] Lys. 22.5-6. See n.19, above.

[34] Dem. 56.7-9.

[35] Gabrielsen, 'Profitable Partnerships' (n.1, above) 230-31.

[36] Stigler, 'Monopoly' (n.10, above).

[37] A. Bergson, 'On monopoly welfare losses', *American Economic Review* 63 (1973) 853-70; K. Cowling and D. C. Mueller, 'The social costs of monopoly power', *The Economic Journal* 88 (1978) 727-48; D. R. Lee and R. D. Tollison, 'The welfare costs of monopoly are larger than you think', *Managerial and Decision Economics* 32 (2011) 85-89. The advocacy of monopoly became prominent in some circles after the influential contribution of A. C. Harberger, 'Monopoly and Resource Allocation', *American Economic Review* 45 (1954) 77-87, but even Harberger and his adherents agree that monopoly adversely affects consumer welfare; the main matter for debate is the extent of the adverse affect.

[38] Lys. 22.12.

arrangement is temporary and dictated by expediency, the targeted consumer is most often outside the *polis* itself: this is clearly noticeable in the cases of Klazomenai and Selymbria.

Lastly, while the state's income from the 'special products' of the country remained stable and indeed potentially increased, the central role that individuals and groups of investors played in state monopoly operations encouraged private enterprise. At the same time, it served to provide a strong framework against the creation of a private monopoly of the country's most important and valuable products. Hence monopolies in Greek polities in the classical period were used for the creation of wealth, both in terms of public finance and private enterprise. Given the lack of personal (*i.e.* income) taxation in Greek polities, such monopolies, which were generally connected to industries with considerable export potential, not only increased the public and private wealth of the polity, but also stopped wealth from exiting the polity's economy.

Monopolies were understood in the classical Greek world as wealth-creating devices, for states and for individuals alike. However, such creation of wealth was clearly tempered both by attempts to promote the welfare of the citizens and denizens of the state, and by efforts to protect and control products of particular significance to the state, especially in the long term.

University of Wales: Trinity St David

AGELLUS ENTRE LA PAUVRETÉ ET LA RICHESSE

JEAN ANDREAU

Dans la très bonne étude qu'il a consacrée aux gestionnaires des domaines ruraux à la fin de la République et sous le Haut Empire, Jesper Carlsen a été confronté à une inscription funéraire de l'*ager Aequicolorum*, dans le Samnium, dont l'un des dédicants était un *actor*, Hélius. Avec l'esclave femme Legas, et avec la collaboration du *collegius agellanus* (*sic*), il offrait l'inscription au défunt, un esclave lui aussi, Ianuarius.[1] Comme, dans quelques autres documents des IIe et IIIe siècles ap. J.-C., l'*actor* semble avant tout chargé du contrôle des tenanciers, tandis que le *vilicus* se rencontre davantage dans des domaines ayant une main d'œuvre servile, J. Carlsen a conclu que le *collegiu(m) agellanu(m)* était une sorte d'association des tenanciers du domaine concerné.

Plus récemment, Nicolas Tran s'est intéressé, lui aussi, à cette inscription, et il n'a pas été convaincu par cette conclusion. Certes, l'expression est un hapax, et est donc extrêmement délicate à interpréter. N. Tran s'est toutefois davantage orienté vers un sens funéraire d'*agellus*, parce que d'autres inscriptions attestent l'emploi du mot pour désigner un enclos funéraire,[2] tandis qu'il n'est jamais utilisé dans le sens de 'tenure', de 'terre en location'. Il propose donc de reconnaître dans ce *collegium agellanum* un collège à vocation notamment funéraire, et qui 'disposait d'un terrain dont la structure n'était sans doute pas très différente de celle d'un *hortus* ou d'un *hortulus*'.[3] *Agellus*, à son avis, n'est pas seulement appliqué à des réalités agraires et agricoles, mais aussi à des contextes funéraires. Il ne nie en aucune façon le sens agraire d'*agellus*, mais montre que ce n'est pas le seul emploi du mot.

*

En réfléchissant sur l'article de N. Tran, je me suis convaincu qu'*agellus* pouvait en effet désigner soit un petit champ cultivé, soit un enclos funéraire, comme il l'a écrit. Mais il m'a semblé en outre que, dans une bonne partie des textes disponibles, le mot s'appliquait aux représentations sociales de la pauvreté et de la richesse, et non point au domaine agraire et agricole proprement dit. Comme chacun sait, *agellus* est un diminutif de *ager*, qui se rencontre plus rarement qu'*ager*, mais qu'on trouve toutefois dans plusieurs dizaines de textes (environ quatre-vingts passages, si je ne me trompe pas). En tant que diminutif d'*ager*, on pourrait s'attendre à ce qu'il désigne un petit territoire, une petite terre, un

---

[1] *CIL* 9.4129 = *ILS* 7300 b. Voir J. Carlsen, *Vilici and Roman estate managers until A.D. 284* (Rome 1995) 121-42, et surtout 132-33.

[2] N. Tran mentionne trois inscriptions dans lesquelles *agellus* a le sens d'enclos funéraire, ou pourrait avoir ce sens: *CIL* 6.26259; *CIL* 5.715 (Trieste); *CIL* 10.6720 (Antium). Voir N. Tran, '*Collegius Agellanus*: Désignation collégiale et espace communautaire sur une épitaphe de l'*Ager Aequiculorum*', *Cahiers du Centre Gustave Glotz* 15 (2004) 121-33 (125-26 et notes 27-29).

[3] Tran, '*Collegius Agellanus*' (n.2, cit.) 127.

petit domaine. C'est en partie le cas, mais seulement en partie, et d'une manière qu'il vaut la peine d'analyser. D'abord, *agellus* ne s'applique jamais, sauf erreur, au territoire d'une communauté, d'une cité; il est toujours en rapport avec des biens appartenant à des particuliers, ou exceptionnellement à un espace dont le propriétaire et le statut ne sont pas précisés. D'autre part, puisqu'il désigne des terres appartenant à des particuliers, on pourrait s'attendre à ce qu'il désigne un petit *fundus*, – à ce qu'il soit employé comme un équivalent de *fundus*, mais pour des terres plus petites. Sauf exception, ce n'est pas le cas.

Agellus n'est pas synonyme de *fundus*, et, en règle générale, il n'est pas employé dans les mêmes genres de textes que *fundus*. Par exemple, il n'est jamais employé dans le traité agronomique de Caton l'Ancien; il n'apparaît que deux fois dans celui de Varron[4] et qu'une fois dans celui de Columelle.[5] Au contraire, *fundus* se rencontre 22 fois dans le *De Agricultura* de Caton, 30 fois dans le *De re rustica* de Columelle et 95 fois dans celui de Varron. Des fréquences aussi différentes ont évidemment une signification. Une des explications réside dans le fait qu'*agellus* est souvent davantage lié à la propriété et au patrimoine qu'à l'agriculture et à l'exploitation du sol. Souvent, au singulier ou au pluriel, il désigne plutôt les biens fonciers du propriétaire, dans leur globalité, qu'une terre précise et bien individualisée, comme nous allons le voir. Autre explication, encore meilleure à mon sens: dans la plupart des textes où se trouve *agellus*, c'est sur la valeur symbolique et emblématique de la terre qu'est mis l'accent, et non pas sur son rendement économique. Quand on veut parler d'une parcelle d'un point de vue technique ou dans le cadre d'un raisonnement plus ou moins économique, c'est *fundus* qui est employé, et non point *agellus*. Il y a des exceptions, mais elles sont peu nombreuses.

Commençons par plusieurs autres remarques préliminaires. D'une part, nous verrons, certes, que, dans un texte, l'*agellus* concerné a probablement coûté environ 15,000 sesterces, que dans un autre il a coûté 60,000 sesterces, et dans un troisième 100,000 sesterces.[6] Mais il serait stupide de fixer des seuils, de prétendre par exemple qu'un *agellus* ne peut jamais dépasser tant de jugères ou un prix de tant de sesterces (parce que, sans cela, on ne l'appellerait pas *agellus*). Même si, en principe, le mot désigne une petite terre (mais nous verrons qu'en pratique, les choses sont sensiblement plus compliquées), il ne permet jamais d'avancer des chiffres, qu'il s'agisse de chiffres de prix ou de surface. Le mot ne conduit pas à des conclusions quantitatives.

Deuxième remarque: aucune des valeurs, aucune des nuances que j'ai signalées ou que je vais signaler dans la suite de l'article ne suffit, à elle seule, à rendre compte de tous les usages du mot. Certaines de ces valeurs sont plus rares que d'autres, mais toutes sont attestées, peu ou prou.

En outre, je vais être amené à séparer les emplois du mot dans son sens propre, au premier niveau, et ceux qui relèvent des représentations, de la connotation. Mais cet exercice de séparation n'est qu'en partie légitime. Il est légitime parce qu'il permet de clarifier le propos. Il est légitime parce qu'il va montrer que le mot *agellus* se situe presque toujours du côté de la connotation, du signe emblématique, des représentations, et que les valeurs qu'il connote concernent l'opposition entre richesse et pauvreté. Mais, en même temps, cet exercice de séparation n'est que partiellement légitime, parce que le mot peut prendre à la fois, dans le même passage, son sens propre et un de ses sens figurés, ou plusieurs de ces

---

[4] Varro, *Rust.* 3.12.1 et 3.16.10-11.

[5] Colum. *Rust.* 3.3.14.

[6] Hor. *Ep.* 1.7.80-81; Apul. *Apol.* 101.6; Plin. *Ep.* 6.3.1.

sens figurés. Dans la même phrase, il arrive qu'il soit à la fois du côté de la dénotation et de la connotation.

Autre remarque: certains des textes disponibles sont d'interprétation difficile, voire presque impossible. C'est le cas de l'une des deux occurrences d'*agellus* dans les Satires de Juvénal. Juvénal parle d'*agellus paternus* qu'il est prêt à céder si une certaine femme reste vertueuse, mais on ignore si cet *agellus* lui appartient, ou s'il s'agit d'une formule proverbiale; ce passage a été beaucoup commenté, mais sa signification demeure obscure.[7]

Enfin, il faut noter que les occurrences d'*agellus* ne se répartissent pas de la même façon que celles des diminutifs les plus répandus, telles que les a analysées R. Hakamies.[8] On ne le trouve jamais chez Plaute, qui est pourtant très amateur de diminutifs; on en trouve un exemple chez Térence, qui, lui, au contraire, en est très avare. Chez Catulle (qui emploie 44 diminutifs substantifs et 26 diminutifs adjectifs et adverbes), il ne se rencontre jamais. Chez Caton et Vitruve, qui apprécient les diminutifs 'minoratifs' ou désignant la partie d'un tout, il ne se rencontre pas non plus. Cette situation s'explique en partie par le fait que les diminutifs ayant rapport à la richesse, à l'argent, au gain, ont une valeur spécifique, que R. Hakamies appelle la 'fonction atténuante': ils permettent à celui qui parle de donner l'impression qu'il prend de la distance par rapport aux intérêts matériels, et notamment à ses propres intérêts matériels. La correspondance de Cicéron, par exemple, contient beaucoup de diminutifs de ce type (*hortuli, mercedula, possessiuncula, praediolum, pratulum, quaesticulus, raudusculum*), que signale R. Hakamies.[9] *Agellus* fait partie de ces diminutifs qui sont en rapport avec la richesse, l'argent et le gain. Mais nous allons voir qu'il ne prend la 'fonction atténuante' que lorsqu'il est utilisé par des riches. Dans les cas où il désigne des biens de pauvres, il souligne l'exiguïté des terres concernées; il remplit alors une fonction 'minorative' plutôt qu'une 'fonction atténuante'.

*

Cependant, dans un petit nombre de textes et d'inscriptions, *agellus* est en rapport étroit avec les réalités les plus matérielles de la propriété foncière et de l'agriculture. Ainsi, dans une inscription de Volcei, il est question de deux *agelli,* dont l'un est dit *sup(erior)* et l'autre *inf(erior).* Dans une autre inscription, que cite également N. Tran, un collège a reçu des *agelli* dont les revenus agricoles doivent financer des cérémonies funéraires.[10] Ainsi encore, dans un fragment de Q. Cervidius Scaevola qu'on lit dans le Digeste,[11] il désigne des terres faisant l'objet d'un legs et adjointes à une autre terre qualifiée de *fundus*. Il y a d'un côté, dans ce texte, le *fundus Titianus*, et de l'autre l'*agellus Sempronianus*.

Quant aux textes littéraires, un très bel exemple d'un tel usage se trouve dans une fable de Phèdre. Phèdre y évoque un testament qu'Ésope était parvenu à tirer au clair. Dans ce testament, tous les éléments nécessaires à l'exploitation d'un domaine sont énumérés.

---

[7] E. Courtney, 'Juvenalia', *Bulletin of the Institute of Classical Studies* 13 (1966) 38-43, à 40; J. Gérard, *Juvénal et la réalité contemporaine* (Paris 1976) 10-11; G. Highet, *Juvenal the Satirist* (Oxford 1960) 297 n.20; A. Thierfelder, 'Juvenal 6.57', *Hermes* 76 (1941) 317-18.

[8] R. Hakamies, *Étude sur l'origine et l'évolution du diminutif latin et sa survie dans les langues romanes* (Helsinki 1951).

[9] Cic. *Att.* 4.8.1; 9.9.4; 12.6.2; 13.11.1; 13.23.3; et Cic. *Fam.* 2.16.2 ; 7.23.3; 9.16.7. Voir Hakamies, *Étude* (n.8, cit.) 23-24.

[10] *CIL* 10.407 = *Inscr. Italiae* 3.1.17 = *AÉ* 1988, 412 (Volcei); *CIL* 5.4489 = *Inscr. Italiae* 10.5.280 = *ILS* 8370 (Brescia); voir Tran, '*Collegius agellanus*' (n.2, cit.) 125 et notes 24-25.

[11] *Dig.* 33.7.27.3 et 5 (Scaev. *lib. VI digestorum*).

Agellus s'y applique à la terre, tandis que *villa* désigne les bâtiments et que les mots *pecora, operarii, boves, iumenta, instrumentum rusticum* figurent aussi dans l'énumération.[12] 'The items of a farm-property', notait très justement W. E. Heitland.[13] Il est plaisant de noter qu'un des emplois les plus 'réalistes' du mot *agellus* se rencontre précisément dans une fable! Ce n'est probablement pas un hasard. Dans cette énumération, des mots comme *pecora, iumenta* ou *instrumentum* produisent incontestablement un effet de réel, ils plantent en quelque sorte le décor agricole et foncier. Mais il faut aussi que le lecteur se rende compte qu'il se trouve dans une fable. *Agellus*, qui, nous allons le voir, fonctionne en général dans le registre de la connotation, remplit cette fonction.

Ce texte de Phèdre n'est d'ailleurs pas le seul où *agellus*, dans son sens matériel, se trouve intégré, d'une manière ou d'une autre, à l'univers de la fable. Dans un passage d'une Épître d'Horace, le mot désigne aussi un «vrai» petit champ dont les caractéristiques sont évoquées et considérées comme connues, mais dans un contexte qui n'est nullement réaliste.[14] C'est le fameux passage relatif au crieur public Volteius Mena, que le sénateur L. Marcius Philippus avait persuadé d'acheter des terres (*persuadet ut mercetur agellum*), en lui donnant sept mille sesterces, et en lui promettant un prêt de sept mille autres sesterces. Horace ne nous dit pas la superficie de la terre ainsi achetée, mais, vu son prix, elle était manifestement modeste. Elle ne pouvait guère dépasser une dizaine de jugères, deux hectares et demi ou trois hectares. Malgré cela, Horace présente ce changement de vie comme une sorte de promotion sociale. *Parvum parva decent*, 'aux petits conviennent les petites choses',[15] pour expliquer que Mena ne se soit pas habitué à cette nouvelle existence. En cas de succès, cette petite exploitation agricole pouvait probablement permettre des gains plus importants. Malheureusement, la vie de petit propriétaire foncier n'a pas du tout satisfait Volteius Mena, qui s'est trouvé beaucoup plus énervé et angoissé par elle que par son ancienne existence de *praeco* dans la grande ville. L'activité agricole, dans son *agellus*, est ressentie par Volteius Mena comme une source de stress difficile à supporter, et moins enviable que son ancienne vie urbaine. Le contexte fait penser à l'univers du conte ou de la fable, puisqu'il s'agit d'une petite histoire, vraie ou fictive, mais racontée pour en tirer une leçon, et il rapproche le passage d'Horace de celui de Phèdre dont nous venons de parler.

On peut encore citer un petit nombre de textes dans lesquels *agellus* désigne une petite terre précise et réelle, dans un contexte clairement agricole ou foncier, mais ils ne sont pas nombreux. Il y a le passage de Varron dans lequel il fait allusion aux frères Veianii du territoire Falisque, qui avaient hérité de leur père une petite villa et un *agellus* ne dépassant pas un jugère, et qui se lancèrent dans l'apiculture.[16]

Il y a aussi celui des *Épîtres* d'Horace où il est question des terres qu'Horace lui-même possède en Sabine.[17] De ces terres, s'occupe un *vilicus*, elles sont cultivées par cinq familles de colons, et l'épître est censée adressée à ce régisseur. Il serait évidemment facile de montrer que, dans un tel passage, le sens d'*agellus* ne relève pas seulement de la dénotation. W. Heitland, par exemple, a insisté sur le désaccord entre Horace et le *vilicus* qu'indique

[12] Phaedr. 4.5.23.

[13] W. E. Heitland, *Agricola. A study of agriculture and rustic life in the Greco-Roman world from the point of view of labour* (Cambridge 1921) 243.

[14] Hor. *Ep.* 1.7.81.

[15] Hor. *Ep.* 1.7.44.

[16] Varro *Rust.* 3.16.10-11.

[17] Hor. *Ep.* 1.14.

l'épître.[18] Le désaccord vient de ce qu'Horace cherche avant tout un endroit où se retirer et où s'abstraire de l'agitation de la ville de Rome, tandis que le *vilicus* souhaiterait un domaine plus profitable. On voit combien le mot *agellus* exprime une réalité qui, pour Horace, n'est pas avant tout agricole, même s'il y a des colons et un régisseur. Mais enfin, il s'agit d'un véritable champ, ou d'un champ présenté comme véritable par le poète. Faute de mieux, on utilise même cette épître comme document relatif à la fortune et au patrimoine du poète.

Parlons aussi de l'*Apologie* d'Apulée. Elle contient deux occurrences d'*agellus*, et qui, si on les considère ensemble, sont assez caractéristiques des emplois du mot. La seconde fait référence à un terrain existant, il est donc du côté réaliste d'*agellus*, mais avec une part non négligeable de connotation.[19] Apulée est accusé de magie par Aemilianus, frère du premier mari de son épouse Pudentilla. On lui reproche notamment d'avoir acheté un vaste domaine (*pulcherrimum praedium*), sous son nom, avec l'argent de son épouse. Il répond que c'est un tout petit domaine, *exiguum herediolum*, qui a coûté 60,000 sesterces, et que c'est sa femme qui l'a acheté (*Pudentillae nomen in tabulis esse*). Le domaine est qualifié d'*agellus* au singulier, en plus d'*herediolum*. Laissons de côté la question de savoir qui a acheté le domaine, Pudentilla ou Apulée. Le domaine existe en lui-même, mais la manière dont il est nommé met bien en évidence un des enjeux de l'opposition entre Apulée et ceux qui l'accusent: s'agit-il d'un très beau domaine (*pulcherrimum praedium*) ou bien, au contraire, d'un *exiguum herediolum*, d'un *agellus* ?

*

Avec l'autre passage de l'*Apologie*, on entre de plain pied dans le domaine des représentations. En ce cas, l'*agellus* est le signe de la pauvreté, l'attribut symbolique de la pauvreté, – que les pauvres en question soient de 'vrais' pauvres ou des pauvres mythiques. Il ne s'agit plus de parler d'un petit champ et de son exploitation ou de sa vente, mais de la pauvreté, dont il est l'indice évident. Dans le passage d'Apulée dont je n'ai pas encore parlé, Il s'agit pour l'auteur de déconsidérer Aemilianus, et pour cela de montrer qu'il était né très pauvre, et qu'il est parvenu à s'enrichir par des pratiques peu reluisantes, par exemple en recevant un certain nombre d'héritages, ce qui lui avait valu le surnom de Charon, selon Apulée. Son père ne lui avait laissé, pourtant, qu'un petit champ qu'il labourait en trois jours avec un âne.[20] C'est un texte d'autant plus intéressant que la pauvreté y est dévalorisée, ce qui n'est pas tellement fréquent dans la rhétorique antique. Mais il est vrai que nous sommes ici en présence d'un vrai pauvre (si l'on en croit Apulée), et non pas de l'image du pauvre, ni du mythe du pauvre. Il est plus facile de valoriser l'image abstraite de la pauvreté qu'un vrai pauvre. Aemilianus lui-même ne se prive pas de critiquer les pauvres pour leur pauvreté, semble-t-il.[21] Mais Aemilianus n'est pas seulement un vrai pauvre, c'est un pauvre qui s'est

---

[18] Heitland, *Agricola* (n.13, cit.) 217: 'To Horace, the estate with its quiet homestead and the five tenants of the outlying farms is an ideal property: he wants a retreat, not urban excitements. To the steward, it seems that there is 'nothing doing', while the grandeur of a great estate is lacking. So the master is contented, while the slave is discontented, with this five-farm property looked at from their different points of view'.

[19] Apul. *Apol.* 101.4-5.

[20] Apul. *Apol.* 23.6.

[21] Apul. *Apol.* 23.6.

enrichi, et cet enrichissement peut donner lieu à toutes les explications, même les plus désobligeantes.

Dans d'autres textes, l'emploi d'*agellus* au singulier est lié à l'image d'un 'vrai'pauvre, qu'on peut rencontrer dans la vie quotidienne, et qui n'est pas nécessairement valorisée, ni dévalorisée. C'est le cas d'un passage d'Horace dont je n'ai pas encore parlé: il imagine les rêves de paysans ou de petits propriétaires désireux de s'enrichir, – rêves auxquels il échappe lui-même, parce qu'il est content de son sort. Si cette terre voisine s'ajoutait à la mienne (*agellus*)! Après ce petit propriétaire, les vers suivants concernent un ouvrier agricole (*mercennarius*) qui rêve de découvrir un trésor.[22] C'est aussi le cas des provinciaux, dont parle Juvénal dans le long passage de la huitième satire où il est censé donner des conseils à Ponticus, jeune homme (fictif ou non) de la *nobilitas*: une fois que les provinciaux ont été privés de leur *agellus*, il ne leur reste plus que quelques bœufs et chevaux, sans compter, parfois, des armes dont il faut se méfier.[23]

Quand il est question de la figure sociale du pauvre, dans sa généralité, et par opposition avec celle du riche, la figure du pauvre est le plus souvent valorisée. C'est par exemple le cas dans l'une des *Declamationes* de Quintilien, dans laquelle un pauvre apiculteur se trouve attaqué en justice par un riche voisin, qui reproche aux abeilles du pauvre de venir manger le pollen de ses fleurs. La description de l'*agellus*, que le pauvre a reçu de son père, a tout pour susciter la compassion: *est mihi paternus agellus, sane angustus et pauper, non vitibus consitus, non frumentis ferax, non pascuis laetus, ieiunae modo glebae atque humilis thymi.*[24] On perçoit dans cette phrase une ouverture vers les réalités agricoles, mais ce qui domine, c'est l'image du pauvre, défendant son point de vue face au riche. Le pauvre, en ce cas, n'est pas heureux, puisqu'il est en butte aux attaques du riche voisin, mais on peut dire que sa pauvreté est globalement valorisée.

Quand il s'agit des grands ancêtres de l'Histoire romaine, ou parfois de ceux de l'Histoire grecque, ou des grands philosophes, la pauvreté est aussi valorisée, évidemment. Dans ces cas-là, le mot *agellus*, s'il est utilisé, constitue un signe, un emblème, de cette pauvreté que l'on admire et à laquelle on prétend aspirer. Il ne s'agit pas de savoir à quoi ressemblait la terre en question, et encore moins de préciser quel était son rendement. La pauvreté est exprimée et représentée par l'*agellus*, par le champ, qui est petit et unique: le fait qu'il s'agisse d'un diminutif souligne le caractère réduit de la propriété, et le mot est employé au singulier. Les exemples disponibles sont nombreux. Le plus célèbre de ces grands ancêtres de l'Histoire romaine est M. Atilius Regulus, héros de la première guerre punique, dont le régisseur était mort pendant qu'il se trouvait à la guerre, et qui n'avait plus les moyens d'entretenir sa petite terre. Il est question de lui dans Tite-Live,[25] Valère Maxime,[26] Frontin[27]

[22] Hor. *Sat.* 2.6.8-9 et 10-13.

[23] Juv. *Sat.* 8.109.

[24] Quintil. *Decl. Maior.* 13 (*Apes pauperis*), 2 et 4: 'I have just a little plot of land, left to me by my father, rather cramped and poor, neither planted in vines, nor productive enough for grain, nor luxuriant in pasture. It is just a holding of barren soil and low-lying thyme' (trans. L. A. Sussman).

[25] Liv. *Per.* 18.7.

[26] Val. Max. 4.4.6.

[27] Frontin. *Strat.* 4.3.3.

et Apulée.[28] Une autre personnalité bien connue, et dont le patrimoine foncier a été qualifié d'*agellus*, n'est autre que le fameux L. Quinctius Cincinnatus.[29]

De ces héros de l'Histoire romaine, il faut rapprocher le Grec Phocion, auquel rendent hommage Cornelius Nepos et L. Ampelius. Lui aussi se piquait de se contenter d'un *agellus,* et il refusa l'argent que lui proposait le roi Philippe pour qu'il passe de son côté, en disant: si mes enfants sont bons, ces biens [que je possède] leur suffiront; si au contraire ils sont mauvais, rien ne leur suffira.[30] Mais de tels modèles se rencontraient aussi en dehors des élites politico-sociales. Pline l'Ancien cite le cas de l'affranchi C. Furius Chresimus, qui obtenait de meilleures récoltes avec un petit domaine que ses voisins dans leurs très grandes propriétés, et faillit être condamné, parce que ses voisins, envieux, l'accusèrent de maléfices.[31] Du côté grec, il y a également l'exemple de l'Arcadien Aglaüs de Psophis, qui n'avait qu'un *agellus* et que l'oracle d'Apollon Pythien déclara pourtant plus heureux que Gygès.[32]

Quand Pline le Jeune parle dans une lettre de l'*agellus* qu'il a donné à sa nourrice et qui valait alors cent mille sesterces, il est évidemment question d'une terre précise et réelle. Il voudrait en confier la gestion au destinataire de la lettre, un certain Vérus.[33] D'après les prix habituellement attestés de la terre, A. N. Sherwin White pensait qu'elle devait compter entre 40 et 50 jugères, et je suis d'accord avec cette estimation.[34] L'emploi du mot *agellus* s'explique par les dimensions relativement réduites de la terre, mais aussi par le fait que Pline veut insister sur le caractère modeste de son cadeau, et par la personnalité sociale de la nourrice, - l'importance du bienfait étant en relation avec le statut de la bénéficiaire (ou, dans d'autres cas, du bénéficiaire). Ce n'est pas par hasard s'il emploie, trois ou quatre lignes plus loin, un autre diminutif, *munusculum*, 'mon petit présent'.[35]

Martial est l'auteur qui emploie le plus fréquemment le mot *agellus*. On en trouve dix exemples dans ses poèmes.[36] Sept de ces exemples concernent les terres de Martial lui-même (ou en tout cas du personnage qui parle à la première personne),[37] et trois les terres d'autres hommes.[38] On lit *agellus* au pluriel dans un seul de ces passages, et ce sont les terres de Martial qui y sont concernées.[39] Pourquoi Martial, quand il parle de ses biens fonciers, emploie-t-il six fois sur sept *agellus* au singulier, et une seule fois au pluriel? Dans tous les autres, l'emploi du mot au singulier semble viser à présenter l'auteur comme un homme vraiment pauvre (bien qu'il appartienne à l'ordre équestre). Dans celui où on lit *agelli* au pluriel, le dédicataire est Manius (ou Marcus?) Aquilius Regulus, souvent mentionné par Martial, un redoutable délateur qui était parvenu à une très grande richesse.[40] Il n'est pas

---

[28] Apul. *Apol.* 18.11.

[29] Val. Max. 4.4.7.

[30] Corn. Nép. *Phoc.* 1.4 et Ampel. *Lib. memor.* 15.17.4.

[31] Plin. *Nat.* 18.8.41.

[32] Val. Max. 7.1.2.

[33] Plin. *Ep.* 6.3.1.

[34] A. N. Sherwin White, *The letters of Pliny. A historical and social commentary* (Oxford 1966) 358.

[35] Plin. *Ep.* 6.3.2.

[36] Mart. 1.116.5; 2.32.3; 7.31.8; 7.91.1; 7.93.5; 10.61; 10.92; 12.16; 12.25; 12.72.1.

[37] Mart. 2.32.3; 7.31.8; 7.91.1; 7.93.5; 10.61; 10.92; 12.25.

[38] Mart. 1.116.5; 12.16; 12.72.1.

[39] Mart. 7.31.8.

[40] Y. Rivière, *Les délateurs sous l'Empire romain* (Rome 2002) 508-09, no. 6.

exclu que Martial, en lui écrivant, tout en jouant au modeste, ne veuille tout de même pas lui apparaître comme plus pauvre qu'il n'est réellement. Car si la pauvreté peut être valorisée au niveau de l'idéal, cela n'empêche pas le pauvre d'être méprisé.

Il n'est peut-être pas inutile de rappeler que, dans la tradition gréco-romaine, le vocabulaire de la pauvreté est toujours ambivalent, et doublement ambivalent. Il est ambivalent, parce que les mêmes mots peuvent exprimer à la fois une pauvreté digne et satisfaite et une insupportable misère. Il est aussi ambivalent, parce que la pauvreté est à la fois refusée et enviée, dévalorisée et valorisée. Une telle ambivalence se constate dans le cas d'*agellus,* quand il symbolise l'idée même de pauvreté, quand la taille réduite de la terre disponible devient le signe flagrant de la pauvreté. Dans tous les cas, il s'agit d'un jeu de représentations, de connotations liées à la pauvreté, ou à l'absence de richesse, ou à une relative médiocrité dans l'aisance. Les textes dans lesquels on trouve le singulier *agellus* visent certainement à souligner davantage la modestie ou même la pauvreté de la personne. Et cette pauvreté est présentée de façon très ambivalente: enviable en un sens, valorisée, mais socialement attristante, dignes de compassion (ou de mépris).

*

Le plus étrange est qu'*agellus* peut, très indirectement, devenir aussi un signe de la richesse. En même temps que l'image de la pauvreté, il peut symboliser celle de la richesse, mais indirectement. Cela se produit parce que le riche ou le très riche a tendance à minimiser sa richesse, surtout quand il la présente aux autres. Ses terres très vastes ou même immenses, deviennent alors, dans sa bouche, des *agelli*. Remarquons qu'alors le mot est employé par le propriétaire lui-même, et non pas par d'autres, et qu'il est toujours employé au pluriel. Ce qui sépare *agellus* signe de pauvreté d'*agellus* signe de richesse, c'est la forme du mot: au singulier, il symbolise la pauvreté, au pluriel la richesse, mais une richesse que le riche cherche à ne pas afficher et à ne pas mettre en avant.

Pline le Jeune est l'exemple le plus typique de ce phénomène. Il utilise à plusieurs reprises le mot *agellus*; c'est avec Horace et Martial un des auteurs qui l'emploient le plus souvent.[41] Et, trois fois, il l'emploie pour désigner ses propres domaines.[42] On connaît l'ampleur des terres de Pline le Jeune, dont le patrimoine a fait l'objet de plusieurs études.[43] Il est impossible de considérer qu'il n'est propriétaire que de modestes petites terres.

De la part de Pline le Jeune, on peut expliquer ce vocabulaire de plusieurs façons, qui ne s'excluent pas nécessairement. Ou il cherche à demeurer humble et réservé, et ne souhaite pas étaler sa richesse quand il écrit à des proches, qui de toute façon la connaissent déjà. Ou bien il considère que, par rapport à d'autres sénateurs, ses moyens sont relativement limités (tout est relatif); c'est d'ailleurs ce qu'il écrit explicitement dans l'une des trois lettres dont

---

[41] Plin. *Ep.* 1.24.1 et 3; 2.4.3; 5.14.8; 6.3.1; et 8.15.2.

[42] Plin. *Ep.* 2.4.3; 5.14.8; 8.15.2.

[43] Voir par exemple: R. Martin, 'Pline le Jeune et les problèmes économiques de son temps', *Revues des Études Anciennes* 69 (1967) 62-97; G. G. Tissoni, 'Nota sul patrimonio immobiliare di Plinio il Giovane', *Rendiconti dell'Istituto Lombardo* 101 (1967) 161-83; P. W. de Neeve, 'A Roman landowner and his estates: Pliny the Younger', *Athenaeum* 78 (1990) 363-402 et *id.*, 'A Roman landowner and his estates: Pliny the Younger', *Studi Italiani di Filologia Classica* s. 3, 10 (1992) 335-44; D. P. Kehoe, 'Allocation of risk and investment on the estates of Pliny the Younger', *Chiron* 18 (1988) 15-42 et *id.*, 'Investment in estates by upper-class landowners in early Imperial Italy: the case of Pliny the Younger', in *De Agricultura. In Memoriam Pieter Willem de Neeve*, éd. H. Sancisi-Weerdenburg (Amsterdam 1993) 214-37.

je parle en ce moment.[44] Cela peut être aussi une manière de suggérer qu'il est détourné de ses plus nobles activités (la culture et la politique) par des préoccupations bien terre à terre, et, somme toute, bien modestes, telles que les plaintes des paysans et le contrôle de la comptabilité. Il oppose d'ailleurs explicitement les écritures comptables à d'autres écrits, à une autre littérature dont il est connaisseur.[45]

L'usage du diminutif, dans de tels textes, peut aussi être un procédé d'affectivation, une manière d'exprimer l'affectivité qui lie Pline à ses terres.[46] Je n'ai pas observé, à vrai dire, qu'*agellus* ait souvent cette valeur; d'autres diminutifs la prennent beaucoup plus fréquemment. On la trouve cependant dans certains des *Carmina Priapea*, dans lesquels des éléments de la nature ou de la vie rurale peuvent être rapprochés (explicitement ou non) de détails érotiques.[47] Mais, dans les *Carmina Priapea*, *agellus* est employé au singulier, et non au pluriel; en outre, les lettres de Pline ne relèvent évidemment pas du même genre littéraire que ces *Carmina*!

Mais la manière dont Pline le Jeune utilise ce diminutif n'est pas l'apanage exclusif de cet auteur. On la retrouve par exemple dans le *Satyricon*, quand Trimalcion parle de ses *agelli* d'Italie, qu'il veut joindre à la Sicile.[48] On la retrouve aussi chez Columelle, dans le passage où il vante le rendement et les mérites de la viticulture,[49] et également, à deux reprises, chez Sénèque.[50] Il faut admettre qu'*agelli*, au pluriel, est une manière possible de parler de patrimoines fonciers immenses sans en avoir l'air, en les réduisant à des proportions beaucoup plus modestes. Mais entre un patrimoine pauvre (ou modeste) et un très gros, il y a une nuance, celle qui sépare le singulier du pluriel. Tout dépend de la façon de présenter les choses!

*

Dans une étude comme celle-ci, la société rurale se partage entre ceux qui possèdent beaucoup d'*agelli* et ceux qui n'ont qu'un pauvre *agellus*. Mais il ne faut pas oublier la troisième fraction de cette société rurale, fraction qui doit être encore plus pauvre que la deuxième: celle des paysans libres qui ne possédaient aucune terre. Il ne faut pas non plus oublier une autre fraction de la société, composée de ceux qui n'avaient pas de terres, mais possédaient d'autres biens. Ce n'est certes pas à partir du mot *agellus* que nous pouvons appréhender ces deux autres fractions, – la troisième, très mal connue de nous dans l'ensemble, – et la quatrième, le monde des commerçants et artisans, sur laquelle une plus large documentation est disponible.

Le mot *agellus* et son pluriel *agelli* ne sont pas très intéressants comme révélateurs des réalités de la société rurale, puisqu'ils prennent rarement place dans un contexte franchement social ou agricole. C'est sur le plan des représentations, des symboles, de l'image, ceux de la pauvreté et de la richesse, qu'ils présentent un intérêt. Ils montrent l'importance du patrimoine foncier dans la manière dont le monde romain se représentait la

---

[44] Plin. *Ep.* 2.4.3.

[45] Plin. *Ep.* 5.14.8.

[46] Sur cette valeur des diminutifs, voir par exemple J. Marouzeau, *Traité de stylistique appliquée au latin* (Paris 1935) 151-55.

[47] *Priapea* 15.2; 16.7; 82.1; 82.5.

[48] Petr. 48.3.

[49] Col. 3.3.14.

[50] Sen. *Ben.* 2.28.3 et 5.24.3.

richesse ou l'absence de richesse. Ils montrent aussi combien on passe facilement du mythe, de la représentation utopique ou rêvée, à des façons de parler qui essaient de rendre compte des possessions des uns et des autres. L'*agellus*, c'est à la fois le petit lopin de L. Quinctius Cincinnatus ou de M. Atilius Regulus et le patrimoine de chevaliers comme Horace ou Martial, qui, l'un et l'autre, ont tendance à se présenter comme pauvres. Attitude qu'ils ont en commun avec Pline le Jeune, mais que ce dernier exprime par un pluriel. Un mot comme *agellus* montre à la fois comment la propriété de la terre creuse des gouffres entre les divers niveaux de la société romaine, et comment ces gouffres sont brouillés, atténués, au moins en apparence, par des manières de parler, par le biais du discours et des nuances du vocabulaire.

École des hautes études en sciences sociales, Paris

MIDDLE CLASSES IN LATE ANTIQUITY:
AN ECONOMIC PERSPECTIVE

FILIPPO CARLÀ

A binary system?

Under the *Constitutio Antoniana* (212 CE), all free inhabitants of the Empire, with the sole exception of *laeti* and *dediticii*, became Roman citizens;[1] juridical status thereby ceased to be a way of distinguishing between *ingenui* in Roman territory. It is generally accepted that 'internal, social divisions became stronger' as a result.[2] Scholars accordingly often presume that another distinction – its emergence often dated to the second century CE – had gradually arisen in Roman law: that between *honestiores* and *humiliores*.[3] Despite the prominence of this distinction, we do not even have a definition of what constituted a *honestior*; the decisive elements for membership in this category appear to have been *honos*, *dignitas*, and *condicio*, all rather vague concepts, and not clearly defined in the sources.[4] The only passage that has been interpreted as an attempt to classify *honestiores* does not use the term; in terms of substance, it only provides examples of persons against whom *iniuria* is qualified as *atrox*.[5] The *humiliores* also had widely differing social statuses and economic means. The sources generally have no interest in defining these categories;

---

[1] Slaves are intentionally excluded from this paper: the divide between free and unfree remained the most important distinction between individuals in Late Antiquity, as had always been the case; Gai. *Inst.* 1.9 expresses this in the clearest possible way. See D. Grodzynski, 'Tortures mortelles et catégories sociales. Les *summa supplicia* dans le droit romain aux IIIᵉ et IVᵉ siècles', in *Du châtiment dans la cité. Supplices corporels et peine de mort dans le monde antique* (Rome 1984) 393-96.

[2] C. R. Whittaker, *Rome and its frontiers: the dynamics of empire* (London and New York 2004) 207.

[3] F. M. De Robertis, 'La variazione della pena *pro qualitate personarum* nel diritto penale romano', *RISG* 14 (1939) 59-110, at 65-86; G. Cardascia, 'L'apparition dans le droit des classes d'*honestiores* et d'*humiliores*', *Revue historique de droit français et étranger* 28 (1950) 305-337, 461-85, at 319-20; P. Garnsey, *Social status and legal privilege in the Roman empire* (Oxford 1970) 260-71; F. Jacques and J. Scheid, *Rome et l'intégration de l'Empire, 44 av. J.-C. – 260 ap. J.-C.. Tome I: Les structures de l'Empire romain* (Paris 1990) 301-303; R. De Castro-Camero, 'Consecuencias jurídicas de la dicotomía social honestiores-humiliores', *Studia et Documenta Historiae Iuris* 65 (1999) 333-43, at 333-35. F. J. Navarro, *La formación de dos grupos antagónicos en Roma:* honestiores *y* humiliores (Pamplona 1994) 164 speaks of 'una fuerte tendencia a la polarización'.

[4] Garnsey, *Social status* (n.3, above) 223-27 and 234-35; R. Teja, '*Honestiores* y *humiliores* en el Bajo Imperio: hacia su configuracion en clases sociales de una division juridica', *Memorias de Historia Antigua* 1 (1977) 115-18, at 115-16; Navarro, *Formación* (n.3, above) 22. According to De Castro-Camero, 'Consecuencias' (n.3, above) 341-43 the determinant concepts were *auctoritas* and *dignitas* (342). Wealth was not included; Cardascia, 'Apparition' (n.3, above) 317, 'néanmoins, qui dit *honestior* ne dit pas nécessairement *locuples*'. On *dignitas* and *honos*, see also H. Löhken, *Ordines dignitatum. Untersuchungen zur formalen Konstituierung der spätantiken Führungsschicht* (Cologne and Vienna 1982) 2-4, 23-24.

[5] *PS* 5.4.10 (to be compared with Gai. *Inst.* 3.225). Cardascia, 'Apparition' (n.3, above) 317-19 and 327-28; De Castro-Camero, 'Consecuencias' (n.3, above) 337-41 has indeed tried to extract a more precise definition of *honestior* from this text.

instead, they were meant to be defined by the criminal justice system on a case-by-case basis. Even though Cardascia, to take one example, recognises the fluidity of these categories, he concludes that '*Honestior, humilior* ne sont pas des catégories juridiques', but rather social definitions and could unproblematically be assimilated to modern social classes.[6]

The distinction between *honestiores* and *humiliores* – independent of the fact that these specific terms are conventionally used today – appears to be a peculiarity of the pseudo-Pauline *Sententiae*; its real significance in Roman law has been much discussed.[7] The categories have been thought to blur progressively in Late Antiquity in response to two distinct developments: one towards greater homogeneity of penalties and the other a growing 'economic' distinction between rich and poor,[8] that is, a gradual convergence of the different classifications (be it social, economic, or legal) and a general identification of the poor – the powerless – as those without dignity.[9] De Robertis believed that the main difference between the Principate and Late Antiquity consisted precisely in the fact that the latter took wealth rather than honour into consideration.[10]

The notion that thus came to be widespread among scholars was that middle imperial and, even more so, late antique society had a binary character:[11] a upper stratum contrasted with a lower one; a middle level would have been substantially absent, and political, economic and judicial power would have coincided much more than before, allowing a further concentration of power and wealth in the hands of the members of the upper layers.[12] This paradigm was sometimes replaced by a tripartite system in which *curiales* held a middling position, distinct from both the lower strata and the upper levels and therefore sometimes interpreted as a 'middle class':[13] *CTh* 13.5.5 separates the holders of a *potior*

---

[6] Cardascia, 'Apparition' (n.3, above) 326-37.

[7] Cardascia, 'Apparition' (n.3, above) 324-26; Garnsey, *Social status* (n.3, above) 221-22; R. Rilinger, *Humiliores – honestiores. Zu einer sozialen Dichotomie im Strafrecht der römischen Kaiserzeit* (Munich 1988) 35-37. Once again, the *Pauli Sententiae* propose rather a tripartition, adding slaves to *honestiores* and *humiliores* (*ibid.* 65-82), but see n.1.

[8] Rilinger, *Humiliores* (n.7, above) 22; Navarro, *Formación* (n.3, above) 28 and 259 (who dates the origin of this process to the second and third century). G. Bravo, 'Cuestiones metodologico-historicas en la renovación de la problematica tardoantigua: la elaboracion de los conceptos 'relaciones de clase', 'clases sociales', 'conflictos', *Memorias de Historia Antigua* 1 (1977) 119-25, at 121 classifies two variants of 'binary' late antique social distinctions, 'sociological' distinctions, *i.e.* slave/free and *honestior/humilior*, and 'socioeconomic' distinctions, setting the rich and powerful against the poor and powerless. It is important to emphasise that Bravo does not at all believe these distinctions perfectly mirror late antique society.

[9] Teja, *Honestiores* (n.4, above) 117; G. Alföldy, *Römische Sozialgeschichte* (Stuttgart 2011[4]) 141.

[10] De Robertis, 'La variazione' (n.3, above) 94-97. But this reconstruction was already rejected by Cardascia, 'Apparition' (n.3, above) 478-82.

[11] Rilinger, *Humiliores* (n.7, above) 18-19.

[12] In consequence to this image of late antique society, Teja, *Honestiores* (n.4, above) 117 defines *honestiores* and *humiliores* as social classes in a Marxist sense, capitalists and landlords being equivalent to the former and workers being equivalent to the latter. See also *e.g.* K. Christ, 'Grundfragen der römischen Sozialstruktur', in *Studien zur antiken Sozialgeschichte. Festschrift Friedrich Vittinghoff*, eds W. Eck, H. Galsterer and H. Wolff (Vienna 1980) 197-228, at 216.

[13] R. L. Anderson, *The rise and fall of middle-class loyalty to the Roman Empire. A social study of Velleius Paterculus and Ammianus Marcellinus* (Diss. Berkeley 1962) 80-82; Alföldy, *Römische Sozialgeschichte* (n.9, above) 284. Anderson, *Rise and fall*, 80-182 even identifies the 'middle class' in Late Antiquity with curial status *tout court* (having identified the 'middle class' in the time of Augustus with the *equites*) and consequently reads Ammianus, a curial, as a source that perfectly transmits the condition and feelings of that status group ('we no doubt see the authentic emotions of the middle class in Ammianus': 151), and thus its decline and that of its loyalty to the Roman state. It is clear that such a position is untenable. Moreover, it has already been repeated many times that the concept of a 'middle class', like that of an 'upper' and 'lower' class, can only have a relative

dignitas from *decuriones* and *plebei*, and Ammianus also distinguishes between *honorati*, *urbium primates* and *plebei*.[14] But even in these cases we have a distinction based on formal membership in the *ordines* that does not correspond to a division into classes.

Another example seems significant: *CTh* 12.1.72 (370) states that someone in possession of *aliquorum praediorum* (that is, 'some amount of land', clearly specified by other regulations), may be appointed a member of a municipal *curia*. Again, it is not general wealth that is indicated here, but only a specific form of it, landed propriety, the 'moral superiority' of which in the Roman value system need not be discussed further.[15] It is no coincidence that subject of this law is precisely the fiscal obligations of a merchant who has acquired landed property. We thus are not surprised to find an additional category, *possessores*, as an alternative to *decuriones* and *plebei* in *CTh* 9.31.1 (409). But *possessores* cannot be considered a 'middle class', because they include all those who possess landed property, irrespective of its size, and the category here has legal (and fiscal) rather than social significance.[16] *CTh* 11.1.18 even makes it clear that *possessores* may have any *dignitas*, from *maxima* to *infima*. The word could also potentially indicate landowners not belonging to other defined ranks.[17] The only problematic law is *CTh* 12.13.2 (364), in which it seems that all *possessores* are either senators or *curiales* – here we have to assume that the term means 'big landed proprietors', who were, as stated in *CTh* 12.1.72, automatically registered in the *curiae*.[18]

This statement is confirmed by *CTh* 12.1.33, from 342. Under this law all people who privately own at least 25 *iugera* of land and additionally control a large amount of land owned by the *res privata* are to be appointed *curiales*. But even those who possess a smaller amount of land and control less territory of the *res privata* should 'be assigned to the municipal council'.[19] The point at stake is therefore not wealth, but rather the connection to the imperial *res privata*: even in this case we have an 'institutional' definition. It thus emerges that late antique legislative texts confront us with a variety of different, complementary

---

meaning: a group of people identifiable as 'middle class' in the local context of a city would undoubtedly have belonged to the 'lower class' in a pan-imperial perspective or even in a larger, more commercially active city (*e.g.* Christ, 'Grundfragen' [n.12, above] 215-16; S. Roda, 'Classi medie e società altoimperiale romana: appunti per una riflessione storiografica', in *Ceti medi in Cisalpina*, ed. A. Sartori and A. Valvo [Milan 2002] 27-36, at 34). It is therefore necessary to underline explicitly that this paper takes only the general imperial perspective into consideration, knowing full well that many of the persons described here as belonging to an intermediate social level probably held leading positions in their local communities (an obvious case could be Iulianus Argentarius, on whom see *infra*).

[14] Amm. 14.7.1.

[15] See still J. H. D'Arms, *Commerce and social standing in ancient Rome* (Cambridge, Mass. 1981) and *infra*.

[16] *E.g. CTh* 7.7.4 (415); 9.19.2 (320?); 10.10.31 (422); 11.1.2 (313?); 11.1.6 (354?); 11.1.26 (399); 11.3.5 (371); 11.5.4 (436); 12.6.15 (369); 12.6.23 (386). See R. Delmaire, *Largesses sacrées et res privata. L'aerarium impériale et son administration du 4ème au 6ème siècle* (Rome 1996) 60; J. H. G. W. Liebeschuetz, *The decline and fall of the Roman city* (Oxford 2001) 114; G. A. Cecconi, '*Honorati, possessores, curiales*: competenze istituzionali e gerarchie di rango nella città tardoantica', in *Le trasformazioni delle élites in età tardoantica*, ed. R. Lizzi Testa (Rome 2006) 41-64, at 51-54.

[17] Thus in *CTh* 11.7.12 (383), the context of the law makes it clear that *possessores* are landed proprietors who are not *decuriones*, just as in *CTh* 16.2.31 (409); this is also the case in *CTh* 11.22.2 (385), where the *ordines* are distinguished from the *reliqui possessores*. See also *CTh* 15.9.2 (409). *Possessores* could of course also belong to other, different categories: *clerici possessores* are the subject of *CTh* 16.2.15 (359?).

[18] One might add that if the term *possessores* indicated the sum of *curiales* and senators, this definition would clearly be even more institutional, like those already analysed.

[19] *Illo etiam curiae similiter deputando* (trans. C. Pharr).

categorizations that do not easily map onto one another, in contrast to what has long been believed to be the case.

In general, even though the social, economic and political domains were of course closely intertwined in Late Antiquity, as in any other society,[20] the conceptual distinction between wealth, power and authority was still strong, and these different categories remained distinct. They coincided most at the lowest level of the different scales (the poor were also powerless and without any *dignitas*), but this coincidence, which occurs much less frequently at higher social levels, does not entail overlapping and confusion, even less a simplification of social stratification. As Nicolet has shown, in order to describe the entire social history of Antiquity a model is needed that presents 'une hiérarchisation sociale relativement indépendante des données économiques. Non que celles-ci, jusque et y compris dans les promotions militaires romaines, n'accompagnent les promotions politiques ou administratives', but indeed social status and wealth, even when coinciding in the same person, are not necessarily related and are clearly differentiated from a conceptual standpoint.[21]

Nonetheless, modern scholars have not considered this conclusion valid for Late Antiquity. In particular, the pseudo-Pauline terminology has been considered to encompass this evolution, through its semantic expressions:[22] *CJ* 4.40.4, for example, speaks of *honestiores*, but as opposed to *inferiores ... vilioresque*. The 'Pauline' distinction indeed stands alongside another one in the sources, that between *potentiores* and *tenuiores*. This pair is often understood as a parallel distinction, whereby, according to the traditional interpretation, power supposedly was based on one's property.[23] Therefore, contrary to the views of Cardascia, these categories have also been considered as 'real' social classes in contrast to *honestiores* and *humiliores*.[24] This interpretation, however, is as problematic as the previous one: the categories *potentiores* and *tenuiores* are not defined any better than the previous two and also show possible points where they overlap. Additionally, the word *potentiores* in legal texts implies reprehensible behaviour and the abuse of a position of power to violate the law and the rights of other members of society.[25] In this sense, *potentiores* and *tenuiores* are legal and moral/moralizing categories rather than social categories.

The main source of this 'traditional' reconstruction of late antique society is a famous passage in the anonymous *De rebus bellicis*, which apparently uses *tenuiores* and *pauperes*

---

[20] M. I. Finley, *The ancient economy* (Berkeley and Los Angeles 1985[2]) 50; Bravo, 'Cuestiones' (n.8, above) 123.

[21] C. Nicolet, 'Introduction', in *Recherches sur les structures sociales dans l'Antiquité classique*, ed. C. Nicolet (Paris 1970) 1-18, at 14-15.

[22] In the Theodosian and Justinian Codes, the terms also continue to appear on account of the prestige the *Pauli Sententiae* enjoyed in Late Antiquity; as is well known, this source was declared universally valid in the Law of Citations (*CTh* 1.4.3, 426).

[23] But these terms are not as clear as is often presumed: *Dig.* 1.18.6.2 *e.g.* contrasts *potentiores* with *humiliores*. For the 'traditional' image of *potentiores*, see J. Gagé, *Les classes sociales dans l'Empire romain* (Paris 1964) 417-24.

[24] A. Wacke, 'Die *potentiores* in den Rechtsquellen. Einfluß und Abwehr gesellschaftlicher Übermacht in der Rechtspflege der Römer', in *Aufstieg und Niedergang der römischen Welt* II, 13 (Berlin and New York 1980) 562-607, at 578-80. See also Cardascia, 'Apparition' (n.3, above) 308-10; Rilinger, *Humiliores* (n.7, above) 25-26; De Castro-Camero, 'Consecuencias' (n.3, above) 341 (who thinks *honestior* and *potentior* are substantially equivalent). On the use of *potens* during the Principate as opposed to *humilis*, see Navarro, *Formación* (n.3, above) 235-36.

[25] E. Patlagean, 'La pauvreté byzantine au VIe siècle au temps de Justinien: aux origines d'un modèle politique', in *Études sur l'histoire de la pauvreté*, ed. M. Mollat (Paris 1974), I, 59-81, at 61 speaks rather contradictorily of a 'classement social' that 'conservait en tout état de cause une finalité civique'. See Wacke, 'Die *potentiores*' (n.24, above).

as synonyms. But references to poverty in legal sources are generally either rhetorical or meant to explain the reasons for committing a crime. The Constantinian constitution *CJ* 4.43.2 (329), for instance, describes parents selling their children *propter nimiam paupertatem egestatemque victus*. Similarly, *CTh* 9.42.5 (362), speaks of people who *per egestatem abiecti sunt in faecem vilitatemque plebeiam* and who must be punished more severely (*i.e.*, with death, while the rich, *locupletes*, are proscribed); the crime is once more an economic one, that is, stealing wealth from proscribed persons.[26]

A passage by Hermogenian is also very famous. The question asked is who was not allowed to initiate an accusation: 'Some on account of poverty, such as those who possess less than fifty *aurei*'.[27] We cannot be completely sure whether this amount of money had already been established by Hermogenian, at the end of the third century, as commonly assumed, or whether it had been changed by the editors of the *Digesta*; what we know is that this 'poverty threshold' is still defined in the same way in the *Procheiros Nomos* (27.22) and in the *Epanagogé* (12.8). This persistence is due largely to the stability of prices expressed in gold throughout the late antique period.[28] Patlagean thought this threshold extremely high, since she imagined it as a simple monetary or movable asset, excluding immovable property. But this position must be abandoned, not only on account of the value of houses and lands, which was not so high as to be necessarily excluded,[29] but also because it is unreasonable to suppose that the capacity to initiate a prosecution would be limited in such a way. Fifty gold coins are the 'capital' available to the accuser – and of course Hermogenian's ruling had no bearing on the definition of *humiliores*, as Duruy thought.[30]

Can we say, following Patlagean, that this ruling turned an economic threshold into a mark of social differentiation?[31] This interpretation should also be rejected. Social class is not defined by one's ability to act as an accuser in a court of law: other exclusions affected slaves and freedmen (forbidden to accuse their owners), women and children, persons already condemned or persons paid to initiate an accusation, and even magistrates and soldiers.[32] They therefore are not categories connected to economic standing and only partially characterised by low social status. There is indeed no way to demonstrate that the prohibition to accuse applied to *humiliores* generally and that poverty had therefore come to be considered as one of the reasons for belonging to this category. The rule only partially seems intended to prevent frivolous accusations made only for the sake of monetary gain, and rather to ensure that the persons liable give sound guarantees of their property and

---

[26] The concept of 'poverty' is, of course, also anything but easy to define, and it is important to distinguish mere economic poverty, the main concern here, from social poverty and even from the forms of deviance and marginality. On all this, see of course E. Patlagean, *Pauvreté économique et pauvreté sociale à Byzance (IVe-VIIe siècle)* (Paris 1977) and V. Neri, *I marginali nell'Occidente tardo antico. Poveri, 'infames' e criminali nella nascente società cristiana* (Bari 1998), esp. 7-30, with the literature cited there.

[27] *Dig.* 48.2.10; trans. A. Watson: *nonnulli propter paupertatem, ut sunt qui minus quam quinquaginta aureos habent.*

[28] Patlagean, 'La pauvreté' (n.25, above) 66. The transition from Diocletianic *aurei* to later *solidi* was surely not a problem: F. Carlà, *L'oro nella tarda antichità. Aspetti economici e sociali* (Turin 2009) 117.

[29] Carlà, *Oro* (n.28, above) 117-18.

[30] Rilinger, *Humiliores* (n.7, above) 15.

[31] A. Čekalova, 'Fortune des sénateurs de Constantinople du IVe au début du VIIe siècle', in *EYΨYXIA. Mélanges offerts à Hélène Ahrweiler*, eds M. Balard *et al.* (Paris 1998) I, 119-30, at 119 even speaks of a 'correspondance naturelle existant entre richesse et situation élevée, évidente dans toute société'.

[32] *E.g. Dig.* 48.2.8-11. For a general synthesis of the definition of the right to accuse during the Principate, see Rilinger, *Humiliores* (n.7, above) 93-113.

take responsibility if their accusation should prove unfounded. This question could only be solved by quantifying the accuser's property, but it is doubtful whether the general social position of such persons was affected by their inability to make accusations in court.

The monetary component

Similarly for economic classes as for legal structures, traditional interpretations of late antique society hypothesised a phenomenon of simplification, whereby one group of rich people always became richer, and another group of poor people always became poorer (and were the victims of the former). This idea was elevated to the *Rangordnung* of the Empire by Jean Gagé, who envisioned Late Antiquity as a 'caste' society with almost non-existent social mobility and moreover precisely defined economic groups that Gagé erroneously called 'classes'.[33] A. H. M. Jones contradicted Gagé's theories, claiming that 'the legal caste system [...] was by no means all-embracing, and in practice was not rigorously enforced' (and was also not a late antique innovation), but Jones still adopted the same terminology and even described the legal 'system of castes' as 'one of the most repellent features of the later Roman Empire'[34].

Gagé's theories are obsolete today, but the view that late antique society was economically bipartite with reduced social stratification still survives at least in part. This idea, transmitted by many Christian writers who discuss wealth with rhetorical exaggeration,[35] again finds support in the anonymous *De rebus bellicis*:

> This store of gold meant that the houses of the powerful were crammed full and their splendour enhanced to the destruction of the poor, the poorer classes of course being held down by force (*De reb. bell.* 2.2; trans. E. A. Thompson).[36]

This passage creates far more problems than it solves – problems that have been widely discussed. It is clear that this statement is highly rhetorical and cannot be taken literally. Its broader context is an attack on excessive imperial *largitas* – and in particular on Constantine as emblematic of excessively generous emperors who squander gold on the military without sufficiently considering the 'productive' strata of society.[37] The author enriches this primary topic with reflections on the history of money and coinage, the problem of coin counterfeiting and the substitution of bronze for gold (the famous statement *aurum pro aere vilibus commerciis adsignavit*) – a highly moralistic story, largely the product of literary *topoi*.[38]

What the anonymous author of *De rebus bellicis* clearly shows is a conception of society as divided into two groups corresponding to two metals, gold and bronze. This is not a mythological, 'Hesiodic' interpretation: the difference is between receiving and

---

[33] Gagé, *Classes* (n. 23, above) 335-437.

[34] A. H. M. Jones, 'The caste system in the later Roman empire', *Eirene* 8 (1970) 79-96, at 79 = Jones, *The Roman economy. Studies in ancient economic and administrative history* (Oxford 1974) 396-418, at 396.

[35] *E.g.* Bas. Magn. *Hom.* 6.

[36] *ex hac auri copia privatae potentium repletae domus in perniciem pauperum clariores effectae, tenuioribus videlicet violentia oppressis.*

[37] So *e.g.* Jul. *Caes.* 335 b. See Carlà, *Oro* (n.28, above) 126-28.

[38] As Lucr. 5.1269-80. On the 'monetary history' and its agreement with Pliny and Cassiodorus, see *e.g.* D. N. Sánchez Vendramini, 'Die 'Münzgeschichte' in der spätantiken Schrift *de rebus bellicis*', *Historia* 55 (2006) 125-28, at 127-28.

having gold and receiving and having fractional denominations in bronze. Silver – as has been noticed – appears neither in the more 'technical' numismatic parts of the work nor in the coin drawings attached to the third chapter. This in fact corresponds to the dominant trait of the late antique monetary system: the existence of two parallel currencies, in gold and in fractional denominations, which had no fixed exchange *ratio*, but rather fluctuated independent of one another.[39] Inflation almost exclusively hit the fractional currency and therefore the persons who held and used it in their transactions. In contrast, prices in gold remained stable over the centuries, which meant that the groups that held their capital in this metal did not lose their purchasing power.

This phenomenon would indeed attest to a binary society, in which poor people, exposed to inflation, always become poorer, while the rich, who already have gold, at least maintain their capital unchanged. But this first impression is misleading. The smallest gold coin, the *tremissis*, introduced ca. 384, was definitely too valuable to be used by anyone in daily life (it corresponds to a month's income for a non-specialized worker or the price of *c.* 30 litres of wine);[40] we thus should not imagine that *honestiores/potentiores*/rich, powerful people went around with only gold coins in their purses. Money (*i.e.* not physical coins) could be calculated in gold units, or indeed fractions of gold units, even when the amount involved was small, and this avoided a loss of purchasing power.[41] This practice was already widespread in the fourth century, particularly in the second half. The incomes of functionaries and soldiers, for example, were not always particularly high but were calculated in gold (the form in which they were actually paid is another matter). The salaries of officials in the newly conquered and reorganized African prefecture under Justinian are a good example: people working in the first four *scrinia* received 7 *solidi* per year and 9 in the other *scrinia*; only the *semissales* received *emolumenta* of 2.5 *solidi* per year.[42] It was thus normal for a wide group of people to use gold whenever possible in accounting so as not to lose capital – or indeed purchasing power. These people, who probably also held part of their capital in the most precious monetary metal, can be regarded as living at a 'middle level' of wealth.

Following upon new reflections on and redefinitions of the society of the Principate, which is now recognized as having consisted primarily of persons belonging to this 'mid-level',[43] it has indeed been stressed in recent years that late antique society was likewise more complex. To quote just one example, A. Demandt, in the chapter on late Roman society of his handbook on Late Antiquity, only deals with senators and slaves, as respectively 'the highest' and 'the lowest' levels, and includes some discussion of women and foreigners at every social level. He then adds that the 'middle classes' must be covered separately according to their occupations, farmers in the chapter about agriculture, merchants and artisans in the chapter on industry and trades.[44] But a middle class composed of farmers, merchants and artisans frankly defies all definition and cannot be a useful hermeneutic tool

[39] Carlà, *Oro* (n.28, above) 474-79 (and the bibliography cited and discussed there).

[40] Carlà, *Oro* (n.28, above) 283-90.

[41] Carlà, *Oro* (n.28, above) 131-37.

[42] *CJ* 1.27.1.22-38. This was presumably not these functionaries' only source of income (as we will see, the *semissales* would be living far below the subsistence level), but rather was supplemented by *sportulae*, gifts, and fees of various kinds. Carlà, *Oro* (n.28, above) 324-25.

[43] P. Veyne, 'La plèbe moyenne sous le Haut-Empire romain', *Annales HSS* 55 (2000) 1169-99, at 1179-80. *Cf.* E. Mayer, *The ancient middle classes: urban life and aesthetics in the Roman Empire, 100 BCE-250 CE* (Cambridge, Mass. and London 2012) 8-14.

[44] A. Demandt, *Die Spätantike. Römische Geschichte von Diocletian bis Justinian 284-565 n. Chr.* (Munich 2007²) 329.

for understanding late antique society. This is highly problematic, especially if we consider that according to John Chrysostom, for example, the 'middle classes', in his 'internal' (and emic) experience, were indeed the majority in society:

> For in proof that we do sow sparingly, let us inquire, if it seem good, which are more numerous in the city, poor or rich; and which they, who are neither poor nor rich, but have a middle place. As, for instance, a tenth part is of rich, and a tenth of the poor that have nothing at all, and the rest of the middle sort. Let us distribute then amongst the poor the whole multitude of the city, and ye will see the disgrace how great it is. For the very rich indeed are but few, but those that come next to them are many; again, the poor are much fewer than these. Nevertheless, although there are so many that are able to feed the hungry, many go to sleep in their hunger, not because those that have are not able with ease to succor them, but because of their great barbarity and inhumanity. For if both the wealthy, and those next to them, were to distribute amongst themselves those who are in need of bread and raiment, scarcely would one poor person fall to the share of fifty men or even a hundred (Joh. Chrys. *Hom. Matth.* 66.3).[45]

A matter of definitions: distinguishing rank and class

To proceed further, it is therefore necessary to define the terminology adopted here more precisely, and in particular the concepts of 'class' and 'middle class'. 'Middle' social positions can be defined from several different perspectives: 1) a legal perspective; 2) a 'formal' perspective, connected to the *Rangordnung* of imperial structures and independent of the legal perspective: the most typical example for the Principate are the *seviri* and the *seviri Augustales*;[46] or 3) an economic perspective, directly connected to wealth and the ability to display it (*e.g.*, in the form of luxury goods).[47] These three definitions often intersect and overlap (for instance, richer people may reach 'functional' higher positions[48] more easily or, on the contrary, persons with a recognised function may earn money from it, more or less legally), but on a theoretical level they must remain distinct.[49]

It is thus necessary to draw a distinction between 'rank' and 'class': both terms relate to a recognised position in society from an etic perspective, but the former introduces a legal

---

[45] Anonymous English translation from http://www.documentacatholicaomnia.eu/04z/z_0345-0407__Iohannes_Chrysostomus__Homilies_on_The_Gospel_Of_Matthew__EN.pdf.html (last viewed 12.09.2014). See P. Brown, *Poverty and leadership in the Later Roman Empire* (Hanover, NH 2002) 14-15.

[46] A. Abramenko, *Die munizipale Mittelschicht im kaiserzeitlichen Italien. Zu einem neuen Verständnis von Sevirat und Augustalität* (Frankfurt 1993); E. Buchi, 'Il sevirato nella società della *regio X*', in *Ceti medi in Cisalpina*, ed. A. Sartori and A. Valvo (Milan 2002) 67-78. From this perspective H. Hill, *The* Roman middle class *in the Republican period* (Oxford 1952) and H. Hill, 'The *Equites* as a Middle Class', *Athenaeum* 33 (1955) 327-32 defined the equestrian order under the Republic as 'middle class', for which he received much criticism.

[47] B. Cohen, 'La notion d'*ordo* dans la Rome antique', *Bulletin de l'Association Guillaume Budé* (1975) 259-82, at 260-61; Roda, 'Classi medie' (n.13, above) 31. Among analyses of the middle classes, G. Bandelli, 'I ceti medi nell'epigrafia repubblicana della Gallia Cisalpina', in *Ceti medi in Cisalpina* (n.13, above) 13-26 is an example of the application of this last category to Republican society, while, in the same volume, S. Giorcelli Bersani, 'Ceti medi e impiego pubblico nella Cisalpina Occidentale: il caso degli *apparitores*', 59-66 uses the second meaning.

[48] Buchi, 'Sevirato' (n.46, above) 75.

[49] See W. G. Runciman, 'Class, Status and Power?', in *Social stratification*, ed. J. A. Jackson (Cambridge 1968) 25-61, at 37-41.

and legally formalised hierarchy, while the latter does not require such institutionalization. In contrast to the 'realistic' definition, this 'nominalistic' definition of class implies that:

1. boundaries between different classes tend to blur;
2. the number and dimensions of classes can vary;
3. the interdependence of different classes is less relevant, as also is their capacity to act as a unitary subject.[50]

In connection with (3), it is also clear that, in the ancient world, we are dealing only with 'classes in themselves', groups of persons who are in analogous situations *de facto* and not 'classes for themselves', whose members also share an awareness of belonging to the same class and an interest in developing common strategies. Accordingly, the 'nominalistic' definition, integrated with the concept of 'rank', seems much more suitable to describe ancient society than the traditional 'realistic' definition.[51] This does not mean that we need an 'empirical' definition of class as opposed to a 'functionalistic' one,[52] but rather simply that the constituent elements of a class were not clearly defined by the persons involved. According to this definition, a class is not a group, and consists of people sharing an analogous position with regard to property, labour, acquisition, and means, independent of formally and legally accorded privileges; there exists a strong degree of unity and eventually an awareness of the analogousness of one's own position to that of others.[53] Marx's definition of a class as a group of persons occupying the same position with respect to the process of production can thus be broadened, substantially rescuing and broadening Weber's categories: 'class situation' means the typical probability of (1) acquiring goods; (2) winning a position in life; and (3) finding inner satisfaction, a probability derived from their control of goods and skills and from their income-producing uses within a given economic order. 'Class' means all persons in the same 'class situation'.[54]

A 'rank' could also of course have been defined by property: for instance, Roman *equites* had to have at least 400,000 sesterces and decurions, at least in Comum, needed 100,000 sesterces, while, according to the *lex Irnitana* 5,000 sesterces were needed to be chosen as a judge by the *duoviri*.[55] But this does not mean that property was the most important indicator of 'rank': it was just one of the elements of a formalized definition, indicating only the lower limit of the scale. Decurions could indeed be richer than some senators.[56] There therefore will have been different 'classes' within a 'rank': Pliny the Elder distinguished, for example, between *plebs media* and *plebs humilis*.[57]

'Rank' must also be distinguished from 'status',[58] which should be broadly conceived in a more 'individualized' way as someone's standing in regard to other persons, according

---

[50] L. Gallino, *Dizionario di sociologia* (Turin 2006²) 115-16.

[51] See *e.g.* Christ, 'Grundfragen' (n.12, above) 216.

[52] C. Gonzalez Roman, 'Las clases sociales. ¿Un problema terminologico o ideologico en las investigaciones sobre la Antiguedad?', *Memorias de Historia Antigua* 1 (1977) 33-40, at 34-35.

[53] Gallino, *Dizionario* (n.50, above) 116.

[54] M. Weber, *Wirtschaft und Gesellschaft* (Tübingen 1922); Engl. trans. *Economy and society. An outline of interpretive sociology*, eds G. Roth and C. Wittich (Berkeley 1968) 302.

[55] Plin. *Ep.* 1.19; *Lex Irnit.* 86.

[56] Jacques and Scheid, *Rome et l'intégration de l'Empire* (n.3, above) 311-14.

[57] *Nat.* 26.1.3. See Veyne, 'La plèbe moyenne' (n.43, above) 1170-74.

[58] Runciman, 'Class, Status and Power?' (n.49, above) 31. Status should in any case be understood in a performative

to norms accepted by all parties involved, as 'an effective claim to social esteem in terms of positive or negative privileges', and from 'caste', which implies a transcendental or religious normative order.[59] For instance, Weber distinguished between class, based on production, and status, based on consumption; Runciman explains the former in terms of wealth and the latter in terms of prestige, which, together with power, constitute the 'three dimensions' defining social standing.[60] Class and rank are also independent of 'groups' or, to be precise, 'interest groups', that is, informally organized clusters of people united by common interests and a sense of common identity (ethnic, religious, familial, *etc.*).[61]

Thus, if we accept a definition of 'rank' in the 'legal' and 'formal' perspectives, 'class' takes on a broader sense that does not imply a formal hierarchy or distinction;[62] defining the 'middle classes' in Late Antiquity thus requires us to adopt an economic perspective. This is further justified by the fact that while *honestiores* and *humiliores* have been the focus of several scholarly works (even if the complexity of the sources makes firm conclusions impossible),[63] just as the evolution of curial rank in Late Antiquity or the structure of bureaucracy also have been studied,[64] far less attention has thus far been paid to aspects of wealth and to one's position in society according to their economic standing.

It has already been repeatedly stressed – and here need only briefly be recalled – that the ancient world responded to the concept of class in a very different way to the modern Western and capitalistic world. Roman society was structured according to social and political functions, around *ordines* – and therefore around what we define as rank.[65] Nonetheless, economic aspects were present and deeply embedded in society: the Roman world knew a dynamic system of different elements that interacted continuously to define an individual's social position. In this sense, wealth played an important role, sometimes influencing even political and ideological affiliations.[66] The holders of 'economic capital', to use Bourdieu's terminology,[67] can of course create 'social capital' through forms of generosity, exchange

---

rather than static sense: see the reflections on the use of this concept in N. Morley, in S. Knippschild (ed.), *Just for Show? Displaying Wealth and Performing Status in the Ancient and Medieval World* (forthcoming).

[59] Weber neglected this last distinction and considered *e.g.* Indian castes as an example of 'status groups'.

[60] Weber, *Economy and society* (n.54, above) 305-07; Runciman, 'Class, Status and Power?' (n.49, above) 26. See also Finley, *Ancient Economy* (n.20, above) 46-47 and G. Halsall, *Settlement and social organization: the Merovingian region of Metz* (Cambridge 1995) 22-24.

[61] A. Cohen, *Two-dimensional man* (London 1974) esp. 121-23.

[62] See also Nicolet, 'Introduction' (n.21, above) 13-17.

[63] *E.g.* Rilinger, *Humiliores* (n.7, above).

[64] I will not discuss the details of the *Rangordnung* of late antique society here, which, as is well known, placed great importance on precisely defining such positions (even specifying the clothes that identified senators) – a topic that has received a thorough discussion very recently: see S. Schmidt-Hofner, 'Ehrensachen. Ranggesetzgebung, Elitenkonkurrenz und die Funktionen des Rechts in der Spätantike', *Chiron* 40 (2010) 209-43 and the bibliography given there. See also Löhken, *Ordines dignitatum* (n.4, above) esp. 1-30.

[65] Roda, 'Classi medie' (n.13, above) 29. Belonging to a particular *ordo* indeed always depended on meeting specific requirements: 'An order or estate is a juridically defined group within a population, possessing formalised privileges and disabilities in one or more fields of activity [...] and standing in a hierarchical position to other orders' (Finley, *Ancient Economy* [n.20, above] 45). On Roman *ordines* see C. Nicolet, *L'ordre équestre à l'époque républicaine (313-43 av. J.-C.). Tome 1: Définitions juridiques et structures sociales* (Paris 1966) 167-76; Cohen (1975); C. Nicolet, 'Les ordres romaines: définition, recrutement et fonctionnement', in *Des ordres à Rome*, ed. C. Nicolet (Paris 1984) 7-21; Jacques and Scheid, *Rome et l'intégration de l'Empire* (n. 3, above) 303-07. F. Kudlien, *Die Stellung des Arztes in der römischen Gesellschaft* (Stuttgart 1986) 40-42 interprets the word *ordo* in Latin sources as similar to what we call *status* here.

[66] Veyne, 'La plèbe moyenne' (n.43, above) 1169-70.

[67] See especially P. Bourdieu, 'Ökonomisches Kapital, kulturelles Kapital, soziales Kapital', in *Soziale*

and performance; and these in turn may multiply their economic capital: 'the different types of capital can be derived from economic capital, but only at the cost of a more or less great effort of transformation, which is needed to produce the type of power effective in the field in question'.[68] As Bourdieu himself observed, 'the volume of the social capital possessed by a given agent thus depends on the size of the network of connections he can effectively mobilise and on the volume of capital (economic, cultural or symbolic) possessed in his own right by each of those to whom he is connected'.[69] This means that as people belonging to a class with elevated economic capital in a given society network with one another, they increase their social capital.

Hence, even if 'class consciousness' was obviously lacking,[70] one's general 'social consciousness', that is, the perception of one's position in society, which defined one's identity and behavioural models, also took economic aspects into consideration. This allowed for the complicated interplay of various memberships and identities on different, more or less formal levels of class, group and rank. To cite only some well-known and easily understandable examples, poor freedmen did not constitute as much a 'problem' in the social articulation of the Roman Empire as did rich freedmen, who had to be accommodated in the social game with new functions – 'ranks' – such as the *seviri Augustales*, that qualified them legally as 'intermediate citizens' even if they belonged economically, beyond all doubt, to the highest levels of society. At the other end of the spectrum, membership in the Senate was simply impossible below a defined economic threshold. This short-circuit between rank and class also mattered in Late Antiquity, as a simple example will show. The same example will help to cast doubt on the idea of a progressive rapprochement of economic, legal and political distinctions in this period, provided we always bear in mind that none of our sources (including legal sources) are exempt from moralizing discourses, which also play an important role in the definition of status, wealth and their proper use.

A concrete example: rich and poor senators

In order to belong to the senatorial *ordo* (as well as the equestrian order), it was necessary to meet specific property requirements – one of the formal conditions necessary to hold a particular rank. Augustus had fixed the minimal *census* of a senator at one million sesterces.[71] The sources do not tell us how long a minimum amount of property was required to be admitted to and to remain in the senatorial order, but it is clear that some such requirement

Ungleichheiten, ed. R. Kreckel (Göttingen 1983) 183-98; English trans., 'The forms of capital', in *Handbook of Theory and Research for the Sociology of Education*, ed. J. G. Richardson (London 1986) 249-58.

[68] Bourdieu, 'The forms of capital' (n.67) 252.

[69] Bourdieu, 'The forms of capital' (n.67) 249.

[70] Even what Veyne, 'La plèbe moyenne' (n.43, above) 1194 defines as the consciousness of the middle class under the Principate is heavily influenced by rank, *i.e.* by exclusion from the equestrian and senatorial order on the one hand, and by separation from slaves and freemen on the other. Economic elements played a part in this case, particularly to distinguish oneself from the *infima plebs*, but they did not have the most important and most visible role in the structuration of society. Roda, 'Classi medie' (n.13, above) 33-34 instead believes that belonging to the 'middle class' was perceived as a provisional situation, anticipating that social mobility would allow for further movement upwards.

[71] Cass. Dio 54.17.3; this source should be compared to Suet. *Aug.* 41.1, where the *census* is given as 800,000 sesterces. On the general problem of minimal property requirements for senators, which existed 'indirectly' also in Republican time, see still C. Nicolet, 'Le cens sénatorial sous la République et sous Auguste', in *Des ordres à Rome* (n.65, above) 143-74.

remained in force.[72] When a *homo novus* was admitted to the Senate, *iuratores* swore on his behalf that he met the admission requirements, and *laudatores* spoke in his favour; his property was also declared and eventually checked.[73]

Under Constantine a group of the *censuales* was created for this purpose, under the supervision of the *magister censuum*.[74] Directly subordinate to the Urban Prefecture, that is, the 'presidency' of the Senate itself, the *censuales* performed many different tasks, which also changed many times over the decades; above all, though, their work consisted of registering and verifying senatorial property.[75] Men who joined the Senate by imperial *adlectio* immediately had to declare their current property and were punished if they lied on any point.[76] In the speech with which he tried to convince the Roman senators to accept Synesius among them, Symmachus insists on the fact that Synesius had the necessary wealth to fulfil his senatorial obligations.[77] The *censuales* distributed senators into three classes, each paying a different amount of *gleba senatus* (2, 4, or 8 *folles* per year).[78] It was admitted that persons without landed property could sit in the Senate,[79] but those who could not afford to pay the *gleba senatus*, that is, who did not reach the minimum property category, simply had to leave the Senate.[80]

Nonetheless, the problem of 'poor' senators became increasingly serious in the fourth century, especially in conjunction with the entrance of imperial functionaries into the *ordo* and the recruitment of new members for the Senate of Constantinople. This problem is illustrated by a letter written by Libanius to Themistius, who had personally overseen the expansion of the assembly:[81]

> Although you have no need for power, she [*scil.* Constantinople] does need a good
> leader, and who in her view could have priority over you, through whom she's

[72] L. Cracco Ruggini, 'Il Senato fra due crisi (III-VI secolo)', in *Il Senato nella storia: il Senato nell'età romana* (Rome 1998) 223-375, at 246, 275. It is immaterial here whether a distinction still existed between belonging to the senatorial *ordo* and to the Senate in Late Antiquity, as scholars generally think (*e.g.* C. Lécrivain, *Le Sénat romain depuis Dioclétien à Rome et à Constantinople* [Paris 1888] 10-15; A. Chastagnol, 'L'évolution de l'ordre sénatorial aux IIIᵉ et IVᵉ siècle de notre ère', *Revue Historique* 94 [1970] 305-14, at 311-12; Cracco Ruggini, 'Il Senato' [above] 274-75), or whether the two were by then identical, as P. Garbarino, *Ricerche sulla procedura di ammissione al Senato nel tardo Impero romano* (Milan 1988) has sought to prove.

[73] Garbarino, *Ricerche* (n.72) 218-19, 352-53. But here Garbarino says that the property declaration was made only for fiscal reasons and was not directly connected to admission. It will be shown below, however, that paying the *gleba senatoria* was a necessary requirement for admission to the Senate (with the few exceptions of the exemptions accorded), and therefore the two things are not separate as the Italian scholar thought.

[74] The first known *magister censuum* is C. Caelius Saturninus (*CIL* 6.1704), who perhaps held this office before 314. F. Elia, 'Nuove osservazioni sull''officium' del 'magister census'', *Quaderni catanesi di studi classici e medievali* 6 (1984) 337-53 and Delmaire, *Largesses* (n.16, above) 374 reject the dating of the institution to the age of Constantine; see F. Carlà, 'Tassazione sociale ed aristocrazia senatoria: la *gleba senatus*', in *Droit, religion et société dans le Code Théodosien*, ed. J. J. Aubert and P. Blanchard (Geneva 2009) 179-211, at 181, and the literature cited there.

[75] Löhken, *Ordines dignitatum* (n.4, above) 118; Carlà, 'Tassazione sociale' (n.74, above) 182-83.

[76] *CTh* 6.2.13 (383); Symm. *Rel.* 46.

[77] Symm. *Or.* 7.6 (before 388).

[78] Alföldy, *Römische Sozialgeschichte* (n.9, above) 288-89; Carlà, 'Tassazione sociale' (n.74, above) 184-86.

[79] This already was an important innovation: Cracco Ruggini, 'Il Senato' (n.72, above) 275.

[80] *CTh* 6.2.13 (383). This constitution acknowledges the possibility that senators might not own landed propriety (*etiam si possessiones forte non habeant*); regardless, such senators had to pay the 2 *folles* that were set as the lowest possible payment.

[81] Cracco Ruggini, 'Il Senato' (n.72, above) 296.

become greater in men, some of whom possess virtue with wealth, while others have no money but a nature superior to money? May it be your wish, good sir, that poor men of this sort make up the complement of the Senate; but if anyone should require gold of them, you'll prevent it, so that sharing in the blessings among you doesn't become for them a source of evils'.[82]

After some pressure from within the Senate itself, a lower 'level' was granted in 393; its members only had to pay 7 *solidi* per year. Once again it is stated that whoever could not afford to pay had to renounce his senatorial rank:[83]

In reply to the complaints of those persons who testify that they are not able to bear the burden of the glebal tax, it has been decreed by the Council of the Most August that seven *solidi* should be paid annually for his portion by each man who is not able to fulfill the payment of the folles. By this law We confirm this decree of the aforesaid council to the extent that if the property of any man should be meager and if this tax payment is not displeasing to him, he shall have the free choice, in contemplation of the resources of his patrimony, and he shall not withdraw from his fellowship in this Most August Order; but if the tax payment seems burdensome, that is, ruinous, he shall not seek to retain the Senatorial rank.[84]

In a famous fragment, Olympiodorus relates the average incomes of Western senatorial families, quantifying them very precisely:[85] 'Many of the Roman households received an income of four thousand pounds of gold per year from their properties, not including grain, wine and other produce which, if sold, would have amounted to one-third of the income in gold. The income of the households at Rome of the second class was one thousand or fifteen hundred pounds of gold'.[86] These figures, which, to my knowledge, are unparalleled in other texts that might have inspired them, seem extremely 'artificial' in their roundness and give the appearance of being officially defined income levels. It is possible that what Olympiodorus presents here were indeed the limits of the senatorial income categories in use at the beginning of the fifth century: senators with registered incomes over 4,000 gold pounds would have to pay the *gleba senatus* in the highest bracket; those with an income of at least 1,000-1,500 pounds in the second category (or perhaps those over 1,500 in the second category and those between 1,000 and 1,500 in the third).

I have addressed these problems elsewhere, in particular the contradiction between the form of land tax affecting the first three categories and the sort of 'poll tax' that applied to the fourth group, whose payment is defined *septem solidorum functio*. The two taxes are always clearly distinguished in the legal sources – and generally also in the literary ones.[87] This point is not immediately relevant here – what matters is that the introduction of this fourth category reveals the existence of a short-circuit between class and rank: since 393 the ability to sit in the Senate was independent of other limitations or definitions of wealth and tied

[82] Lib. *Ep.* 40.1-2 (358-359); trans. S. Bradbury.

[83] A. H. M. Jones, *The Later Roman Empire, 284-602. A social, economic and administrative survey* (Oxford 1964) 555-56.

[84] CTh 6.2.15 (393); trans. C. Pharr.

[85] Carlà, *Oro* (n.28, above) 420-21.

[86] Olymp. *Fr.* 41.2 Blockley; trans. R. C. Blockley.

[87] Carlà, 'Tassazione sociale' (n.74, above) 186-89.

only to one's ability to pay seven *solidi* annually, a quite substantial but not extremely high amount of money.[88] One could thus say that this payment *tenuissimos senatorum adsolet obligare*,[89] while use of the word *tenuis* for senators shows why schematic interpretations of late antique society must be abandoned.

Membership in the Senate by this date was almost completely severed from economic standing and had instead become purely a matter of rank. This was connected to the introduction of functionaries from the imperial bureaucracy to the senatorial class, who possessed more modest economic means.[90] The arrival of these newcomers made it necessary to redefine 'senatorial identity'. This had until the mid-fifth century repercussions[91] – already well studied by scholars – on the 'old' senatorial aristocracy.[92] It is worth noting that Olympiodorus, an Easterner, refers with some surprise to the numbers mentioned above as something typical of the West: the problem of 'poorer' senators was indeed more pronounced in the East, and it is even possible that the fourth, lowest bracket was introduced only for the Constantinopolitan Senate.[93]

It thus must be recognised that, far from confusing or confounding the economic and the social spheres, or identifying poverty with lack of dignity, Theodosius introduced an important reform in the opposite direction. His attention to the problem of poor senators within the senatorial order is also attested by his decision to raise the number of praetors to eight, in effect halving the costs they faced in the compulsory organization of games.[94]

The division of the senators by census according to wealth has nothing to do with another form of stratification introduced to the senatorial order that divided them into *illustres*,

---

[88] In Carlà, 'Tassazione sociale' (n.74, above), esp. 199-203, I propose that income from the *gleba senatoria* did not go to the *sacrae largitiones* but to the Senate itself, being intended therefore as a sort of yearly admission fee. The risk of expulsion was real: we at least know of the case of Valerius Fortunatus (Symm. *Ep.* 5.55; *Or.* 8), which also shows that, once they recovered the required property level, such persons could be reintegrated in the senatorial order by imperial decree (Symm. *Ep.* 4.67); see Garbarino, *Ricerche* (n. 72, above) 87-95; S. Giglio, *Il tardo impero d'Occidente e il suo Senato: privilegi fiscali, patrocinio, giurisdizione penale* (Naples 1990) 153-56, 178.

[89] *CTh* 6.2.23 (414). It is important to stress that exemption from the payment of the 7 *solidi* was granted in some cases. See Carlà, 'Tassazione sociale' (n.74, above) 192-97.

[90] Carlà, 'Tassazione sociale' (n.74, above) esp. 205-207.

[91] At this moment, the admission procedure became entirely bureaucratic. See Garbarino, *Ricerche* (n.72, above) 60-62. It is no coincidence that the 'senatorial tax' was abolished under Marcian: Carlà, 'Tassazione sociale' (n.74, above) 206-207.

[92] Lécrivain, *Le Sénat* (n.72, above) 23; Gagé, *Classes* (n.23, above) 355-57; Jones, *Later Roman Empire* (n.83, above) 545-52; Chastagnol, 'Évolution' (n.72, above); Alföldy, *Römische Sozialgeschichte* (n.9, above) 291-92; S. Roda, 'Nobiltà burocratica, aristocrazia senatoria, nobiltà provinciali', in *Storia di Roma* III, 1, eds A. Momigliano and A. Schiavone (Turin 1993) 643-74, at 650-55.

[93] Roda, 'Nobiltà burocratica' (n.92, above) 650-53; Čekalova, 'Fortune' (n.31, above) 120-21; Cracco Ruggini, 'Il Senato' (n.72, above) 295-97; Carlà, *Oro* (n.28, above) 319; Carlà, 'Tassazione sociale' (n.74, above) 190. Olympiodorus also describes, with surprise, the houses of Western aristocrats (*Fr.* 41.1 Blockley), surprise that is confirmed by Paulinus of Milan, when he says that the two biggest sources of admiration for Eastern visitors to Italy were Ambrose's wisdom and Petronius Probus' house (*Vita Ambr.* 25.1-2). The existence of 'tension' also in the Western Senate is in any case clear in our sources for the second half of the fourth century, especially in connection with the promotion of persons of humble origins to the senatorial order (Jones, *Later Roman Empire* [n.83, above] 144). A symptom of this is *e.g.* the interpretation of the prodigy of the blossoming brooms in Amm. 28.1.42. Nonetheless, the conflict in the Western Senate seems to have involved different groups of aristocrats and only later to have been (under Theodosius) reinterpreted in this sense by Symmachus and Ammianus: see R. Lizzi Testa, 'Quando nella curia furono viste fiorire le scope: il senato di Valentiniano I', in *Le trasformazioni delle élites in età tardoantica*, ed. R. Lizzi Testa (Rome 2006) 239-76.

[94] *CTh* 6.4.25 (384). See A. Chastagnol, 'Observations sur le consulat suffect et la préture du Bas-Empire', *Revue Historique* 82 (1958) 221-53, at 247-50; Cracco Ruggini, 'Il Senato' (n.72, above) 297; H. Leppin, *Theodosius*

spectabiles and simple *clarissimi*.[95] This distinction was connected to the hierarchy of office-holding and established a further ranking system that defined the upper social strata in relation to the functions that they performed. Belonging to these 'sublevels' of the senatorial order was therefore also exclusively personal: the son of an *illustris* was a *clarissimus* until he managed to obtain the appropriate office to climb the internal hierarchy. A famous law of 412 CE differentiates penalties according to the social position of the offender, and sets out the following fines for the members of the senatorial order:[96]

illustres	50 pounds of gold
spectabiles	40 pounds of gold
senatores	30 pounds of gold
clarissimi	20 pounds of gold

Should we presume that *illustres* were richer than other members of the Senate? The answer must be in the negative. The definition of penalties is not connected to anticipated wealth, but rather to the 'social' gravity of the crime:[97] in this case adhering to the Donatist movement was simply considered far more inappropriate and shameful for persons of higher social standing. A law issued two years later in fact states this explicitly, using a phrase that had already been typical of classical and post-classical jurisprudence: *damna quoque patrimonii poenasque pecuniarias evidenter imponimus viris mulieribus, personis singulis et dignitatibus pro qualitate sui quae debeant irrogari*.[98]

An economic perspective

The senatorial example shows quite clearly the complicated interaction of rank, status and class and also the fact that these different elements were not (and never are) static or fixed, but undergo a continuous, dynamic process of reciprocal influence and redefinition. If we read further in the above-mentioned law about Donatism, we find an example of how

---

der Große (Darmstadt 2003) 116. Complaints against the burden of this contribution had already been raised in past years (*CTh* 6.4.13; Symm. *Rel.* 8), and a reflection of them is found in Zos. 2.38. Indeed the organization of games was problematic, since it was decreed in Constantinople in 361 that praetors should be designated ten years in advance in order to have sufficient time to deal with this problem: *CTh* 6.4.12-13. This rule was subsequently introduced also in Rome (*CTh* 6.4.21, 372).

[95] Jones, *Later Roman Empire* (n.83, above) 528-29; Alföldy, *Römische Sozialgeschichte* (n.9, above) 289.

[96] *CTh* 16.5.52. See Garbarino, *Ricerche* (n.72, above) 265-70.

[97] De Robertis, 'La variazione' (n.3, above) 90.

[98] *CTh* 16.5.54 (414).

society below the senatorial rank could be schematically represented – in a way appropriate to the specific circumstances dealt with by that legal text:

sacerdotales	30 pounds of gold
principales	20 pounds of gold
decuriones	5 pounds of gold
negotiatores	5 pounds of gold
plebei	5 pounds of gold
circumcelliones	5 pounds of silver
servi	master's admonition
coloni	lashes

Of course, one might stress that this social stratification differs significantly from that under the Early Empire.[99] But in this case we are dealing only with ranks and 'groups' (such as the *circumcelliones*, whose presence here is clearly connected to the religious subject of the law) and not with classes, and it is impossible to recognise 'middle levels' in this classification. *Decuriones*, who in many respects were members of the élite, pay the same fine as merchants and *plebei*. It is clear that different distinctions by rank coexisted and were used differently according to specific problems and needs. Sometimes a division into two broad categories was considered necessary; sometimes the classification could go into detail, as presented here.

Yet, according to the definition of 'class' provided in this paper, the 'middle classes' must be identified from an economic perspective, independently of 'rank'. This also happened in Antiquity, as is clear in the passage by John Chrysostom quoted above, but it had been so already since the fourth century BCE.[100] One example, drawn from the pseudo-Plutarchan life of Isocrates, will suffice:

> Isocrates was the son of Theodorus of Erchia, a citizen of the middle class (τῶν μετρίων πολίτων), an owner of slaves who made flutes, through whom he gained a competence, so that he paid for a public chorus and gave his children an education... ([Plut.], *Mor.* 836 E; trans. H. N. Fowler).

This is admittedly again an oversimplification that attaches maximum importance to wealth and neglects others aspects; but every description of so complex a structure as a society must choose central categories adequate to its present purposes and produce a model that is by its very nature simpler than the object described. By adopting this 'economic perspective', which the definitions provided, as the ancient sources themselves enable us to do, we can identify which groups might have been considered 'middle classes'; comparing this data to the *Sozialordnung* based on rank then enables us to gain deeper insight into late antique society and to discuss the potential problem of the progressive assimilation of wealth, power and status on firmer ground.

Such a perspective necessarily entails a quantitative approach, with all the problems connected to quantitative analysis of the ancient world. This quantitative approach itself, moreover, must be 'residual': a 'middle class' is defined only by defining and subtracting upper and lower classes, as is implicit in the concept 'middle' itself. While Marx, in his

---

[99] Alföldy, *Römische Sozialgeschichte* (n.9, above) 281-82.

[100] Roda, 'Classi medie' (n.13, above) 27-28.

description of society as consisting only of landlords, capitalists and workers, did not recognise any 'middle class', Weber always distinguished 'positively' and 'negatively' privileged' classes; it was only later that he went on to define what fell in between, on the basis of the distinctions he had already drawn.[101] Even Paul Veyne, who attempted to define the 'middle-class' of the Principate as free persons who did not belong to any order but were economically well-to-do, speaks of an 'image neutre, non "marquée": ils n'étaient ni miséreux, ni personnages publics, ni dévalorisés par la tare de la naissance servile; on parlait d'eux sans plus de mépris que de révérence'.[102] It is necessary to avoid excesses such as those found in some archaeological works, which try to classify, for example, the social status of the occupants of graves, making claims such as 'middle-class burials were defined as those containing between five and fifteen objects; upper-middle-class burials, as those containing between sixteen and fifty objects'.[103] Nonetheless, integrating literary, epigraphic and papyrological sources can permit some analysis of different levels of wealth and income in Late Antiquity. Where such information is available, it indeed constitutes precious data that allows us to understand the respective position of different social agents and to compare that to their standing in the rank system. It must be emphasised that this is the aim of the analysis, and definitely not 'to ascertain the distribution of income, or wealth, and then to fit it to the Pareto or longnormal or whatever is the most appropriate curve',[104] which is simply impossible[105].

In recent years, a 'poverty threshold' – starting from the bottom – for the late antique period has been defined with a good degree of certainty. Beginning with the passage of Hermogenian cited above, Jean-Michel Carrié placed this threshold at a notional yearly income of four *solidi*, which coincides with calculations, made possible by papyri, of the cost of living in late antique Egypt.[106] We must therefore conclude that four to five *solidi* per year was an income that guaranteed subsistence:[107] according to Morelli, three *solidi* would have allowed one worker to survive, and five a small family.[108] This is consistent with the data we have about salaries.[109] To cite some examples: functionaries in the civil service and

[101] Weber, *Economy and society* (n.54, above) 303-04.

[102] Veyne, 'La plèbe moyenne' (n.43, above) 1178. See also Christ, 'Grundfragen' (n.12, above) 220 (who emphasises the importance of the quantitative economic aspect in the definition of the 'middle classes'); J. P. Sodini, 'Archaeology and Late Antique social structures', in *Theory and practice in Late Antique archaeology*, ed. L. Lavan and W. Bowden (Leiden 2003) 25-56, at 42-48.

[103] M. R. De Maine, I. Lazar and V. V. Perko, 'Middle-class burials in three provincial Roman cemeteries: Emona, Celeia, Šempeter', in *Life of the average Roman. A symposion*, eds M. R. De Maine and R. M. Taylor (White Bear Lake 1999) 35-49, at 41.

[104] Runciman, 'Class, Status and Power?' (n.49, above) 41-42.

[105] A final disclaimer: it is true that the data presented are drawn from a very broad chronological range, from the fourth to the seventh century. But if such economic data are quantified in units of value connected with gold, the extraordinarily stable purchasing power of this metal in the period under consideration ensures that this comparison is not void of scientific value.

[106] J.-M. Carrié, '*Nihil habens praetor quod ipso die vestiebatur. Comment définir le suil de pauvreté à Rome?*', in *Consuetudinis Amor. Fragments d'histoire romaine (IIe-VIe siècle) offerts à Jean-Pierre Callu*, ed. F. Chausson and E. Wolff (Rome 2003) 71-102, at 91-95. On subsistence levels under the Principate, see Jacques and Scheid, *Rome et l'intégration de l'Empire* (n.3, above) 309-11.

[107] Leont. *V. Joh. Eleem.* 5. H. Gelzer, *Leontios' von Neapolis Leben des Heiligen Johannes des Barmherzigen Erzbischofs von Alexandrien* (Freiburg and Leipzig 1893) *ad loc.* in fact considers a salary of three *solidi* per year very low.

[108] F. Morelli, *Olio e retribuzioni nell'Egitto tardo (V-VIII d.C.)* (Florence 1996) 181.

[109] Carlà, *Oro* (n.28, above) 117-21.

soldiers received four *solidi* per year, subsequently adjusted in various ways; four *solidi* minus five carats was the salary of a *tabularius* on the *cursus publicus*.[110] At the other end of the scale, we have Olympiodorus' senators, with a yearly income of at least 1,000 pounds of gold (and a further third of that amount consisting of products from their estates), and generally those persons who could record their accounts in *centenaria / kentenaria*, units of 100 pounds of gold in use since the fifth/sixth century CE for large sums of money.[111]

We are thus left with all the people 'in between', as Weber would say, whose property fell somewhere between tens and several hundred pounds of gold, and whose yearly income could oscillate between 5-10 and several thousand *solidi*. One such example might be the *possessor – ktetor* from Alexandria whose property, according to the life of John the Almsgiver, was worth 200,000 *modii* of wheat and 108 pounds of gold.[112] It is possible to introduce a series of case studies on groups that should be analyzed and understood from this point of view. In particular, the sources allow us to recognise professional categories that fall within these very broad limits; this is particularly interesting, since it permits comparison with their social standing and potentially also their 'rank' (indeed often very stratified). Space constraints make it impossible for me to linger on such examples here, which range from specialized workers,[113] to functionaries,[114] to merchants and bankers[115]. I will pick only one concrete case study to show the opportunities that such an approach opens up for the researcher: physicians.

The position and potential social mobility of physicians has already been the subject of discussion for earlier periods.[116] It was long thought, and still is often proposed, that doctors were generally well-to-do, or even rich, and that free or freed physicians found their profession an important means of social advancement, even if it was admitted that they did not reach the decurionate.[117] More 'minimalistic' theories presume that physicians did not enjoy high social standing and had very limited chances of mobility: doctors only very rarely would have reached levels of economic comfort or social recognition (*e.g.* by nomination to the sevirate).[118] Only a limited number could be considered as having belonged to the 'middle classes'.[119] Medicine frequently was not even recognised as one of the *artes liberales*, as Isidore of Seville still underlines – naturally, because doctors had

---

[110] *PGot.* 9. See R. Rémondon, 'Papyrologica', *Chronique d'Égypte* 41 (1966) 165-79, at 173-78. On the expression *solidi x para keratia y*, see Carlà, *Oro* (n.28, above) 367-78.

[111] G. Dagron and C. Morrisson, 'Le *kentenarion* dans le sources byzantines', *Revue Numismatique* s.6, 17 (1975) 145-62; J.-P. Callu, 'Le *centenarium* et l'enrichissement monétaire au Bas-Empire', *Ktéma* 3 (1978) 301-16; Carlà, *Oro* (n.28, above) 322-24.

[112] Leont. *V. Joh. Eleem.* 26 Gelzer.

[113] I. Milewski, 'Löhne und Preise bei den Kappadokischen Kirchenvätern und bei Johannes Chrysostomus', *Münstersche Beiträge zur antiken Handelsgeschichte* 19 (2000) 48-58, at 51-52; Carlà, *Oro* (n.28, above) 119-21.

[114] Carlà, *Oro* (n.28, above) 324-26.

[115] Carlà, *Oro* (n.28, above) 291-96, 373-76, 400-402.

[116] A huge amount of literature has been dedicated to this topic; the following footnotes will cite only the most recent or most relevant publications, to which one must refer for a more complete overview of relevant studies.

[117] B. Rémy and P. Faure, *Les médecins dans l'Occident romain* (Bordeaux 2010) 65-66. The position of Kudlien, *Stellung* (n.65, above) 210-15, who claims that doctors might even have access to the Senate, is more extreme.

[118] M. Hirt, 'Le statut social du médecin à Rome et dans les provinces occidentales sous le Haut-Empire', in *Archéologie et Médecine* (Juan-les-Pins 1987) 95-107, at 99-100; H. W. Pleket, 'The social status of physicians in the Graeco-Roman world', in *Ancient medicine in its socio-cultural context*, eds P. J. Van der Eijk, H. F. J. Horstmanshoff and P. H. Schrijvers (Amsterdam and Atlanta 1995) 27-34. See also Kudlien, *Stellung* (n.65, above) 35-36.

[119] A. Buonopane, 'Ceti medi e professioni: il caso dei medici', in *Ceti medi e professioni* (n.13, above) 79-92, at 85.

to be paid:[120] 'it seems improbable that more than a few percent of Roman healers could have claimed to practice medicine as a liberal art'.[121] What we must recognise is that the social position of doctors varied along a very broad spectrum, in particular according to the different places where they practised their profession.[122] But there also clearly is confusion between the economic status of doctors (they could be very well paid) and formal social promotion, from which they were generally excluded, even if their social importance was recognised in some other public form (*e.g.*, fiscal immunities).[123] This is made clear by the limited number of Roman citizens who chose the medical profession:[124] Pliny the Elder writes, for instance, that 'medicine is the only one of the arts of Greece, that, lucrative as it is, Roman gravity has hitherto refused to cultivate'.[125] Cicero thinks that *medicina* and *architectura* are honest occupations *iis, quorum ordini conveniunt*.[126]

In Late Antiquity medicine enjoyed, without a doubt, great prestige, and it is often presumed that the profession made progressive gains in importance and status,[127] which led to physicians being admitted to the urban magistracies by Constantine and at the end of the fourth century to the Senate.[128] Indeed, the state became increasingly interventionist in defining the status and privileges of doctors, who were previously dependent on the urban *curiae*.[129] Physicians were differentiated into *medici* and *archiatri*: the second term indicates

---

[120] *Dig.* 50.9.4.2; *Isid. Etym.* 4.13.1: but Isidore indicates the cause in the fact that medicine is placed on a higher level, as *secunda philosophia* (4.13.5). On the contradictory assessment of medicine in Late Antiquity, see B. Lançon, 'Les itinéraires de la guérison en Occident dans l'Antiquité Tardive', in *Archéologie et Médecine* (n.118, above) 39-53, at 43-44. See also K. H. Below, *Der Arzt im römischen Recht* (Munich 1953) 56-60; F. Kudlien, 'Medicine as a liberal art and the question of the physician's income', *Journal of the History of Medicine and Allied Sciences* 31 (1976) 448-59; Kudlien, *Stellung* (n.65, above) 154-81; J. André, *Être médecin à Rome* (Paris 1987) 37-39, 133. A. Bernard, *La rémunération des professions libérales en droit romain classique* (Paris 1936) 83-84 tried to solve this problem by supposing that the Latin word *medicus* indicated two different groups of persons, 'real' physicians, whose art was liberal, and 'handworkers', such as the surgeons. This explanation is not convincing, because Greek and Latin never differentiate between such groups, but rather solely between 'private', 'public' and 'official' doctors, as will be shown below.

[121] R. P. G. Jackson, 'Roman medicine: the practitioners and their practices', in *Aufstieg und Niedergang der römischen Welt* II.37.1 (Berlin and New York 1993) 79-101, at 90. It is important to note that 'education does not by definition stratify society, it only differentiates it. Polymaths do not constitute a high-ranking stratum in the way that the rich, or the social aristocracy, or the holders of governmental office do' (Runciman, 'Class, Status and Power?' [n.49, above] 33).

[122] Hirt, 'Statut social' (n.118, above) 102-103.

[123] Below, *Artz* (n.120, above) 22-55; M. Kobayashi and F. Sartori, 'I medici nelle epigrafi, le epigrafi dei medici', *Acme* 52 (1999) 249-58. It is important to remember that Caesar granted citizenship to all physicians working in Rome (Suet. *Jul.* 42).

[124] Bernard, *La rémunération* (n.120, above) 69-70; Alföldy, *Römische Sozialgeschichte* (n.9, above) 148-49; Kudlien, *Stellung* (n.65, above) 34; André, *Être médecin* (n.120, above) 36-38.

[125] Plin. *Nat.* 29.17; trans. J. Bostock and H. T. Riley. On the profitability of the medical profession, see also Galen. *Meth. Med.* 1.1. Scholars who think that doctors had or could have had a higher social position under the Principate refer to these passages as 'anachronistic'; see Kudlien, *Stellung* (n.65, above) 39.

[126] Cic. *Off.* 1.151. A 'positive' evaluation of this definition is found in Bernard, *La remuneration* (n.120, above) 71 and in Kudlien, *Stellung* (n.65, above) 39-40, but it is not convincing.

[127] It is important in any case to underline that scientific interest in medicine and recognition of its cultural importance are not necessarily connected to a high social position of doctors, as realised already by G. Baader, 'Der ärztliche Stand in der römischen Republik', in *Acta conventus XI Eirene* (Wrocław 1971) 7-17, at 17.

[128] André, *Être médecin* (n.120, above) 38-39; J. Korpela, *Das Medizinalpersonal im antiken Rom. Eine sozialgeschichtliche Untersuchung* (Helsinki 1987) 143-44 (explicitly connecting this transformation to the Christianization of society); C. Vogler, 'Les médecins dans le Code Théodosien', in *Droit, religion et société dans le Code Théodosien*, ed. J. J. Aubert and P. Blanchard (Geneva 2009) 327-73, at 339-40.

[129] *Dig.* 50.9.1.

the 'recognised' doctors, whether attached to the court (*archiater sacri palatii*) or to other groups and communities: a law of CE 368 establishes fourteen of them in Rome, one for each urban region, with additional *archiatri* for *Portus*, *Xystus* and for the Vestal virgins; an *archiater* of *Hippo Regius* is mentioned by Augustine in *Ep.* 41.2.[130] They also were in charge of teaching medicine: *archiatri* were permitted to join the senatorial order.[131] Their selection was subject to precise rules.[132] Constantine's laws imposed respect for doctors – one may not commit violent acts against them and had to pay their salaries.[133] Doctors' salaries, divided into *mercedes*, the money paid directly by the patient, and *salaria* paid to 'public' doctors by cities or the court, were indeed very high.[134] The above mentioned law of 368 CE declares that, 'knowing that their subsistence allowances are paid from the taxes of the people, [*archiatri*] shall prefer to minister to the poor honorably rather than to serve the rich shamefully. We allow these physicians also to accept those offerings which healthy persons offer them for their services, but not those offerings which persons in danger of death promise them for saving their lives'.[135]

Doctors' salaries were considered excessive already under the Principate (and sometimes led to legal proceedings), and the few quantitative data we find in late antique sources show that indeed little had changed.[136] Attested yearly salaries range from 35 to 99 *solidi*: for example, Flavius Phoebammon, the city doctor of Antinoopolis, whose will is dated to 570, earned 60 *solidi* per year.[137] Prices for single treatments also appear to have been high, ranging from 5 *solidi* for a cataract in the Visigothic Kingdom to the 100 *solidi* mentioned for the East by John Chrysostom (if that is not an exaggeration).[138] These high prices do not clash with the fact that *liberalitas* and *philanthropia* were considered essential elements of the profession. The Greek idea that the best doctor, who comes from a wealthy family and does not practise medicine to earn money,[139] cures for free quickly gave way to the Christian *topos* of the doctor healing the poor without asking for a fee.[140] Ausonius states that his father used to cure the poor for free,[141] and, according to the hagiographical legend,

---

[130] *CTh* 13.3.8. See Below, *Artz* (n.120, above) 49-51; V. Nutton, '*Archiatri* and the medical profession in antiquity', *Papers of the British School at Rome* 45 (1977) 191-226, at 197-98; 204-205; 208-10.

[131] H. F. Frings, *Medizin und Arzt bei den griechischen Kirchenvätern bis Chrysostomos* (Bonn 1959) 31-32; Jones, *Later Roman Empire* (n.83, above) 1012; André, *Être médecin* (n.120, above) 106-10; Vogler, 'Les médecins' (n.128, above) 338-39, 357-58.

[132] *CTh* 13.3.9 (370); Symm. *Rel.* 27.

[133] *CTh* 13.3.1.2 (321 or 324). Below, *Artz* (n.120, above) 43-44; Vogler, 'Les médecins' (n.128, above) 344.

[134] R. Herzog, in *Reallexicon für Antike und Christentum, s.v. Arzthonorar*: vol. 1, 724-25; André, *Être médecin* (n.120, above) 133-39; Vogler, 'Les médecins' (n.128, above) 353-56.

[135] *CTh* 13.3.8.pr.-1; trans. C. Pharr. See André, *Être médecin* (n.120, above) 110-15.

[136] Carlà (n.29, above) 121. See also Frings, *Medizin und Artz* (n.131, above) 91-92; Korpela, *Medizinalpersonal* (n.128, above) 149.

[137] *PCairoMasp* 67151. See Jones, *Later Roman Empire* (n.83, above) 1012.

[138] *Lex Visig.* 11.1.5; Joh. Chrys. *In paral.* 4; *CJ* 1.27.1.41 (534). Also Joh. Chrys. *In cap. V et VI Gen. Hom. XI* (*PG* 53.184). On further references to the price of physicians in John Chrysostom, see also Milewski (2000) 49-50.

[139] Kudlien, *Stellung* (n.65, above) 452-54.

[140] See *e.g.* Philostorg. *Hist. Eccl.* 3.15. Frings, *Medizin und Artz* (n.131, above) 92.

[141] Auson. *Epiced.* 11-12. M. Albana, '*Archiatri... honeste obsequi tenuioribus malint quam turpiter servire divitibus (CTh 13, 3, 8)*', in *Poveri ammalati e ammalati poveri*, eds R. Marino, C. Molé and A. Pinzone (Catania 2006) 253-79, at 258-64.

Saints Cosmas and Damian, protectors of doctors, refused to accept any recompense for their services.

In the case of *archiatri* and 'official' doctors, who enjoyed social recognition and also a long list of privileges,[142] their high salary undoubtedly corresponded to their high social standing. Antoninus Pius had already granted a pre-existing *immunitas* enjoyed only by the 'official' doctors of every city, whose maximum number was now also fixed.[143] Constantine granted *medici*, together with *grammatici* and *professores*, further immunity (but not from the *munera curialia*); they moreover could not be forced to hold public office (*honores*).[144] Immunity from *munera curialia* seems to have been conferred later by Julian.[145] *Archiatri*, on the contrary, were freed from the duties of curials, senators and *comites*.[146] Macrobius' Dysarius, a *vir clarissimus* who appears uninvited at the symposium and is simply said to be the best doctor of Rome, had high social standing; from Symmachus we know that he held the most senior position among the professors of medicine, that is, the Roman *archiatri*.[147] Symmachus' friend Dionysius must also have belonged to this 'aristocracy' of doctors,[148] as also must have Gregory of Nazianzus' brother Caesarius.[149] Ausonius' father, as already mentioned, was also a doctor, described by his son as *primus arte medendi*.[150] He was a member of the *curiae* of both Bordeaux and Bazas, but was exempt from the corresponding *munera*, which hints at a position as *archiater*.[151] This could explain his higher social standing, compatible with his appointment as praetorian prefect of Illyricum in 377.[152] Even if we admit a good deal of rhetorical spin in this case, it is interesting that he is said to have been *non opulens nec egens*.[153] Even Avitus' letters do not show that physicians generally enjoyed high social status:[154] in one letter (11) he simply mentions that a blind bishop, Maximian, is going to Arles to find a better ophthalmologist; in another (38) he expresses the hope that the deacon Helpidius will be able to cure Ceretius' son. Rather

[142] Bernard, *La rémunération* (n.120, above) 67-68; André, *Être médecin* (n.120, above) 140-42. Korpela, *Das Medizinalpersonal* (n.128, above) 138-42 speaks of a bipartition of the Late Antique physicians in a 'privileged' group (the *archiatri*) and the 'not privileged' one (the normal *medici*), mostly following the general idea of a bipartition of Late Antique society. Additionally, the doctors would also have, like society as a whole, become more structured in a fixed hierarchy.

[143] *Dig.* 27.1.6.2; 8. See Below, *Artz* (n.120, above) 34-40.

[144] *CTh* 13.3.1 (321 or 329), confirmed by 13.3.3 (333). See also 13.3.10 (370) in reference to the city of Rome.

[145] Jul. *Ep.* 75b. See also Lib. *Ep.* 723.

[146] *CTh* 13.3.2 (326 [354]), confirmed by 13.3.4 (362). See also 13.3.12 (379) on the extension of privileges to the heirs of *archiatri* operating at the imperial court. Further confirmations include 13.3.13-19 (387; 393; 414; 427; 428).

[147] Macr. *Sat.* 1.7.1: *Evangelum adesse nuntiat cum Dysario, qui tunc Romae praestare videbatur ceteris medendi artem professis.* Symm. *Ep.* 3.37: *Dysarius clarissimus vir, qui inter professores medendi summatem iure obtinet locum...* Dysarius is presented as a young professor of medicine already in Symm. *Ep.* 9.44. A. Pellizzari, *Commento storico al libro III dell'epistolario di Q. Aurelio Simmaco* (Pisa 1998) 145-46 proposes that Dysarius was one of the fourteen *archiatri* of the city of Rome.

[148] Symm. *Ep.* 8.64; 9.4.

[149] *PLRE* I, *s.v. Caesarius 2*:169-70.

[150] Auson. *Epiced.* 1-2.

[151] See *CTh* 13.3.1-4.

[152] *PLRE* I, *Iulius Ausonius 5*: 139.

[153] Auson. *Epiced.* 7.

[154] So *e.g.* L. Di Paola, *'Naturalis siquidem cura est aegris dare laetitiam*: medici e malattie, cure naturali e terapie mediche nella testimonianza di alcuni autori tardoantichi', in *Poveri ammalati e ammalati poveri* (n.141, above) 281-97, at 294-96.

than reveal the high social standing of these doctors, he admits the 'inadequate medical care or lack of specialists in Vienne'.[155] Helpidius, also a friend of Ennodius,[156] was indeed apparently a famous doctor in Ostrogothic Italy and also attended the court of Theoderic, to whom he was probably bound by personal friendship;[157] the king apparently agreed to authorize building repairs at Spoletium at his request and at the end of his life told him about his vision of the dead Symmachus.[158] But Helpidius' potential proximity to the king and his presence at court implies only an informal, personal high position (a 'status') and says nothing about the social standing of doctors generally. Ultimately, Helpidius himself was a deacon and apparently never had any other institutional recognition or function.[159]

Indeed, defining the social standing of 'simple' doctors is not so easy. Even leaving aside slaves who worked as doctors,[160] we nonetheless can still observe, as Rilinger stressed, that legal texts punish physicians in forms that generally do not apply to *honestiores*, thus revealing that the 'lawgiver' almost automatically excludes them from the category of privileged persons.[161] In conclusion, what we know is that some doctors, and in particular *archiatri*, had greater chances to attain higher social positions than their colleagues; ordinary physicians occupied very different places in society, and their wealth and income were not directly related to their 'rank' or even their 'status'.

The long march of the economy

As mentioned above, traditional interpretations of Roman society stressed the progressive simplification of social stratification in Late Antiquity and the general convergence of economic poverty and social poverty or the lack of authority and power. But the concrete examples and source material presented thus far have shown that this model is substantially misleading, and that 'rank' and 'class' were far from overlapping completely; on the contrary, they seem to remain conceptually distinct – even if in discourse they often tend (vaguely) to be mapped onto one another. Additionally, it has been shown that the available quantitative information about wealth and salaries allows us to recognise a broad and complex stratification of wealth that runs on a continuous spectrum throughout late antique society and is far from endorsing the idea of a progressive disappearance of the 'middle classes'.

Some details, however, particularly questions of chronology, require further discussion. It has been claimed that the sixth century witnessed an important social development whereby wealth rose to become the indicator of social status *par excellence*, supplanting

---

[155] D. Shanzer and I. Wood, *Avitus of Vienne. Letters and Selected Prose* (Liverpool 2002) 359.

[156] Ennod. *Ep.* 7.7; 8.8; 9.14; 9.21.

[157] *PLRE* 2, *Helpidius 6*: 537.

[158] Cassiod. *Var.* 4.24; Proc. *BG* 1.1.38.

[159] *Medicus diaconus* in the definition of *Vit. Caes.* 1.41.

[160] See n.1. Slave doctors are mentioned in this period, *e.g.* by Jul. *Contr. Heracl.* 207 c-d; *CJ* 6.43.3.1; 7.7.1.5.

[161] *PS* 5.22.3; Rilinger, *Humiliores* (n.7, above) 71.

and marginalizing the ranks discussed above. Patlagean viewed this process as culminating in the age of Justinian:

> La législation de Justinien fait donc explicitement place aux pauvres, comme à une catégorie sociale dont le statut juridique est déterminé per une estimation qui s'affirme, en fin de compte, de plus en plus clairement dans l'ordre économique.[162]

In fact, according to Patlagean, this development, progressing more rapidly in the East than in the West, will have been nearly complete in the former already towards the end of the fifth century.[163] In her opinion, a law such as *CJ* 5.5.7 (454), which clearly explains the difference between a poor girl and a humble and sordid one, illustrates the effort to reassert a legal distinction in the face of a social evolution that was moving towards assimilation and would ultimately emerge victorious in the Greek laws of the end of the century. But the examples introduced to the discussion are largely irrelevant: the fact that poor people who could not afford to pay fines (or finish a job they had been paid for) were to be punished corporally, as stated in *CJ* 8.10.12.5e and 9 (474-479), is nothing new: corporal punishment in the event of an unpaid monetary fine had already been envisaged in the third century, for example, by Modestinus.[164] On the contrary, this constitution could illustrate another case in which a professional category – here architects – had rather low social standing (being subject to flogging and expulsion from the city, which *honestiores* would have been spared),[165] yet was expected to be able to pay relatively large amounts of money: the fine was indeed 10 pounds of gold.

Nothing new is offered by *CJ* 11.41.7 (457-467), in which conviction for pimping carries the penalty of banishment to the *metalla* or exile for the *euteles* and the loss of rank and wealth for those who 'have a *militia* or an honourable profession'. Close scrutiny of this second category, defined only by rank and lacking any reference to economic wealth, shows that *euteles* here must be intended as equivalent to Latin *humilior* or *tenuior* – a meaning that is well attested for this word. Even Justinian's legislation fails to show any clear movement in the direction suggested by Patlagean. The distinction between *honesti* and *humiles* proposed for differentiating penalties in the *Institutions* neither departs from the categories already in use nor shows any positive approach to rank and class[166]. Furthermore, when in *Nov.* 90.1 (539), concerning the right to testify, it is stated that 'witnesses shall be men of good reputation and who, by reason of their rank (dignity), position of state-service, wealth or honourable occupation, are above any accusation of perjury' (trans. J. F. Blume), this merely reiterates in simplified form the complex interaction of the many

---

[162] Patlagean, 'La pauvreté' (n.25, above) 67.

[163] Patlagean, 'La pauvreté' (n.25, above) 62-63.

[164] *Dig.* 2.4.25. Already De Robertis, 'La variazione' (n.3, above) 61-62 stressed the necessity of distinguishing between the existence of different punishments according to the person of the criminal and variation due to the impossibility of applying the penalty established by the law; see also De Robertis, 'La variazione' (n.3, above) 100-102.

[165] *Dig.* 48.19.28.2.

[166] *Inst.* 4.18.4.

different factors we have seen operating in the fourth century, which had already been enforced for centuries.[167]

Agapetus' claims that no one should take pride in the nobility of his ancestors and that 'all men have clay as forefather of their race: those who flaunt themselves in purple and fine linen; those invested with the diadem, [and those lying exposed, seeking alms]' also clearly have no bearing on the subject to hand, since these propose, following a well-known *topos*, a radical image of society, with a mainly moral significance.[168] Agapetus also highlights only the economic aspects, and his reference to purple is meant to indicate wealthy people rather than persons of high rank, as comparisons with another passage in his work confirms.[169] Thus, also in the case of the symbolic use of purple, political, social, and economic categorizations can be confounded or differentiated as dictated by the needs and requirements of a single author.

We have to wait until the *Procheiros Nomos* (27.22) to read that 'the poor (*penetes*) do not testify'. The difference with Hermogenian's threshold of 50 gold coins is evident: Hermogenian sought to define the property conditions that qualified someone to initiate an accusation, being potentially liable to pay if it proved wrong; here the poor person is simply delegitimized as a possible witness. This rapprochement of economic and social categories in fact seems to be the product of a development that took place much later than Patlagean thinks. In the *Ecloga Isaurica*, published in 740, different punishments for the same crime are structured on a tripartite system based on wealth, composed of the rich, people of lesser fortune (*endeesteros*) and the destitute poor (*penes kai aneuporos*).[170] Even later, the law of the Macedonian dynasty separates proprietors entirely from the poor, who are now called *ptochoi*.[171]

The new proximity of the poor and humble, of the lack of wealth and social discrimination, resulting in its formal establishment in the legal texts, far from being typical of Late Antiquity, is a product of Byzantine developments and became entrenched only two centuries after Justinian. That Justinian's legislation paid particular attention to the poor, their activities and their assistance is another problem, which does not directly interest us here, and which Patlagean has excellently discussed.[172] But once again this in no way implies a shift in social definitions towards the construction of a binary social classification poor/rich, which existed no more in the sixth century than it did in the fourth.

The evaluation of the middle classes

As is well known, Greek philosophers developed a high assessment of the middle classes. Already in the archaic period, voices could probably be heard claiming the superiority of the middle classes from a moral point of view, or at least from the perspective of individual happiness – a fragment of Phocylides known through Aristotle points in this direction.[173] In

[167] On the right to give testimony under the Principate, see Rilinger, *Humiliores* (n.7, above) 114-36.

[168] Agapet. 4; trans. P. N. Bell. The words in brackets are missing in two manuscripts.

[169] Agapet. 16. At 53 and 60, Agapetus presents charity and care for the poor as a necessary quality of the emperor. This also adds nothing to the argument proposed.

[170] *Ecl. Isaur.* 17. Patlagean, 'La pauvreté' (n.25, above) 65.

[171] Patlagean, 'La pauvreté' (n.25, above) 77-78.

[172] Patlagean, 'La pauvreté' (n.25, above) 67-72.

[173] Phocyl. 10 Hiller-Crusius.

423-21 BCE, Euripides may have expressed this sentiment in his *Hiketidai* – if the verses in question are authentic, since there is strong suspicion of interpolation:

> There are three classes of citizens: the rich are useless and always lusting for more; the poor, who lack their daily bread, are dangerous, for they assign too great a place to envy and hurl their stings at the rich, being deceived by the tongues of wicked leaders; of the three classes the one in the middle preserves states by keeping to the disciplines that the city establishes[174].

Plato completely agreed, when around the mid-fourth century BCE he wrote his *Laws* and discussed the moral value of property he regarded as neither too big nor too small:

> The same holds true for the possession of money and property; honor should be bestowed on this according to the same scheme. Excesses of each of these create enmities and civil strife both in cities and in private life, while deficiencies lead, for the most part, to slavery.[175]

Aristotle went further, not only by restating that the optimal individual condition is that of one who has moderate wealth, but also by elaborating a political theory centred on the concept of 'middleness' and aimed at giving to this 'middle class', as the most balanced, control over the state:

> Now in all states there are three elements; one class is very rich, another very poor, and a third is middling. It is admitted that moderation and the mean are the best, and therefore it will clearly be best to possess the gifts of fortune in moderation; for in that condition of life men are most ready to listen to reason. [...] So that the one class [the excessively rich] cannot obey, and can only rule despotically; the other [the excessively poor] knows not how to command and must be ruled by slaves. Thus arises a city, not of freemen, but of masters and slaves, the one despising, the other envying. [...] But a city ought to be composed, as far as possible, of equals and similars; and these are generally the middle classes. Wherefore the city which is composed of middle-class citizens is necessarily best governed; they are, as we say, the natural elements of a state. And this is the class of citizens which is most secure in a state, for they do not, like the poor, covet their neighbours' goods; nor do others covet theirs, as the poor covet the goods of the rich; and as they neither plot against others, nor are themselves plotted against, they pass through life safely. Wisely then did Phocylides pray – 'Many things are best in the mean; I desire to be of a middle condition in my city'. Thus it is manifest that the best political community is formed by citizens of the middle class, and that those states are likely to be well-administered, in which the middle class is large, and larger if possible than both the other classes, or at any rate than either singly; for the addition of the middle class turns the scale, and prevents either of the extremes from being dominant.[176]

As is evident, a monetary definition was always at stake, which generates further moral, social, and thus also political considerations and categorizations. It is obvious that neither

---

[174] Eur. *Suppl.* 238-45; trans. D. Kovacs.
[175] Plat. *Leg.* 5.728e-729a; trans. T. L. Pangle.
[176] Arist. *Pol.* 1295 a-b; trans. B. Jowett, slightly modified.

these philosophical theories nor the effective position of individuals in daily life could ever lead to the rise of something recognizable as 'class consciousness' in the ancient world. Nonetheless, it must be acknowledged that economic standing was extremely important in defining one's personal role in society. Holding 'economic capital' – to use Bourdieu's terms – was recognized as essential to acquiring 'social capital' or even 'cultural capital'.

But in spite of John Chrysostom's 'quantitative' observation, the Roman world never developed – not even in Late Antiquity – such a 'myth' that the middle classes were morally superior and more apt to undertake the administration of the state, even if some sources acknowledge their existence.[177] The reasons are extremely difficult to pin down: it has been suggested that the 'middle class' was generally perceived as a temporary situation in the Early Imperial period, thanks to elevated levels of social mobility. An alternative to this answer may lie in the greater importance placed on 'rank' rather than 'class' and wealth in the construction of 'status'. It certainly has nothing to do with the later appearance, in some Christian writers, of the moral exaltation of poverty; this, coupled with maxims from the Gospels and sometimes also with an idealized image of the poor and virtuous Roman Republic,[178] is not an expression of a concrete political philosophy, but is generally based on hyperbolic and highly rhetorical *topoi*.

For Late Antiquity the traditional explanation is that the middle classes would have progressively disappeared to make way for a society constituted on a rigid binary system. But it should be clear by now that the economic classification and stratification of 'classes' do not at all show the progressive simplification and reduction of society to two large groups as has sometimes been reconstructed. It is therefore necessary to ask whether this kind of reduction applied at least to the definition of 'rank', and whether late antique society ultimately appeared composed of two large groups corresponding to what the legal sources call the *honestiores/potentiores* and *humiliores/tenuiores*. The legal sources indeed give such an impression, but their purpose is certainly not to describe late antique society. Even the normative character of this distinction is not intended to define how society should be (still less to shape it), but only to structure the penal system so as to differentiate between punishments for people belonging to the higher and lower ranks.[179]

On the contrary, in the West the creation and conferral of new titles is attested in the fifth century and the sources seem to define categories that do not belong to the highest imperial élite (below *clarissimi* and *perfectissimi*), but are still distinct from the normal *plebs*. They in fact define a new structuring of the 'middle ranks'. Two titles, attested both by inscriptions and documentary sources, appear particularly relevant: *vir laudabilis* and *vir honestus*. A traditional interpretation associates the first title with decurions and their families, the second with *honestiores* – but the etymological connection is misleading in suggesting that the term might have a specific legal meaning connected to that distinction.[180]

[177] Plin. *Nat.* 26.3 is the most famous.

[178] *E.g.* Salv. *Gub. Dei* 1.10; 3.10.

[179] Cardascia, 'Apparition' (n.3, above) 319-24; R. Villers, 'Le droit romain, droit d'inégalité', *Revue des Études Latines* 47 (1969) 462-81, at 467-68; Löhken, *Ordines dignitatum* (n.4, above) 23-24; Rilinger, *Humiliores* (n.7, above) 263-73; M. Bretone, 'Tra storia sociale e storia giuridica', *Rechtshistorisches Journal* 8 (1989) 35-51, at 49-50; Jacques and Scheid, *Rome et l'intégration de l'Empire* (n.3, above) 303. De Castro-Camero, 'Consecuencias' (n.3, above) 336-37 clearly illustrates the relevance of the distinction in the penal system but, even though he addresses only this topic and clearly shows that all the sources concern inflicting punishment, he still believes that these categories were the 'legal consequences' of a 'social dichotomy'.

[180] O. Hirschfeld, 'Die Rangtitel der römischen Kaiserzeit', *Sitzungsberichte der Berliner Akademie* (1901) 579-610, at 609-10; A. Ferrua, 'Tre sarcofaghi importanti da S. Sebastiano', *Rivista di Archeologia Cristiana* 27 (1951)

It is difficult to establish when these words are used in a 'technical' sense, indicating a precise title, and when they are merely honorific adjectives.[181] There is, for example, no attestation of *laudabilis* in the *CTh* that can securely be considered an example of the 'official' title.

Hirschfeld's theory that *laudabilis* was potentially an additional title for *spectabilis* is no longer tenable. According to Sannazaro, the title originally applied to the senatorial *ordo* but later, from the end of the fourth century, became an honorific title for members of municipal *curiae*.[182] A *laudabilis vir* is *curator rei publicae* in Madauros under Julian:[183] since he also describes himself as *ducenarius* it can be excluded that he belonged to the senatorial order. An inscription dated to 383 presents us with a *laudabilis* who is *flamen perpetuus* and *sacerdotalis provinciae* in Africa Proconsularis.[184] In 341 two inscriptions in Ocriculum honoured the patron of the town, Sextus Cluvius Martinus, *vir laudabilis*, *omnibus honoribus perfunctus*:[185] this is a reference to civic magistracies. The title is attested also in an inscription from 408 CE celebrating M. Sentius Redemptus, the *primarius* of Interamna Lirenas, and in another one from 543 CE, for Paulus, a *decurio* in Cimitile.[186] An honorary inscription from Minturnae celebrates the patron of the city with this title at the end of the fourth or the beginning of the fifth century.[187] In Augustine we find two *comites* described as *laudabiles*, but it is impossible to determine what kind of *comitiva* they held (*comes civitatis*?).[188] Indeed, a sarcophagus from Vicetia presents us with a *laudabilis ex comite* (*civitatis*),[189] while an inscription from Volsinii memorializes a *laudabilis* physician.[190] Either we must presume that he was also a member of the local *curia* (in spite of the immunity granted by Julian), or we have to entertain the possibility that the title *laudabilis* also had a less 'institutionalized' meaning. The same applies to the funerary inscription (dated between 542 and 565) of the *vir laudabilis* Urbicus, an *archiater* from Capua.[191] Another *archiater* and *laudabilis* is Marcellinus from Abellinum, whose funerary

7-33, at 11; M. Sannazaro, '*Viri laudabiles* e *viri honesti* in età tardoantica: alcune considerazioni', in *Ceti medi in Cisalpina* (n.13, above) 281-91, at 284. So *e.g.* F. Grossi Gondi, *Trattato di epigrafia cristiana latina e greca* (Rome 1920) 119 thought that *vir honestus* indicated *honestiores* and members of their families, additionally interpreting *honestior* as someone who held some official post.

[181] *E.g.* Symm. *Ep.* 2.10; 3.32. On this problem in general, see Cracco Ruggini, 'Il Senato' (n.72, above) 247-48.

[182] Sannazaro, '*Viri laudabiles*' (n.180, above) 282. The connection between the title and local *curiae* had already been proposed by P. Koch, *Die byzantinischen Beamtentitel von 400 bis 700* (Jena 1903) 98-99; Grossi Gondi, *Trattato* (n.180, above) 119. In Symmachus *laudabilis* is indeed sometimes added to *clarissimus* as a further specification: *e.g. Rel.* 23.3-4; 26.3. Nothing certain can be said about the *viri laudabiles* in Symm. *Ep.* 1.67 and 7.127. The *vir clarissimus* Taurus, quaestor and praetorian prefect, is also designated *laudabilis* in *CIL* 6.41336 (364-367); the word does not seem used here as a proper title but rather as a generic honorific adjective.

[183] *ILAlg* 1.2100.

[184] *CIL* 8.11025.

[185] *CIL* 11.4096-97.

[186] *CIL* 10.1354; 5349. See also *CIL* 5.7405 (*praepositus et clericus*), 8.15880; 9.1563; 9.2074 (a *curator* from Beneventum, 522 CE); 9.3685. For further examples, see E. De Ruggiero and G. Barbieri, *Dizionario Epigrafico* IV, 1 (Rome 1957) 470-471, *s.v. laudabilis*.

[187] *AÉ* 1989, 137.

[188] Aug. *Ep.* 227 and 244.

[189] *ILCV* 254 = *AÉ* 1980, 504.

[190] *CIL* 11.2835 = *ILCV* 255.

[191] *AÉ* 1989, 165.

inscription is dated to 505:[192] we accordingly must state that this coincidence of medical activity and *laudabilitas* is attested in central Italy. By modifying Sannazaro's chronological scheme, we can conclude that *laudabilis* originally developed from a 'generic' meaning as an additional title and over the course of the fourth century, in tandem with and then instead of the 'senatorial' use, came to identify members of the local élite who did not manage to attain the rank of *clarissimus*.[193] In the Latin papyri from Ravenna many individuals are given the title *laudabilis*; where further details are available, they appear connected to the *curia* and local magistrates, often being *principales*;[194] *laudabilitas vestra* is used to indicate the entire *curia*.[195] The term additionally appears to have a specific ecclesiastical use, which may have been derived from its 'technical' meaning, since in turn it is apparently not attested until the end of the fourth century:[196] Symmachus gives the title *laudabilis* to Damasus, bishop of Rome, but once again it is difficult to understand with what precise meaning.[197]

The use of *honestus* is even more complicated.[198] This term, even if only with a 'generic' meaning,[199] had been applied in Republican times generally to members of the equestrian order.[200] In the imperial period it seems to lose this specificity, being used to designate senators, *equites* and generally persons of high standing also at a local level.[201] From the third century onwards it was used as a title and, according to Pflaum, was applied to *curiales*;[202] however, in many cases he includes funerary inscriptions with the expression *honestae memoriae*, which cannot be considered significant evidence for official titles held by the deceased. Once again it is necessary to distinguish between a generic use, frequent in the literary sources, and a more 'technical' one, generally connected to persons holding a relevant position in their society.

The local nature of both titles *laudabilis* and *honestus* forces us to allow for local variations in exact meaning and use; it will not have escaped attention, for example, that almost all the inscriptions mentioned come from Italy and Africa.[203] Some African inscriptions present us

---

[192] *EDR* 100317 (13.05.2009; A. De Carlo):
http://www.edr-edr.it/edr_programmi/visualizza.php?id_nr=EDR100317, last accessed 13.08.14.

[193] Sannazaro, '*Viri laudabiles*' (n.180, above) 286.

[194] *P. Lat.* 4-5 B IV 6-7; 29.1; 31.iii. See Koch, *Die byzantinischen Beamtentitel* (n.182, above) 98-99.

[195] *P. Lat.* 4-5 B *passim*; 7.9; 10-11 B IV 4. See Koch, *Die byzantinischen Beamtentitel* (n.182, above) 117.

[196] Sannazaro, '*Viri laudabiles*' (n.180, above) 283-84.

[197] Symm. *Rel.* 21.6.

[198] For example, it is difficult to know whether the qualification *honestissimus vir*, attributed to Helpidius at the moment he is sought as patron of Paestum (*CIL* 10.478), is intended in a 'technical' sense as a title or merely as an honorific.

[199] On the 'generic' meaning of *honestus* in Latin culture, see still F. Klose, *Die Bedeutung von honos und honestus* (Breslau 1933) 98-136.

[200] Koch, *Die byzantinischen Beamtentitel* (n.182, above) 96-97; Navarro, *Formación* (n.3, above) 45-63 (excessively schematic in places, and see Klose, *Bedeutung* [n.199, above] 121).

[201] Hirschfeld, 'Rangtitel' (n.180, above) 608-609; Navarro, *Formación* (n.3, above) 165-98 (here too it is necessary to an excessively schematic treatment; additionally, Navarro never takes epigraphic attestations of the term into consideration).

[202] H.-J. Pflaum, 'Titulature et rang social sous le Haut-Empire', in *Recherches sur les structures sociales dans l'antiquité classique*, ed. C. Nicolet (Paris 1970) 159-85, at 183-85. See also Klose, *Bedeutung* (n.199, above) 122.

[203] *RICG* 1.129, probably from the first half of the fifth century, mentions a *laudabilis* in Trier, but the inscription is highly fragmentary.

with *viri honesti* who are also *flamines perpetui*;[204] another inscription, from the year 400-401, records three *honesti*, two of whom had held the office of *curator rei publicae*, while the third was the son of one of them.[205] The members of the *curia* of the city of Reate, who in 557 signed the *gesta municipalia*, were one *spectabilis*, one *laudabilis* (even if the entire *curia* is addressed as *laudabilitas vestra*) and five *viri honesti*.[206] Indeed, we have cases of *viri honesti* who are members of the local curiae and local magistrates, as are two *edilicii* and *duoviralicii*, father and son, from *Africa Proconsularis*;[207] nonetheless, the connection of *honesti* to the *curiae* seems to be less strong than that of the *laudabiles* in the Ravenna papyri as in other sources.[208] What appears particularly relevant is that this title is also gradually given to persons who assumed an important social position on account of their profession, or rather their economic prosperity: since the late fifth to the sixth century, merchants, goldsmiths, and bankers are designated *viri honesti*.[209] Thomas, a *negotiator*, is a *vir honestus* from Mantua in 540 CE;[210] Iohannes, an *argentarius* from Rome, bears the same title in an inscription from 522.[211] In sixth-century Milan we have a *honestus aurifex*, Lucifer.[212] In the Latin papyri from Ravenna we find as *honesti* the *negotiator* Syrus, Iohannes, the *negotiator* Martinus, the *argentarii* Theodorus and Flavius Basilius[213] and even the most famous banker of the city, Iulianus, if he is the same man who signed a papyrus in 539.[214] The title apparently also belonged to local functionaries, such as the *orrearius* Quiriacus, the *adiutor forensis* Iulianus, the *forenses* Iohannes and Vitalis and the *collectarius* Petrus in Ravenna or the *tabellio urbis Romae* Theodorus.[215] *Honesti* therefore appear to belong to a more fluid system that does not, as Pflaum thought, result from social 'petrification' and the decline of social mobility, 'fossilized' by the multiplication of titles.[216] Precisely on the contrary, both titles, and *honestus* in particular, seem to reflect the need to express the dignity and social standing associated with a particular institutional or economic position in society that we would describe as 'middle'.[217] While *laudabilis* appears to refer to a 'middle rank', *honestus* has some characteristics that suggest it may have been the formal designation of a 'middle class'.

The chronological development of this phenomenon has become clear: such titles begin to appear at the end of the fourth century; their meaning and application are clarified over the course of the fifth and then the sixth century. As stated above, these titles were introduced and used only in the Western part of the Empire, and they did not have a univocal translation

---

[204] *CIL* 8.759-60; 1283.

[205] *CIL* 8.969.

[206] *P. Lat.* 7.97-104.

[207] *CIL* 8.12260 = *ILCV* 310.

[208] Sannazaro, '*Viri laudabiles*' (n.180, above) 286-87.

[209] Koch, *Die byzantinischen Beamtentitel* (n.182, above) 96-97.

[210] *CIL* 5.4084 = *ILCV* 673.

[211] *CIL* 6.9162. See also *ICUR* 5.13410, where another anonymous *argentarius honestus* is mentioned.

[212] *Monumenta Epigraphica Christiana* 2.1, X.5.

[213] *P. Lat.* 4-5 B VI 10; 20.123; 25.6-7; 29.2.

[214] *P. Lat.* 30.92.

[215] *P. Lat.* 6; 17.39; 29.8; 31.ii.10; 31.iii.3.

[216] Pflaum, 'Titulature' (n.202, above) 184-85. F. W. Deichmann, 'Giuliano argentario', *Felix Ravenna* 56 (1951) 5-26, at 11 regards it as an honorific title with no official meaning; but its formulaic use in the Ravenna papyri contradicts him.

[217] Deichmann, 'Giuliano argentario' (n.216, above) 11; Sannazaro, '*Viri laudabiles*' (n.180, above) 287.

or equivalent in Greek. Nonetheless, Egyptian papyri in the same period also show a much less clear-cut and organised multiplication of honorary titles, also involving the world of tradesmen and the 'middle-classes', but it is not possible to analyze them on account of space constraints.[218] Löhken was probably right to argue that late antique society was more complicated than that of the Principate;[219] and, as has been shown, within this complicated society there was still room for 'middle classes' and for 'middle ranks'.

University of Exeter

---

[218] *E.g. ellogimotatos, aidesimos, eudokimotatos, thaumasiotatos.* See O. Hornickel, *Ehren- und Rangprädikate in den Papyrusurkunden. Ein Beitrag zum römischen und byzantinischen Titelwesen* (Giessen 1930).

[219] Löhken, *Ordines dignitatum* (n.4, above) 35.

LEGENDARY AND REAL WEALTH
IN THE ARSACID KINGDOM

LEONARDO GREGORATTI

After Crassus' disastrous defeat at Carrhae in northern Mesopotamia (53 BC) and until the early decades of the third century AD, Rome's plans for hegemony in Western Asia were aggressively thwarted by the Parthians. Established in central Asia a few decades after Alexander's death, situated near the remotest borders of the Seleucid Empire, the Parthian Kingdom was able to exploit the disintegration of that huge Hellenistic state by conquering the Iranian plateau, Babylonia, and Mesopotamia as far as the Euphrates river. From that time on the river was the dividing line between the two superpowers struggling for supremacy in Western Asia: Rome and Parthia.[1]

Although the narrative of Rome's political confrontation with the 'barbarians' beyond the Euphrates occupies significant portions of the works of authors like Tacitus, Plutarch, and Cassius Dio amid a general scarcity of oriental sources, modern scholars have pointed out that what Greek and Roman writers tell us about the history and administration of the Parthian Kingdom is incomplete and largely stereotypical.[2]

In 2007, C. Lerouge's book *L'image des Parthes dans le monde gréco-romain* demonstrated that the Romans' perception of the Arsacid Kingdom and its inhabitants, organization, and culture owed much to the characterization of the ancient Persians conceived by the Greek historiographical tradition five centuries before. The vastness of its domains, its exotic luxury, ostentatious opulence, despotic government; the intrinsic weakness and extreme instability of its monarchs and any central authority; the intermingling of private and public life in the secret chambers of the harem where intrigue, seduction, and murder constituted means of political action, are all aspects that had figured in Classical Greek historiography and literature.[3] In many respects Roman historians portrayed the Parthians, Rome's oriental enemies, as the 'New Persians', that is, the heirs of the Achaemenids in

---

[1] In general on the history of the late Parthian Kingdom, see N. C. Debevoise, *A political history of Parthia* (Chicago 1938); K.-H. Ziegler, *Die Beziehungen zwischen Rom und dem Partherreich. Ein Beitrag zur Geschichte des Völkerrechts* (Wiesbaden 1964); K. Schippmann, *Grundzüge der parthischen Geschichte*, (Darmstadt 1980); A. D. H. Bivar, 'The political history of Iran under the Arsacids', in *The Cambridge History of Iran, the Seleucid, Parthian and Sasanian periods*, ed. E. Yarshater (Cambridge 1983), III, 1, 21-99; E. Dabrowa, *La politique de l'état parthe à l'égard de Rome – d'Artaban II à Vologèse I (ca 11 – ca 79 de n. è.) et les facteurs qui la conditionnaient* (Krakow 1983); R. N. Frye, *The history of ancient Iran* (Munich 1984); J. Wolski, *L'Empire des Arsacides* (Leuven 1993); J. Wiesehöfer, *Das antike Persien. Von 550 v. Chr. bis 650 n. Chr.* (Munich-Zurich 1994); M. Rahim Shayegan, *Arsacids and Sasanians: Political ideology in post-Hellenistic and late antique Persia* (Cambridge 2011).

[2] For the sources for the history of the Parthian Kingdom see *Quellen zur Geschichte des Partherreiches*, eds U. Hack, B. Jacobs, and D. Weber (Göttingen 2010).

[3] In Aeschylus' *Persians*, followed by the works of Herodotus, Ctesias of Cnidus, and Xenophon: see E. Hall, *Inventing the barbarian. Greek self-definition through tragedy* (Oxford 1989); J. M. Hall, *Ethnic identity in Greek antiquity* (Cambridge 1997).

the East just as the Roman Empire succeeded to the Greeks in the West. In this context the Parthians, like the Achaemenids, are described as a decadent people, addicted to luxury and pleasure.[4]

In the mainstream Roman imagination, the Parthian Kingdom was considered to be an extraordinarily wealthy state, not unlike the oriental states that had previously dominated Western Asia. In the everyday experience of a Roman citizen, the East was closely connected to exotic luxury goods like silk and spices, which, from the first century BC, began to flow ever more abundantly into Mediterranean markets in response to rapidly increasing demand from the cities' leading classes.[5] The influx of luxury goods from the East along with traditional tales, already widespread in the Greek world,[6] about the fabulous riches of the ancient oriental states, helped to reinforce in Western countries the idea that every Eastern empire, including the Parthian, had a huge amount of wealth at its disposal.

This common opinion found a significant place in the historiography of later centuries. There are numerous references to the legendary riches of the Arsacids in narratives of *res orientales,* the chronicles of Rome's uneasy cohabitation with the 'barbarians' beyond the Euphrates.[7] Already in the years immediately following the Roman defeat at Carrhae, for instance, and in the entire historiographical tradition that followed, one of the explanations given for Crassus' calamitous Oriental campaign, in addition to his quest for personal glory, was his well-known greed.[8]

Historians thus attempted to give a convincing explanation for the unjustified war in the East, an explanation that was instrumental in ascribing personal responsibility for the military campaign and its devastating consequences, including the devastating attacks that the Arsacids later launched on the Roman provinces, solely to Crassus. The historical tradition thus stressed the importance of Crassus' greed in the events that took place. Crassus aimed, as Plutarch states, to reach and take the city of Seleucia on the Tigris, the terminus of sea and overland routes from Central Asia and India and, according to Pliny the Elder, one of the richest and most populous cities outside Roman borders.[9] Of course, this explanation worked perfectly because it fit the widely held idea of a Parthian Kingdom full of fabulous riches ripe for the taking.

There are constant references to the opulence that characterised the Arsacid lifestyle in Roman historians' accounts. Describing Surena, the Parthian general, Plutarch states that he 'was not an ordinary man at all, but in wealth, birth, and consideration, he stood next to the king. [...] He used to travel on private business with a baggage train of a thousand camels, and was followed by two hundred wagons for his concubines, while a thousand mail-clad horsemen and a still greater number of light-armed cavalry served as his escort; and had altogether, as horsemen, vassals, and slaves, no fewer than ten thousand men'.[10] Similar observations are expressed by Cassius Dio in describing the journey that Tiridates, the newly appointed king of Armenia, undertook in AD 66 in order to be confirmed on the throne by Emperor Nero. Dio's epitomiser writes: 'Tiridates presented himself in Rome [...]

[4] C. Lerouge, *L'image des Parthes dans le monde gréco-romain. Du début du Ier siècle av. J.-C. jusqu'à la fin du Haut-Empire romain* (Stuttgart 2007).

[5] For a general view on the topic see E. Choisnel, *Les Parthes et la route de la soie* (Paris 2004).

[6] See *e.g.* Hdt. 5.49; 7.118-20; 9.80-81; Ctesias, *FGrHist* 688, F. 37-40; Xen. *Cyr.* 8.8.3.

[7] Lerouge (n.4, above) 352-56.

[8] Vell. Pat. 2.46.2; Plut. *Crass.* 16.1-3; Flor. *Epit.* 2.13.10-12; App. *BCiv.* 2.18; Cass. Dio 40.12.1.

[9] Strab. 16.2.5; Plut. *Crass.* 32; Plin. *Nat.* 6.122; Paus. 1.6.3.

[10] Plut. *Crass.* 21.6-9; 32.4-5.

his whole retinue of servants together with all his royal paraphernalia accompanied him. Three thousand Parthian horsemen and numerous Romans besides followed in his train. [...] Provisions were furnished them free of cost, a daily expenditure of 800,000 sesterces for their support being thus charged to the public treasury'.[11]

In both the episodes concerning Surena and Tiridates, descriptions of the luxury and opulence of the retinues of the two dignitaries, which no doubt created a sensation among their contemporaries, merged in the later historiographical tradition (third century AD) and were probably revised and enhanced to form part of the consolidated and stereotypical tradition that viewed the Parthians as a people addicted to luxury and ostentation.

These historians' attitude toward Arsacid wealth was shared by writers like Tacitus, for whom the opulence shown during the sumptuous banquets of the Nabatean king was suitable more to the Parthians than to the Romans.[12] Many other such references are scattered throughout Roman imperial literature. In the narrative of Apollonios of Tyana's Eastern travels written by Philostratos (AD 172-247), for example, the Great King's palace in Babylon is described as full of gold and precious carpets. Philostratos' narrative is characterized by extensive use of fictional and novelistic elements. The East described by Philostratos is in fact Herodotus' Persian Empire. The names of places and monarchs are changed to give the work a superficial appearance of historicity, but Apollonios' journey through Parthia is ultimately that of a Greek man at the Achaemenid court.[13]

Similar details can be detected in the works of other authors. A recurrent element in the work of Herodian, for instance, are precious vests that the Parthians supposedly wore. According to Herodian, the Parthians produced valuable textiles and wore long light robes 'embroidered in gold and various colours'[14] that reached their feet, the same garment that the Medes, according to Pompeius Trogus, once wore.[15] Herodian goes on to say that this ostentatious wealth caused the Parthian defeat at the hands of Caracalla: once the Parthians had fallen off their horses or were forced to fight on foot, the skilful Parthian knights were easy prey for the Roman legionaries, since they were hampered by their long robes and unable to flee.[16]

From the beginning, Roman historians who wrote about the Arsacids preferred to adopt, at least in part, patterns and forms of the earlier Greek tradition concerning oriental people. Finding themselves obliged to give their audience a representation of a people that challenged Rome's supremacy over the known world, Roman historians used the same stereotypes that the Greeks had conceived for their enemies, the Persians. A series of familiar ethnographic *topoi* was adopted. The immeasurable, ostentatious wealth of the

[11] Cass. Dio 63.1.1-3; Suet. *Nero* 13; Tac. *Ann.* 15.24; F. Cumont, 'L'iniziazione di Nerone da parte di Tiridate d'Armenia', *Rivista di Filologia e di Istruzione Classica* 61 (1933) 145-54; M. Lemosse, 'Le couronnement de Tiridate. Remarques sur le statut des protectorats romains', in *Mélanges G. Gidal* (Paris 1961) 455-68; A. Stépanian, 'Le traité de Rhandée et le couronnement de Tiridate l'Arsacide à Rome', *Revue des Études Arméniennes* 11 (1975/1976) 205-18; Dabrowa, *La politique de l'état parthe* (n.1, above) 146-47; Frye, *History* (n.1, above) 240; J. Wolski, 'Le couronnement de Tiridate par Vologèse I comme roi de l'Arménie: échec de Néron et de l'empire romain', in *Neronia 3* (Rome 1983) 167-78; Wolski, *Empire* (n.1, above) 169-71.

[12] *Cf.* Tac. *Ann.* 2.57.

[13] Philostr. *Vita Apoll.* 1.25, 30, 33-34.

[14] Hdn. 4.11.3; *cf.* 3.4.8, 9.11; 4.10.4, 11.6.

[15] Pomp. Trog. 41.2.4.

[16] Hdn. 4.15.3.

orientals plays a prominent role in Roman accounts, another element that could explain the weakness and degeneracy of oriental peoples in contrast to the Romans.[17]

On the other hand, the imagined connection between the ancient Persians and the Parthians was not totally unsubstantiated. It is probable that the Parthians, originally a steppe people who settled on the northern periphery of the Seleucid Empire, adopted most of the cultural elements and the characteristics of the peoples they later managed to subdue. Hence, it is very likely that accounts of their ostentatious wealth were not entirely fictional but based on facts that were later reworked and exaggerated, under the influence of stereotypes inherited from the Greek literary tradition. It also is evident that in regard to the Parthians, and to all oriental peoples generally, the Romans always had a very limited interest in learning more about the culture and internal dynamics of the Arsacid state.

Such a view of the East, based as it is on old stereotypes, fails to provide the students of this period with information that would be indispensable to fully understand the historical role of the Parthian Kingdom, its structural versatility, and its ability to withstand Roman attacks. The real forms of Parthian wealth were barely perceived in the West, beyond a very basic understanding of the importance of the oriental trade in goods. Distracted by forms of luxury and ostentation, real or fictional, Roman chroniclers failed to take into consideration a more tangible and important form of the wealth of the Parthian Kingdom: wealth based on the exploitation of territorial resources and trade – a kind of wealth that proved to be a fundamental support for the kingdom and an important factor in the revival of Arsacid royal authority and the consolidation of the government after a period of grave political crisis. In other words, the Roman leadership was probably too heavily influenced by the ideological approach to the Arsacids to observe the political transformation of the Parthian empire that gave the King the economic means he needed to consolidate his state.

At the beginning of the first century AD, when the Parthian confrontation with Rome had already reached a critical phase, the Arsacids experienced a period of severe social and institutional instability. The Great King's leadership had been in fact overruled. Arsacid monarchs were kept on their thrones by aristocratic groups. Members of the royal family were induced to rebel against the ruling king with the sole intent of formally legitimising the power gained and wielded by different sectors of the aristocracy. Parthia was torn apart by rival noble factions that represented the different political orientations coexisting in the kingdom. The aristocrats had a shared interest in weakening the monarch to expand their own power, thus enhancing their independence from the Great King.[18]

During the so called 'expansion' period, when the Arsacids successfully conquered most of the satrapies of the ailing Seleucid empire, the Arsacids rewarded noble collaborators by granting them ownership of large portions of the conquered land. Noble families then gradually began to build their own power on the large estates they had received from the king. The absolute control they enjoyed over the territory and population of Parthia was also the basis of their military strength. They had to fight side by side with the monarch, leading onto the battlefield huge personal armies recruited from the subject population that lived on their lands. Equipped and trained at their lords' expense, these units were the backbone of

---

[17] See above, n.6. For more specific aspects of this topic: L. Gregoratti, 'Parthian women in Flavius Josephus', in *Jüdisch-hellenistische Literatur in ihrem interkulturellen Kontext*, ed. M. Hirschberger (Bern 2012) 183-92 and *id.*, 'Fighting a dying enemy: Western view on the struggle between Rome and the Parthians', in *Myth-making and myth-breaking in History and the Humanities*, eds C. Dobre, I. Epurescu-Pascovici and C. Ghita (Bucharest 2012) 25-36.

[18] J. Wolski, 'La périodisation de l'époque parthe en Iran', *Folia Orientalia* 22 (1981/1984) 13-21.

a typical Parthian army, like Surena's contingent at Carrhae,[19] where in 53 BC Crassus was slain with most of his legionaries.[20]

During the first century BC, the 'expansion' phase gave way to a period of consolidation in which no significant territorial gains were made. In this phase, the king's military and financial dependence on the aristocracy became ever more important.[21] The Great King Artabanus II,[22] who ascended the throne in AD 12 after several years of political crisis and internal strife, eventually devised a solution to this problem. His plan was to find new sources of income that would give the King a degree of economic power, counteracting the overwhelming influence of aristocracy. The highly lucrative long-distance trade network, by both land and sea, that connected East Asia and India with the Mediterranean coast, passing through many of the most important Parthian cities, was a promising solution.[23] Controlling these trade routes and establishing an efficient system of collecting taxes on trade goods would give the king the financial resources he needed. To achieve this, it was essential to cultivate new political and institutional relationships that could connect the king directly to all local subjects who were in a position to exert control over long-distance trade and imperial territory. In other words, the king sought to create a network of new allies responsible for trade and territorial control as an alternative to the nobility.

Artabanus tried to include local political and social subjects in his political project, such as the vassal kings, Jewish communities, and Greek *poleis*, with varying results. Unfortunately, the weakness of the Arsacid state made fulfilling his goals very difficult. Several Roman military initiatives shook Artabanus' reign to its very core, exposing its weaknesses, and the system of alliances he created did not survive his death. After a decade of anarchy, Artabanus' vision was revived by Vologaeses I (AD 51-77/80), who is widely regarded as the restorer of Parthian royal authority. Vologaeses strengthened his political leadership of the kingdom by associating his rule with his two brothers Tiridates and Pacorus, monarchs of Armenia and Media Atropatenes respectively. Moreover, Parthian military successes in Armenia against the Romans, which kept the threat from the West at

---

[19] J. Wolski, 'Remarques critiques sur les institutions des Arsacides', *Eos* 46 (1954) 59-82; *id.*, 'L'état parthe des Arsacides. Éssai de reconstitution de son évolution intérieure', *Palaeologia* 7 (1958/1959) 325-32; *id.*, 'Aufbau und Entwicklung des parthischen Staates', in *Neue Beiträge zur Geschichte der Alten Welt*, I, ed. E. C. Welskopf (Berlin 1964) 379-88; *id.*, 'Le rôle et l'importance des mercenaires dans l'état parthe', *Iranica Antiqua* 5 (1965) 103-15; *id.*, 'L'aristocratie parthe et les commencements du féodalisme en Iran', *Iranica Antiqua* 7 (1967) 134-44; *id.*, 'Les relations de Justin et de Plutarque sur les esclaves et la population dépendante dans l'empire parthe', *Iranica Antiqua* 18 (1983) 145-57; *id.*, 'Die abhängige Bevölkerung im Partherreich', in *Antike Abhängigkeitsformen in den griechischen Gebieten ohne Polisstruktur und den römischen Provinzen*, eds H. Kreißig und F. Kühnert (Berlin 1985) 80-87; *id.*, 'Sur l'impérialisme des Parthes Arsacides', in *Archaeologia Iranica et Orientalis. Miscellanea in Honorem Louis Vanden Berghe*, II, eds L. De Meyer and E. Haerinck (Ghent 1989) 637-50; *id.*, 'Die gesellschaftliche und politische Stellung der großen parthischen Familien', *Tyche* 4 (1989) 221-27.

[20] Plut. *Crass.* 23-32; Vell. Pat. 2.46.4. See J. D. Timpe, 'Die Bedeutung der Schlacht bei Carrhae', *Museum Helveticum* 19 (1962) 104-29 and, most recently, G. Traina, *La resa di Roma. 9 Giugno 53 a.C. Battaglia a Carre* (Bari and Rome 2010).

[21] The criticism voiced by Hauser does not seem to undermine the validity of this model. Hauser nonetheless agrees on the fact that in later times the Parthian kings became much less dependent from the nobility and that some major changes intervened: S. R. Hauser, 'Die ewigen Nomaden? Bemerkungen zu Herkunft, Militär, Staatsaufbau und nomadischen Traditionen der Arsakiden', in *Krieg – Gesellschaft – Institutionen, Beiträge zu einer vergleichenden Kriegsgeschichte*, eds B. Meißner, O. Schmitt, and M. Sommer (Berlin 2005) 163-208.

[22] Flav. Jos. *AJ* 18.48-50. See U. Kahrstedt, *Artabanos III. und seine Erbe* (Bern 1950); M. Karras-Klapproth, *Prosopographische Studien zur Geschichte des Partherreiches auf der Grundlage antiker literarischer Überlieferung* (Bonn 1988) 28-34.

[23] U. Ellerbrock and S. Winkelmann, *Die Parther, die vergessene Grossmacht* (Mainz 2012) 169-72.

bay, created the ideal conditions for the realization of Vologaeses' plans for the revival of Arsacid power.[24]

Connections and alliances with local subjects were accordingly intensified. In contrast to Artabanus' effort, the creation of a network of alliances aimed at controlling trade was part of a broader policy of reasserting royal authority over the land. The consolidation of the kingdom went hand in hand with the king's claim to the land and its resources.

The urbanization measures enacted by Vologaeses I and his son Pacorus II (AD 77/80–110) must be interpreted in this context. Pacorus II inherited and continued his father's policy; he was perhaps the Arsacid monarch most involved in the administration of trade routes.[25]

Territorial control was of primary importance in Vologaeses' new system of rule; it was achieved through the deep-set presence of the King's men who protected communication routes and economically vital points. In consequence, new cities began to spring up in Mesopotamia, and many existing cities were enlarged and outfitted with impressive fortresses.[26] For the first time after more than a century and a half of Arsacid domination in Mesopotamia, the Parthian monarchs put in action a massive and systematic programme to repopulate the areas and settlements that had been left totally abandoned or seriously depopulated since the Achaemenid era.

In order to overcome the profound institutional crisis that afflicted it, the Arsacid state was forced to evolve. The Parthian Kingdom assumed the character of a sedentary state, gradually developing more direct and stable forms of territorial occupation and administration. It is fair to suppose that the changes that occurred during the reigns of Vologaeses and his successors significantly influenced the perception of Arsacid royal authority and raised its level of visibility. The palpable presence of structures and people connected to royal power in the cities as well as in areas of economic interest contributed to the spread of a common feeling of belonging to the Iranian Arsacid state among the lowest social classes and new and old local elites, while the previous system, largely dependent on government representatives who were often closely linked to the life and the intrigues of the court, had naturally been unable to evoke the same response.

The monarch himself gave his name to his most famous and most successful foundation: Vologaesias. The precise geographical location of this city is still debated. However, it must have been located in central Mesopotamia, where the Euphrates and Tigris Rivers are at their closest and connected by a series of canals.[27] Such a location is well suited to

---

[24] Debevoise, *Political history* (n.1, above) 176-77; Bivar, 'Histoire politique' (n.1, above) 79; Ziegler, *Beziehungen* (n.1, above) 66; Karras-Klapproth, *Prosopographische Studien* (n.22, above) 192-99; Dabrowa, *La politique de l'état parthe* (n.1, above) 132; Wolski, 'Couronnement' (n.11, above) 165; M. J. Olbrycht, 'Das Arsakidenreich zwischen der mediterranen Welt und Innerasien, Bemerkungen zur politischen Strategie der Arsakiden von Vologases I. bis zum Herrschaftsantritt des Vologases III. (50-147 n. Chr.)', in *Ancient Iran and the Mediterranean world*, ed. E. Dabrowa (Krakow 1998) 123-59, at 125.

[25] G. Košelenko, 'La politique commerciale des Arsacides et les villes grecques', in *Studi in onore di Edoardo Volterra*, I (Milan 1971) 761-65; E. J. Keall, 'Parthian Nippur and Vologases' southern strategy: a hypothesis', *Journal of the American Oriental Society* 95 (1975) 620-32, at 624.

[26] Keall, 'Parthian Nippur' (n.25, above) 623-24; M.-L. Chaumont, 'Études d'histoire parthe III. Les villes fondées par les Vologèse', *Syria* 51 (1974) 75-81; E. Dabrowa, 'Die Politik der Arsakiden auf dem Gebiet des südlichen Mesopotamiens und im Becken des Persischen Meerbusens in der zweiten Hälfte des I. Jahrhunderts n. Chr.', *Mesopotamia* 26 (1991) 150-53; Olbrycht, 'Das Arsakidenreich' (n. 24, above) 129-30; Frye, *History* (n.1, above) 227-28.

[27] Plin. *Nat.* 5.89-90; 6.120, 122-123; Ptol. 5.20.1-2, 20.6; Amm. Marc. 23.6.23, 25; Steph. Byz. *Ethn. s.v.* Βολογεσσιάς, p. 175 Meineke; Zosim. 3.23; J. H. Schmidt, 'L'expédition de Ctésiphon en 1931-1932', *Syria* 15

Vologaeses' plan to regain control of southern Mesopotamia and its commercial routes. The reasons for Vologaeses' Mesopotamian policy, a region as economically vital as it was socially and politically important, were simple: royal authority was to be re-established not through dialogue with local elites of Semitic or Greek origin, a strategy adopted by Artabanus that had proven unsuccessful, but by means of local presence and direct control exercised by the state authority and its representatives.

Naturally, this could be achieved only at the expense of aristocratic groups of Greek origin, who were unwilling to accept the conditions of royal control and government of the cities. The ruling classes of the cities had remained strong both inside and outside their enclave at Seleucia on the Tigris, a wealthy commercial metropolis, by virtue of the control they continued to maintain over the trade that reached their cities.

In regard to Seleucia, the core of the Greek presence in Babylonia, the Parthian monarch sought to obtain dominance over the enormous commercial interests that gravitated toward the city and sustained its wealth, political strength and influence. Actual control of the city was not the king's chief interest, but it would ensue regardless once the financial factors on which the city's autonomy depended were eliminated. The only feasible means of undermining Seleucia's power lay in the unstable and changing nature of the caravan trade itself, which varied strongly with the geopolitical conditions of the territories involved, besides commercial motives of expediency, and the collaboration of the ruling authorities of the state formations the trade routes crossed.

Vologaeses' idea was to create an alternative and competitive trade network in which his royal authority and representatives could not be hindered by the monopoly of the Greek traders. This was the ultimate purpose of the founding of Vologaesias: the creation of a new Seleucia – open to foreign commerce, free of Hellenistic mercantile factions, and a place where the ruling was class connected with the court and faithful to the monarch and strongly encouraged the presence of non-Greek merchants.

Vologaeses obtained the desired results with this shrewd initiative. He gradually was able to supplant Seleucia as the most important Mesopotamian station along the route to Characene and the harbors of the Persian Gulf, the terminus of the sea routes from India.[28] Gradually excluded from the trade routes toward northern Mesopotamia and deprived, at least in part, of the huge profits it had made via trade activity, the life blood of its economy and true foundation of the political and social power wielded by the Greek ruling classes, Seleucia fell into a period of economic and cultural decline.[29]

This change in commercial traffic seems to be confirmed by information found in the only epigraphic sources that explicitly refer to the movements of men and goods in southern Mesopotamia in the first three centuries of the Christian era: the corpus of caravan inscriptions from the city of Palmyra. Of the nearly 34 documents that attest the extent and intensity of the trade interests of the city's entrepreneurial classes, perhaps only the oldest,

---

(1934) 1-23; Chaumont (1994) 77-81; A. Maricq, 'Classica et Orientalia 7. Vologésias, l'emporium de Ctésiphon', *Syria* 36 (1959) 267-71; A. Oppenheimer, 'Babylonia Judaica in the Talmudic Period', *Tübinger Atlas des Vorderen Orients*, Reihe B, Beihefte, no. 47 (Wiesbaden 1983) 456-61; M. Negro Ponzi, 'Al-Madā'in: problemi di topografia', *Mesopotamia* 40 (2005) 145-69, at 147-49. Ptolemy mentions some other foundations connected to the royal house, such as Pacoria and Tiridata: 5.18.7.

[28] M. Schuol, *Die Charakene. Ein mesopotamisches Königreich in hellenistisch-parthischer Zeit* (Stuttgart 2000); L. Gregoratti, 'A Parthian port on the Persian Gulf: Characene and its trade', *Anabasis. Studia Classica et Orientalia* 2 (2011) 209-29.

[29] Košelenko, 'Politique commerciale' (n.25, above) 764-65.

dating back to AD 19,[30] mentions the city of Seleucia; from the first half of the first century AD, however, several texts mention the presence of Palmyrenes in Vologaesias.[31]

The foundation of Vologaesias and the logistical advantages it offered would not have been possible without the widespread presence of royal officials in the territory responsible for policing and overseeing the trade routes. Under Vologaeses I and his son Pacorus II,[32] vast areas of southern Mesopotamia were reoccupied. Large fortresses were built everywhere, such as the fortified complex on top of Tell Babil in Babylon,[33] or Kish (Tell Bandar), Tell Irsheideh ibn Alwan (Hamrin), Tell Abu Su'ud and Tell al-Khubari,[34] all exhibiting similar architectural features.[35] The fortified centre about which we are best informed is that at Nippur.[36] Between AD 70 and 80, the pre-existing temple terraces were reused as the foundation for the construction of a mighty fortress. The structure was erected in three different construction phases, none of which, however, according to the findings of the archaeological survey, was completed. It was certainly frequented from the reign of Pacorus II (AD 77/80–110) until approximately AD 175, with its greatest prosperity falling in the period between AD 80 and 130,[37] the same years that witnessed the rise of Palmyra and the intensification of merchant trade along the Lower Euphrates.[38]

In the same years that the Arsacids retook possession of the territory in southern Mesopotamia, in the reign of Pacorus II and as the result of a concerted effort by the

[30] *Inv.* 9.6a = *CIS* 2.3924 = *PAT* 270; J. Teixidor, 'Un port romain du désert, Palmyre et son commerce d'Auguste à Caracalla', *Semitica* 34 (1984) 11; M. Gawlikowski, 'Palmyra and its Caravan Trade', in *Palmyra and the Silk Road, Annales Archéologiques Arabo-Syriennes*, 42 (1996) 140; *id.*, 'Palmyra et l'Euphrate', *Syria* 60 (1983) 53-68, at 63; R. Drexhage, *Untersuchungen zum römischen Osthandel* (Bonn 1988) 22-23; J.-B. Yon, *Les notables de Palmyre* (Beirut 2002) 25-26; L. Gregoratti, 'The Palmyrenes and the Arsacid policy', in *Voprosy Epigrafiki: Sbornik statei* 4 (2010) 23-24; J.-B. Yon, *Inscriptions grecques et latines de la Syrie*, 17.1 (Palmyra 2012) 36-38, no. 24.

[31] *Inv.* 10.112; 9.14 = *CIS* 2.3916; 10.124; C. Dunant, *Le sanctuaire de Baalshamin à Palmyre, III. Les inscriptions* (Neuchâtel 1971) n. 45; J.T. Milik, *Dédicaces faites par des dieux (Palmyre, Hatra, Tyr) et des thiases sémitiques à l'époque romaine* (Paris 1972) 12-14; *Inv.* 3.29 = *CIS* 2.3949 and *Inv.* 3.21 = *CIS* 2.3933; *Inv.* 9.15 = *CIS* 2.3917 = *PAT* 263; M. Gawlikowski, *Palmyre VI: Le temple palmyrénien, Etude d'épigraphie et de topographie historique* (Warsaw 1973) 34, 73; Yon, *Notables* (n.30, above) 103-04, 108-11, 121-22; S.R. Hauser, 'Tempel für den palmyrenischen Bel', in *Getrennte Wege?: Kommunikation, Raum und Wahrnehmung in der alten Welt*, ed. R. Rollinger, A. Luther and J. Wiesehöfer (Frankfurt 2007) 228-55; J.F. Healey, *Aramaic inscriptions and documents of the Roman period, Textbook of Syrian Semitic inscriptions*, IV (Oxford 2009) n. 30, 147-50; Yon, *Inscriptions* (n.30, above) 35-36, 39-40, 102-04, 137-40, 159-61, 226-28, nos. 23, 25, 88-89, 127, 150, 246-47.

[32] Karras-Klapproth, *Prosopographische Studien* (n.22, above) 123-25.

[33] B. Haussoulier, 'Inscriptions grecques de Babylone', *Klio* 9 (1909) 352-63; W. Eilers, 'Iran und Babylonien zwischen Alexanderzeit und Islam', *Archäologische Mitteilungen aus Iran* n.s. 17 (1984) 195-219; S. R. Hauser, 'Babylon in arsakidischer Zeit', in *Babylon: Focus mesopotamischer Geschichte, Wiege früher Gelehrsamkeit, Mythos in der Moderne*, ed. J. Renger (Saarbrücken 1999) 207-39, at 216-18, 228-30.

[34] P. R. S. Moorey, 'The city of Kish in Iraq: archaeology and history, ca. 3500 B. C. to A. D. 600', *American Journal of Archaeology* 80 (1976) 65-66; G. Bergamini, 'Parthian fortifications in Mesopotamia', *Mesopotamia* 22 (1987) 195-214, at 203.

[35] Bergamini (n.34, above) 206-08.

[36] J. Knudstad, 'A report on the 1964-65 excavations at Nippur', *Sumer* 22 (1966) 113-14; *id.*, 'A preliminary report on the 1966-67 excavations at Nippur', *Sumer* 24 (1968) 95-106; H. J. Nissen, 'Südbabylonien in parthischer und sasanidischer Zeit', *Baghdader Mitteilungen* 6 (1973) 80-82; E. J. Keall, 'How many kings did the Parthian King of Kings rule?', *Iranica Antiqua* 29 (1994) 263-68; Dabrowa, 'Die Politik' (n.26, above) 151-52.

[37] In those same years (AD 82-130) was built the palace of Abu Qubur by Baghdad: H. Gasche and N. Pons, '*Abū Qubūr 1990, II. Chantier F, le 'bâtiment parthe'*', *Mesopotamia History and Enviroment, Series I, Northern Akkad Project Reports*, 7 (Ghent 1991) 11-34; G. R. H. Wright, 'Abū Qubūr. The 'Parthian Building' and its Affinities', *Mesopotamia History and Environment, Series I, Northern Akkad Project Reports*, 7 (Ghent 1991) 75-91.

[38] E. J. Keall, 'Political, Economic and Social Factors on the Parthian Landscape of Mesopotamia and Western

royal family, Ctesiphon, the capital of the kingdom, began to take on the features of a real city.[39] Soon, a grandiose and organized town arose in the immediate vicinity of Seleucia. Ctesiphon soon became home to the royal court, influenced and shaped the social, economic and cultural life of Seleucia, and finally incorporated it in its slow but sure urban expansion.

It seems legitimate to connect Vologaeses' policy also to the phenomenon of urbanization in the newly acquired Kingdom of Armenia, which his brother Tiridates ruled.[40] We know that Tiridates rebuilt the capital city Artaxata with the financial support of Rome, renaming it Neroneia.[41] An inscription from the city of Garni dating from AD 76 to 77 mentions the construction of a fortress, which almost certainly was carried out by hired craftsmen from Asia Minor.[42] It is not possible, however, to separate Tiridates' construction plans from a larger and more complex project of consolidation of the presence of the king's representatives in the territory of the country. It is significant that analogous building activity has been attributed to Tiridates' successor, Sanatruces.[43] According to predominantly Armenian sources, one of the initiatives of Sanatruces was the founding of the city of Mthsurkh (*Mcurkᶜ*) at the confluence of the Arsanias and Kara-su rivers.[44]

As we have seen both in Armenia and Mesopotamia, two of the best known regions of the Parthian empire, the Great King consolidated his power by intensifying Arsacid presence throughout the territory and effectively managing its resources. The rebirth of the Parthian state, which successfully withstood repeated Roman attacks over the following decades, was based on a form of wealth intimately tied to its geographical location. The exploitation of trade routes, however, was only one aspect of Parthia's territorial wealth, albeit a vital one. The wealth of Parthia was generated by the exploitation of territorial resources, by the urbanization of the land, by trade between old and newly founded settlements, and by manufacturing in highly urbanised areas – in short, by all the activities on the territory that the Parthian state now intended to control directly.

In the late Parthian empire, wealth based mainly on booty and conquest gave way to a much less gaudy form of wealth, wealth produced by cities and trade; in other words, a sort of 'structural' wealth that permeated and influenced the entire government endowed with

Iran: Evidence from Two Case Studies', in *Mountains and Lowlands: Essays in the Archaeology of Greater Mesopotamia*, eds D. L. Levine and T. C. Young (Malibu 1977) 84-86; Keall, 'Parthian Nippur' (n.25, above) 620-32; Keall (1994) 267-72; K. Ciuk, 'Pottery from Parthian, Sasanian, and Early Islamic levels at Nippur, Iraq 1st - 9th century AD', *Bulletin of the Canadian Society for Mesopotamian Studies* 35 (2000) 57-80.

[39] Amm. Marc. 23.6.23; Olbrycht, 'Das Arsakidenreich' (n.24, above) 129.

[40] For a general overview concerning the archaeological data provided by Artashat and other Armenian sites: A.V. Tonikian, 'The layout of Artashat and its historical development', *Mesopotamia* 27 (1992) 161-87; M. H. Zardarian and H. P. Akopian, 'Archaeological excavations of ancient monuments in Armenia 1985-1990', *Ancient Civilizations from Scythia to Siberia* 1.2 (1995) 169-95; A. V. Tonikian, 'Architecture of dwelling houses of Artashat, capital of ancient Armenia (2nd Cent. B.C. – 4th Cent. A.D.)', *Ancient Civilizations from Scythia to Siberia* 3 (1996) 15-37; J. Santrot, *Arménie: Trésors de l'Arménie ancienne, des origines au IVe siècle* (Paris 1996) 178-84, 187-91; Z. D. Khachatryan, 'Archaeological Research in Artaxata. Preliminary Report 2003-2004', *Parthica* 7 (2005) 19-28.

[41] Cass. Dio 63.7.2.

[42] *SEG* 15.836.

[43] Cass. Dio 68.30; Arr. *Parth.* Frgm. 47 = *Suida, s.v.* Σανατρούκης, p. 934 Bekker; P. Asdourian, *Die politischen Beziehungen zwischen Armenien und Rom von 190 v. Chr. bis 428 n. Chr.* (Freiburg 1911) 100-101.

[44] Sebeos; Movses Khorenatzi *P.H.* 2.35-36; pseudo-Pavstos Buzand, 3.1; 4.14 e 24; M.-L. Chaumont, 'L'Arménie entre Rome et l'Iran I. De l'avènement d'Auguste à l'avènement de Dioclétien', in *Aufstieg und Niedergang der römischen Welt* 2.9.1, eds H. Temporini and W. Haase (Berlin and New York 1976) 71-194, at 129-30.

strong historical and political value, a wealth much different from the sheer ostentatious luxury that the Western literary tradition attributed to the Arsacids.

Durham University

'THE EYE OF THE NEEDLE':THE MORALITY OF WEALTH IN THE ANCIENT WORLD

JEREMY PATERSON

> Wealth is not without its advantages and the case to the contrary, although it has often been made, has never proved widely persuasive.
>
> (J. K. Galbraith, *The affluent society*)

Just like the poor, the rich are always with us. To say this, however, is not to assert that there is something natural or inevitable about such a state of affairs. As John Stuart Mill pointed out in his *Principles of Political Economy*, the distribution of wealth 'is a matter of human institution solely. The things once there, mankind individually, or collectively, can do with them as they like'.[1] All societies have had to decide what the distribution should be, what the relationship between rich and poor should be, and to what extent, if any, those with wealth have obligations to those without it.

Pity, or better compassion, for the poor does have some claims to be a basic normal human instinct. For Schopenhauer, for example, it was the foundation of all morality: 'compassion, as the sole non-egoistic motive, is also the only genuine moral one' (*On the Basis of Morality* 19). However, how that sense of compassion should be expressed, and how it should be acted on, raises very serious problems, which through much of history have not been addressed in a very analytical, philosophical, or economic way, as Gordon Tullock, one of the creators of Public Choice Economics, argued powerfully.[2] He pointed to his experience in China and Korea in the aftermath of the Second World War. Here he uncomfortably observed that if he were to redistribute his government income among the poor people he saw, and thus dropped himself to the level of the average Chinese income, he could have saved from starvation about 50 or 60 human beings every year. Yet he did not do it. He had to face up to the fact that he was not willing to impoverish himself in order to prevent a lot of real suffering and death among other people. Further, he experienced another problem familiar to anyone from the West who has travelled in poor countries. Giving to one poor person immediately results in being faced with many others who have equally good claims to my compassion. As a result, many, just like Tullock, give up giving anything to street beggars. Tullock demonstrates that it is no easy matter to construct a philosophically satisfying theory of why the rich should transfer wealth to the poor, although there have been heroic attempts to do so.[3]

There is yet one more complexity, which arises from the widespread perception in the countries, particularly of the West, that in the economic crises of 2008 onwards, the rich

---

[1] J. S. Mill, *Principles of political economy* (1848), Book 2.1.1.

[2] G. Tullock, *The economics of wealth and poverty* (Brighton 1986) 2-4.

[3] Particularly, in recent times, J. Rawls, *A theory of justice* (Cambridge, Mass. 1971) and A. Sen, *The idea of justice* (London 2009).

have been able largely to avoid their share of comparative hardship. Most of the help for the poor comes from the poor or the less well-off themselves, a proportion of whose income is redistributed by a taxation system which the rich are able to avoid. Indeed, it has been observed that compassion possibly declines as individuals become richer and are able to use their wealth to 'insulate' themselves from any sense of dependence on others, for all that they may trumpet their own charitable giving. It will be argued that this is nothing new. The Graeco-Roman world had a strong tradition which recognized the arguments for the rich to be concerned for the poor. However, it has been powerfully argued that the characteristic form of euergetism was limited and led to little in terms of significant redistribution. It is also argued that there was a clear distinction between 'the hard up' who had access to the gifts from the wealthy and the 'penniless' masses who did not (to be seen in the distinction between the Greek terms *penētes* and *ptōchoi*).[4] On the other hand, Christian sources are seen as introducing a wider perception of poverty and a distinctive concept of 'charity'. However, the perceived difference of emphasis on the poor, on compassion, and on charity between Graeco-Roman sources and Christian texts may lie less in any novel or distinctive Christian approach to these matters, and more in the fact that our surviving Graeco-Roman sources reflect mainly the attitudes of the wealthy and comparatively wealthy in society. In contrast, early Christian sources open a window on a sector of society somewhat lower down the economic scale, where self-help, compassion for one's neighbour, and support for those in trouble always had been much more the norm among these sections of the community in general, not just the Christians among them. The lesson to be learned from all this is that at a high philosophical level of analysis the obligations, if any, of the rich towards the poor, are a complex and difficult problem; not only that, once an individual, or society, has decided on a basic position, the implementation of any strategy is also complex and full of ambiguities. You may decide that you have an obligation to use your wealth (or some of it) to help the poor, but how to achieve the best outcome for the poor themselves can be far from clear.

The consequence of all this is that we should expect the responses of individuals and societies in any historical period to the issues of wealth and poverty to be complex, often inconsistent, ambiguous, and extremely varied. Recent work on the classical world has increasingly come to recognize this, but an overly simple analysis still predominates. It is widely argued that the concept of the 'poor' as a distinct category, and of 'charity' by others towards them, is a largely novel creation of Christian thinking.[5] In the Graeco-Roman world euergetism prevailed, but, it is argued, it was limited in scale and it was not motivated primarily by compassion for the really poor (indeed, little of it was designed to reach the poor at all), but was intimately bound up with furthering the image and careers of the wealthy elites.[6]

In, perhaps, AD 362 the emperor Julian wrote to Arsacius, the high priest of Galatia, with orders to 'establish in every city frequent hostels in order that strangers may profit by our benevolence (*philanthropia*); I do not mean for our own people only, but for others also who are in need of money.... It is disgraceful that, when no Jew ever has to beg, and the impious Galilaeans [Christians] provide support not only for their own kind, but ours

[4] W. den Boer, *Private morality in Greece and Rome. Some historical aspects* (Leiden 1979) 162-78.

[5] P. Brown, *Poverty and leadership in the later Roman Empire* (Hanover, N.H. 2002) and *id.*, *Through the eye of a needle. Wealth, the fall of Rome, and the making of Christianity in the West 350-550 AD* (Princeton 2012).

[6] P. Veyne, *Le pain et le cirque. Sociologie historique d'un pluralisme politique* (Paris 1976); English trans., *Bread and circuses: historical sociology and political pluralism* (London 1990).

as well, all men see that our people lack aid from us.' This might be taken as a recognition of the new nature of the Christian approach. But Julian goes on to produce an example from the Graeco-Roman tradition to justify his policy. He quotes Homer *Od.* 14.56, where Eumaeus welcomes Odysseus with 'Stranger, it is not right for me, even if one poorer than you should come, to dishonour a stranger. For strangers and beggars are from Zeus. The gift is small, but it is precious.' The example is an interesting one, because Eumaeus was represented as the son of a king, who had fallen on hard times. Nevertheless it is precious testimony that the practice of hospitality to strangers and to the needy was envisaged as appropriate beyond the class of the nobility. Indeed, Eumaeus' treatment of the disguised Odysseus is contrasted with the abusive welcome Odysseus gets at the suitors' table in the palace.

Julian's letter was a part of his programme to revive traditional Graeco-Roman religious practice by ensuring that it can compete with the attractions of Christian charity (compare his fragmentary *Letter to a Priest*). Julian himself had a Christian upbringing. Yet, contemporary with this, the Christian bishop Basil of Caesarea was arguing for exactly the same end, but in this case he points to the tradition of philanthropy in the broad Graeco-Roman world: 'We lock up what is common to all. We keep for ourselves all that belongs to everyone. That which the Hellenes call philanthropy is fulfilled by a large community sharing one table, common bread, and one hearth' (Basil, *In Time of Famine and Drought* 8). In another of his homilies *To the Rich* 2, while the argument is sustained by quotations from the Old and New Testament, his account of the transgressions of the rich owes much to the long-standing debate on *luxuria* in the Graeco-Roman world (*e.g.* 'baths in town; baths in the country; houses gleaming round with every variety of marble, in one place Phrygian stone, elsewhere tiles from Laconia or Thessaly. And of these houses, some are heated in winter, others are cooled in the summer. A floor decorated with mosaic gems, gold laid out on the roof. And however much of the walls eludes the marble tiling is adorned with choice works of pictorial art.').[7] Both Julian and Basil adopt the same persuasive technique of seeking to spur on and justify change by comparison with the actions of their opponents. But both also draw upon a range of *exempla* from both traditions.

Both the classical and Judaeo-Christian tradition include a view that wealth is an uncomplicated matter of good fortune and the favour of the gods. So in Latin, *beatus* (blessed) can be defined as 'wealthy' (*e.g.* Cicero *N.D.* 2.95 quotes a lost work of Aristotle which states 'people who live in good and notable houses, which are decorated with sculpture and pictures and furnished in every way', and such people are considered *beati*, "blessed"'). As the *Homeric Hymn to Demeter* (488) says, those whom the gods love are blessed, because 'they send Ploutos (the personification of Wealth) to be a guest in their great house, who gives riches to mortal men.' Wealth is the reward for diligent work (*Proverbs* 10.4: 'He becometh poor that dealeth with a slack hand: but the hand of the diligent maketh rich', *cf.* Hesiod *WD* 286-319) and a result of being in a right relationship with the god (or gods) (*Deuteronomy* 15.4: 'There will be no poor among you ... if only you will obey the voice of the Lord your God').

Both traditions also had forms of the myth of the Golden Age at the beginning of history (Hesiod *WD* 111 and Virgil *Georg.* 1.125-28). It has been noted that the distinction between

---

[7] For a convenient modern translation of these homilies see C. Paul Schroeder, *St Basil the Great on social justice* (Popular Patristics Series 38, New York, 2009). On the wider issue of luxury in Roman culture see C. Edwards, *The politics of immorality* (Cambridge 1993); J. P. Toner, *Leisure and ancient Rome* (Cambridge 1995); K.-W. Weeber, *Luxus im alten Rom: Die Schwelgerei, das süsse Gift* (Darmstadt 2003).

rich and poor plays little part in the texts concerned with the early history of the Israelites, and ownership of land following the settlement in Canaan is influenced by the powerful notion that the land was 'the Lord's possession' (*Josh.* 22.19) and had been covenanted to the individual members of the community.[8] Such utopian myths play an important part in subsequent attitudes towards wealth. On the one hand, the myth can back up the role of communistic sharing of property among Plato's ruling class.[9] In the same way the corporate solidarity of the Jews is emphasized repeatedly in the Torah and formed the basis for those groups, like the Essenes who sought to fulfil the utopian ideals of the Torah in their communities.[10] However, these myths also raise the issue of how the utopia was lost and, in particular, how private wealth did come into being in the historical period. In the Classical world this is often represented as part of a decline with the introduction of greed, selfishness, and luxury into society. So Seneca, *Ep.* 90.36: 'There was once a time favoured by fortune when nature's bounty was available to all men's use, before avarice and luxury had broken the bonds that held men together' (*fortunata tempora, cum in medio iacerent beneficia naturae promiscue utenda, antequam avaritia atque luxuria dissociavere mortales*). This linking of wealth and property ownership with decline and corruption found particular favour within Stoic and Cynic philosophy. However, in essence this debate was not about fairness or regard for the poor, but about a desperate attempt by the rich élite to limit the ever spiralling costs for competing successfully in the élite.

In the Jewish tradition there was a powerful recognition that the growth of private wealth threatened the strong communal sense of the people. So it was argued that some are poor *because* others are rich. *Jeremiah* 22.13: 'Woe unto him that buildeth his house by unrighteousness and his chambers by wrong: that useth his neighbour's service without wages, and giveth him not for his work'.

The argument, however, was carried forward in an even more powerful way by suggesting that as a result of the wealthy's oppression of the poor, the poor are to be seen as blessed and righteous, and favoured by God (*Isaiah* 29.19: 'The meek shall obtain fresh joy in the Lord, and the poor among men shall exult in the Holy One of Israel').

This tradition within Judaism has been powerfully exploited by Seth Schwartz.[11] At the heart of his brilliant and wide-ranging approach to the controversy about Judaism and Hellenism, the extent to which Judaism was influenced by and involved in the value systems of the Classical Mediterranean world, Schwartz seeks to set up an opposition between the reciprocity principle of the systems of euergetism, which he sees as a key social characteristic of Mediterranean society, and the concept of giving to the poor in order to preserve the solidarity of the community, which he argues was central to the way the Jewish community evolved. His analysis of the Jewish texts is indispensable, but his claim for the predominance in the Graeco-Roman world of reciprocity within a system of euergetism may be too simplistic, and as a result the contrast between the two systems too stark. As will be argued below, there was a greater range of responses to wealth and poverty in the

---

[8] C. Boersma, *Rich man, poor man – and the Bible* (London 1979).

[9] On this, and the frequent mistake that Plato was advocating a form of communism for the whole community, P. Garnsey, *Thinking about property. From Antiquity to the age of Revolution* (Cambridge 2007) 6-30.

[10] A. Baumgarten, *The flourishing of Jewish sects in the Maccabean era: an interpretation* (Leiden 1997).

[11] S. Schwartz, *Were the Jews a Mediterranean society? Reciprocity and solidarity in ancient Judaism* (Princeton 2010).

classical world than is usually acknowledged and some of them, not just the Christian ones, may be closer to Jewish approaches than Schwartz argues.

It is widely recognized that euergetism in the Graeco-Roman world has significant limitations. Gifts from the wealthy, though they may well be motivated in part by compassion, went in principle to those who in some way could return the favour. Such a principle of reciprocity meant that gifts did not go to the really poor, who could not give anything significant in return, and thus could not have a reciprocal relationship with the élite. Further, the manifest motive for such giving was for display, honour, and political favour.[12] Such euergetism has very distinct limits, which are set out most clearly by Cicero in his discussion in *De Officiis* 1.21-25 of wealth and its obligations. The Stoic influence on this passage is clear.[13] It starts with the standard position that s*unt autem privata nulla natura* ('No property is private by nature', *Off.* 1.21). So how does private property come into existence? Cicero offers a very Roman juridical solution: 'it becomes private by long-established occupation (*vetere occupatione*), as in the case of those who at one time came to a place which was previously unoccupied; or through conquest, as those who take property in war, or by law, agreement, purchase, or allotment'. Cicero never faces up to the potential problem with this solution, which is that if it is a legal convention rather than a law of nature that I have great property; there could equally be a convention that distributes that property in other ways. In *De Finibus* 3.67 he cites the Stoic Chrysippus' analogy of the seat at the theatre. The theatre is *commune* (communal space), but 'it can still be right to say that a seat in it belongs to the man who occupies it; in the same way in the community of the city or the world the law is not opposed to a person having things which belong to them.' But this is no solution at all (as Garnsey has emphasized)[14] and certainly does not help to underpin Cicero's key arguments later (*Off.* 2.73) in defence of property, when he is unequivocal: the man who administrates the state must make it his principle care that 'everyone should have what belongs to him and that there should be no diminution of private property by act of the state (*ut suum quisque teneat neque de bonis privatorum publice deminutio fiat*)'.

On the other hand, Cicero is aware of the issue of communal solidarity, of the need to avoid issues which set rich against poor. He asserts firmly (*Off.* 2.84) that 'action must be taken to ensure that there should be no indebtedness, which could damage the state. This can be guarded against in many ways.' Unfortunately he refuses to give any specific solutions, because his primary requirement is an uncompromising defence of the rights of private property. Indeed, for Cicero the honourable acquisition, maintenance, and enhancement of personal wealth is an obligation (*Off.* 2.87). Cicero does recognize that the wealthy have obligations towards the rest of society, which he sees as fulfilled by acts of euergetism. But for him there are strict limits (*Off.* 1.43-45). Generosity to friends must not harm anyone else. He has in mind the wholesale confiscations of the property of opponents by Sulla. Generosity must be within our means and not be on a scale which significantly diminishes the basic level of wealth which we might bequeath to our heirs; therefore euergetism will result only in marginal redistribution. Finally, gifts should only be given to the deserving, by taking into account their moral character, their attitude towards us, the closeness of the communal and social ties with us and the services which they have in the past done for us (*Off.* 1.45). This last requirement shows that this generosity and marginal redistribution of

[12] Veyne, *Bread and Circuses* (n.5, above) is the classic statement of this approach.

[13] J. Annas, 'Cicero on Stoic moral philosophy and private property' in *Philosophia Togata: Essays on philosophy and Roman society*, eds M. Griffin and J. Barnes (Oxford 1989) 151-73.

[14] Garnsey, *Thinking about property* (n.8, above) 111-18.

wealth, which Cicero accepts as the obligation of all wealthy people, is severely limited to those who are known to the donor. They are not on the same social level as the benefactor, but they come from the sections of society which he would know and have relations with.

It does not follow from this that the wealthy were not seen as having any obligations or concerns to the wider poor. The key passage is Seneca *Ben.* 2.9: 'All philosophers are agreed that certain benefits must be given openly (*palam*), and others secretly (*secreto*) ... those that do not enhance or promote honour, but only help bodily infirmity, poverty, or disgrace (infirmitati, egestati, ignominiae), these must be given quietly, so that they will only be known to those who receive the benefit'. So the rich did recognize compassionate acts in reaction to extreme poverty and distress, but such acts were not considered as part of the processes of euergetism, and mainly go unrecorded. But they must have happened, and happened on a wide scale. It needs to be recognized that the circles affected by acts of generosity by the rich were comparatively small. The number of clients any wealthy individual can have may be counted in the tens or low hundreds. If the number is any larger than this, the clients do not feel they can have a personal reciprocal relationship with the benefactor. The casual acts of small amounts given to the poor or beggars did not count, but may (indeed, must) have been very widespread. The problem is that our sources, mainly from within the élites of Graeco-Roman society, advertise their benefactions and euergetism, but for the reasons given by Seneca ignore the compassionate giving to the poor.[15] Once Christian sources appear, they reveal the views and behaviour of people outside the elites, and hence it may be that they are revealing processes of giving, and of communal help, which always existed in ancient society, but are found only at the fringes of our élite sources. So Schwartz's contrast between the euergetism of the classical world and the Jewish concern for social solidarity may be too stark, because it supposes that élite euergetism was the major, even only significant, approach to the obligations of the wealthy and others towards the poor.

But there is another strand in Graeco-Roman thought: the recognition that the state always had an obligation to help the poor. Social solidarity may be as strong an element of Rome's history as of the Jewish people. Sallust (*Cat.* 33) has the Catilinarian leader Manlius evoke pity for those peasants now risen in arms, describing them as made 'wretched and destitute (*miseri, egentes*)' by the violence and cruelty of the moneylenders, and argue, 'Often your ancestors took pity on the Roman plebs and relieved their *inopia* by their decrees'. This is a theme which can be found throughout Livy's account of Republican history. Right at the beginning of his account of the Roman Republic Livy has the senate seek to meet the needs of the Roman people in order to win their allegiance against any threat from the Tarquins: *multa blandimenta* were granted by the senate in the form of food supplies, measures to control the availability and price of salt, and the *plebs* were freed from paying tolls and taxes. 'Those who could best bear the burden should provide the wealth, while the poor would contribute sufficient service to the state if they simply reared children' (Livy 2.9). Livy commented that this act of *indulgentia* kept the state united (*concordem civitatem*) and no individual in later times ever became so popular (*popularis*) by using *malis artibus* (he is thinking of revolutionary tribunes), as the whole senate did by this act of good ruling (*bene imperando*). The passage is full of the language of the Late Republic – *blandimenta* are what tyrants and monarchs and popular tribunes use to win a following.

---

[15] A. Parkin, '"You do him no service": an exploration of Pagan almsgiving', in *Poverty in the Roman world*, eds M. Atkins and R. Osborne (Cambridge 2006) 60-82.

Indulgentia is the language of gods and autocrats. Nevertheless Livy expresses his approval of state measures designed to preserve and integrate the whole of society.

The reference to the poor's contribution to the state being the rearing of children is exactly the argument ascribed to Tiberius Gracchus by Plutarch and Appian. The poor, ejected from their land by the rapacity of the rich, neglected the bringing up of children (Plutarch *TG* 8.3, while Appian *BC* 1.11 states Tiberius' objective was *euandria*, the rearing of children). Further, Plutarch *TG* 9.5 quotes a powerful rhetorical passage from a speech of Tiberius: 'The wild beasts that range over Italy have every one of them a cave or lair; but the men who fight and die for Italy, have only the air and light, they share nothing else. Homeless, without any where to settle, they wander the world with their wives and children'(ὡς τὰ μὲν θηρία τὰ τὴν Ἰταλίαν νεμόμενα καὶ φωλεὸν ἔχει, καὶ κοιταῖόν ἐστιν αὐτῶν ἑκάστῳ καὶ κατάδυσις, τοῖς δ' ὑπὲρ τῆς Ἰταλίας μαχομένοις καὶ ἀποθνῄσκουσιν ἀέρος καὶ φωτός, ἄλλου δ' οὐδενὸς μέτεστιν, ἀλλ' ἄοικοι καὶ ἀνίδρυτοι μετὰ τέκνων πλανῶνται καὶ γυναικῶν). These could have been described as the provocative statements of a revolutionary tribune; instead, Plutarch describes these words as the product 'of a great mind and of genuine feeling' – another small indication of the strand of thought in Rome which recognized the need for the state to intervene in matters of wealth and poverty to ensure social cohesion. It is notable that the various moments when Livy seems to express a personal opinion in the early books of his history are precisely those when the issue involved is of recognition by the state of the needs of ordinary people: so, for example, at 2.30, in the debate over debt relief in 494 BC, Livy comments on the power of factional and private interests, 'which always have and always will obstruct public decision-making'; then in 2.34 in an early dispute over the need for corn and the demand for the creation of the tribunate to protect the interests of the *plebs*, Livy offers the view that 'it is not easy to say' whether the senate could have avoided the imposition of the tribunate and restrictions they did not want, if only they had conceded to reduce the price of corn; in 4.51, dealing with the consequences of the mutiny which led to the assassination of Marcus Postumius, because of his arrogance over the issue of the distribution of the recently captured land of Bolae, Livy comments that 'this would have been an outstandingly opportune moment to bring forward the distribution of the land of Bolae to soothe people's tempers (*delenimentum animi*), and in this way diminish the desire for an agrarian law which would drive the nobility off state-owned land which they had occupied illegally'.

These comments by Livy are personal and cannot simply be dismissed as slavish copying of the earlier annalists, who allegedly wrote in a *popularis* tradition. Indeed, in many ways Livy expressed hostility to aspects of the popular tribune tradition.[16] But his comments do reflect a tradition in the Republic that the wealthy political élite needed to make concessions to the needs of the poor in order to ensure social cohesion (*concordia* is a frequent term throughout the early books of Livy). Further, Livy was writing at the collapse of the Republic, which may have been in part caused by the failure of the élite to preserve that social cohesion. It could be argued that the Principate was a success in part because

---

[16] R. Seager, '"Populares" in Livy and the Livian tradition', *Classical Quarterly* 27 (1977) 377-90.

it did consciously pursue economic and social policies designed to maintain and enhance social cohesion.[17]

At first sight some of the statements about wealth and its consequences which appear in early Christian texts appear radical. The question is just how unusual and novel they really are. The early Christian community in Jerusalem is attested in *Acts* as pooling its resources:

> *Acts* 4.32-35: Not a man of them claimed any of his possessions as his own, but everything was held in common... for they had never a needy person among them, because all who had property in land or houses sold it, brought the proceeds of the sale, and laid the money at the feet of the apostles; it was then distributed to any who stood in need' (*cf.* more briefly *Acts* 2.44).

Acts then illustrates the process with two examples of Barnabas, and of the fraudulent man and wife, Ananias and Sapphira. These actions are consistent with the attitude to wealth and poverty which forms a strong strand of the gospel of Luke, the author of which is usually and reasonably taken to be the author of *Acts* as well (*Luke* 12.33: 'Sell your possessions and live in charity'; 14.33: 'So also none of you can be a disciple of mine without parting with all his possessions'; *cf. Luke* 12.22, *Mark* 10.21, *Matthew* 19.21). There is little need to doubt the authenticity of this information about the community in Jerusalem, particularly since the process bears a significant similarity to the regulations of the Manual of Discipline of the contemporary Qumran Community.[18] Nor is it an arrangement which would appear particularly odd to a wider Judaeo-Christian audience, aware of the Platonic community of property proposed for the rulers of his ideal city, or the arrangements for mutual self-help among *collegia* and burial clubs in the Graeco-Roman society. But, perhaps, more important than this, is that there is little evidence that other early communities of Christians pooled their resources in the same way. Paul in his second letter to the Corinthians (8-9) praises the contributions by the Christian communities in Macedonia and Achaea to help Jerusalem in ways which suggest that they did not hold all property in common. For all that the idea of property held in common was to be such a feature of later monastic Christianity, it was not necessarily a key feature of the very early church.

Nevertheless, there is no escaping the fierce criticism of wealth as such in parts of the synoptic gospels. Most notorious and uncompromising is the statement attributed to Jesus in response to a wealthy man, 'There is still one thing lacking: sell everything you have and distribute to the poor, and you will have riches in heaven ... How hard it is for the wealthy to enter the kingdom of God. It is easier for a camel to go through the eye of a needle than for a rich man to enter the kingdom of God.' (*Cf.* Luke 6.24: 'But alas for you who are rich; you have had your time of happiness.') This draws on a very strong strand in the Judaeo-Christian sources which sees wealth as hampering or, indeed, making impossible a right relationship with God (*Matthew* 13.22 and *Mark* 4.19 talk of 'the deception of wealth'; much later Basil of Caesarea talks of the 'distraction' (*perispasmos*) of the soul by wealth accumulation (*Regulae brevius tractatae* 91 = Migne, *Patrologia Graeca* 31.1145C-1148A). At the very least, concentration on accumulating wealth is seen as foolish because wealth is often transient and uncertain (*Proverbs* 22.16: 'He that oppresseth the poor to increase his riches, and he that giveth to the rich, shall surely come to want'; *cf. 1Enoch* 94.8: 'Woe

[17] As I have argued in J. Paterson, 'Autocracy and political economy', *Mediterraneo Antico* 7 (2004) 571-89.

[18] B. J. Capper, 'Community of goods in the early Jerusalem Church', in *Aufstieg und Niedergang der römischen Welt* 2.26.2 (Berlin and New York 1995) 1730-74.

to you, ye rich, for ye have trusted in your riches, and from your riches shall ye depart';
Matthew 6.19: 'Do not store up for yourselves treasures on earth, where it grows rusty and
moth-eaten, and thieves break in to steal it. Store up your treasures in Heaven, where there
is no moth and no rust to spoil it, no thieves to break in and steal').

But there is also a stronger theme that the rich man is wicked. The wickedness is linked
to oppression and exploitation of the poor (*Proverbs* 10.2: 'Treasures of wickedness profit
nothing: but righteousness delivereth from death'). This view is summed up much later by
Jerome (*Ep.* 120.1): 'A rich person is either wicked himself or the beneficiary of someone
else's wickedness'. Alongside the emphasis on the wickedness of the rich, there is also the
converse view of the righteousness of the poor, found throughout *Psalms* for example,[19] and
powerfully expressed in the *Magnificat* (*Luke* 1.53: 'The hungry he has satisfied with good
things, the rich sent empty away'). This theme of the 'Great Reversal', where the rich will
be brought low and the poor receive their just rewards, is enlarged upon by the *Epistle of
James* (1.10: 'For the rich man will disappear like the flower of the field', *cf.* 2.5: 'Has not
God chosen those who are poor in the eyes of the world to be rich in faith and to inherit the
Kingdom?').[20]

Yet, for all that the early Christian writings clearly draw primarily from themes about
wealth and poverty in earlier Jewish writings, these concerns about the effects of wealth are
mirrored in the Graeco-Roman world. The philosophical tradition of the Cynics represents
a powerful critique of wealth, that led some to renounce the trappings of wealth and others
to represent themselves as rising above the wealth they had.[21]

There is clearly a set of strands, often interwoven, in the thought about wealth in the
early Christian tradition. However, it is notable that some of our earliest testimony, the
writings of Paul, show very little concern with the problems of wealth and poverty. The
issue does not figure centrally in his writings.[22] The *Letter to the Galatians* 2.9 recounts
Paul's agreement with the leaders of the Christian community in Jerusalem that his mission
should be to wider peoples, while James and his colleagues would concentrate on the Jews;
their only condition, according to Paul, was, 'I should remember the poor, which was the
very thing I ensured that I did'. The collections talked about in the *Second Epistle to the
Corinthians* 8-9 are in part Paul's fulfilment of this requirement. Longeneker argues that
'the poor' in this passage are not, as most early commentators from the fourth century
onwards take for granted, the poor of the Christian community in Jerusalem, but the poor in
general. This seems forced as an interpretation, where the *monon* ('only') in the text is most
naturally taken as an exception to the division of labour between the gentile and the Jews
of Jerusalem. In any case, more generally in Paul's writings, there is little other evidence

---

[19] On all this and on many of the issues central to this chapter see now the exemplary discussion in H. Rhee, *Loving
the poor, saving the rich. Wealth, poverty, and early Christian formation* (Grand Rapids 2012).

[20] P. U. Maynard-Reid, *Poverty and wealth in James* (Maryknoll, NY 1987) and G. K. Hasselhoff, 'James 2:2-7
in early Christian thought', in *Wealth and poverty in early Church and society*, ed. S. R. Holman (Grand Rapids
2008) 48-55.

[21] On the possible influence of Cynic thought on early Christian writing, often posited, sometimes exaggerated, see
J. Moles, 'Cynic influence upon first-century Judaism and early Christianity?' in *The Limits of Ancient Biography*,
eds B. McGing and J. Mossman (Swansea 2006) 89-116.

[22] I maintain this, despite the ingenious arguments of B. Longeneker, *Remember the poor: Paul, poverty, and the
Greco-Roman world* (Grand Rapids 2010).

of the concern for rich and poor, which is such a central issue in the later Christian texts, particularly the Gospels of Luke and Matthew.

Most of the evidence is that the uncompromising radicalism of Jesus' response to the rich man soon came to be seen as a problem in itself, which required reinterpretation. From a vantage point in the Eastern Mediterranean, the apocalyptic vision of the author of *Revelation* emphasized that those who would particularly mourn the fall of Rome, the new Babylon, would be those who fed the luxury demands of the empire: 'the merchants the world over have grown rich on her bloated wealth' (18.3) and there follows a roll call of traders in all sorts of luxury goods: gold, silver, jewels, cloth, spices – a list which comes straight out of the Roman literary critique of *luxuria*.[23] But by the second century the important allegorical work, *The Shepherd of Hermas*, has a truly startling statement: 'Blessed are the rich', which may be considered a remarkable new Beatitude! (*The Shepherd of Hermas, Similitude* 2).[24] The context, which explains the author's meaning, is the comparison of the relationship between the poor and the rich as that between the vine which grows up round the support of the elm tree. The rich are the elm tree and their support is vital, if the vine is to produce grapes: 'Even so the poor praying unto the Lord for the rich, are heard by him; and their riches are increased, because they minister to the poor of their wealth. They are therefore both made partakers of each other's good works.' This is to become one of the standard arguments. The rich can justify their wealth provided it is devoted to supporting the poor.

The transformation is completed by Clement of Alexandria in the later second century in his work, *Quis Dives Salvetur?* (Who is the Rich Man that is to be Saved?). Here he argues (11-13) that when Jesus said to the rich young man, 'Go, sell everything you have and give to the poor' (*Mark* 10.21), this was never intended to be taken literally. 'He does not, as some suppose idly, bid him throw away the wealth he possessed, and abandon his property,' argues Clement, 'but bids him banish from his soul his notions about wealth, his enthusiasm and morbid feeling about it, the anxieties, which are the thorns of existence, which choke the seed of life.' He goes on to point out logically that the person who rids himself of the burdens of wealth 'may none the less still have the lust and desire for money living within him'. Further, the key point is that 'if no one possesses anything, what room would be left among men for giving?' The argument that a society based on reciprocity and gift-giving requires some people to have wealth in order to help those less well-off is one that would be familiar to Cicero (*De Officiis*). The essence of Clement's argument is to be found much earlier in the Pauline pastoral epistle to Timothy (probably dating to the late first century AD): 'Instruct those who are rich in this world's goods not to be proud, and not to fix their hopes on so uncertain a thing as money, but upon God, who endows us richly with all things to enjoy.' (*First Epistle to Timothy* 6.17). The view that it is not the possession of wealth itself, but of one's attitude to wealth, is very much a Stoic argument. Indeed, Clement's case bears close resemblance to Seneca's in his *On the Good Life*, a work which in all probability owes its origins to the attack on Seneca's vast wealth and philosophical pretensions by P. Suillius in his trial in AD 58 (Tac. *Ann.* 13.42.6: 'What sort of learning, what philosopher's precepts enabled Seneca to amass three hundred million sesterces in four years of friendship with the emperor?'). Seneca's response in *On the Good Life* (24-25) is: 'Riches, I say, are not a good thing; for if they were, they would make men good: now since that which is

---

[23] Weeber, *Luxus* (n.7, above).

[24] C. Osiek, *Rich and poor in the 'Shepherd of Hermas': an exegetical-social investigation* (Washington DC 1983); J. A. McGuckin, 'The vine and the elm tree: the Patristic interpretation of Jesus' teachings on wealth', in *The Church and wealth*, eds W. J. Shiels and D. Wood (Oxford 1987) 1-14.

found even among bad men cannot be termed good, I do not allow them to be called so: nevertheless I admit that they are desirable and useful and contribute great comforts to our lives.... Place me as master in the house of a very rich man: place me where gold and silver plate is used for the commonest purposes; I shall not think more of myself because of things which even though they are in my house are yet no part of me. Take me away to the Pons Sublicius and put me down there among the beggars: I shall not despise myself because I am sitting among those who hold out their hands for alms.'

It is easy to be cynical about Clement's case (as, indeed, people were of Seneca also), but Clement does face up to one central problem with the unequivocal views ascribed to Jesus about wealth in some of the gospels. If Jesus' sayings have universal application, which Clement certainly accepts, then if the injunctions to give away wealth are taken literally, the whole social structure was undermined. Therefore for Clement it follows that the sayings cannot be taken literally.[25]

But the most telling argument used by Clement was that those who sought to take Jesus' demand to 'go, sell all you have' literally are following the precepts of traditional classical philosophers ('dead wisdom' in Clement's eyes): 'Nor was the renunciation of wealth and its bestowal on the poor and needy a new thing; for many did so before the Saviour's coming; some in order to have leisure for scholarship, and on account of a dead wisdom; and others for empty fame and vainglory, like the followers of Anaxagoras, Democritus, and Crates' (*i.e.* Cynics). The evolution of Christian thought, although it sought to represent itself as new and distinct, was permeated with the ideas and attitudes of the Classical world. It is true that the issues of wealth and obligations to the poor figure much more prominently in Christian writings than in the Graeco-Roman tradition. But this is not because they reflect a Jewish social tradition which was clearly separate and distinct from the social values of the classical Mediterranean world, as Seth Schwartz argues. Nor is it that the Christians 'invent' the idea of charity and even of the poor as a group. It is rather that the Christian sources reflect the values and views of sections of society, which are not the élite who produced, and were the audience for, so much of classical literature. The arguments of the two traditions permeate each other and share much in common. As with so much thinking about wealth and its obligations in the modern period, so thought in the ancient world was complex, contradictory, often superficial and inconsistent.[26]

The final irony is that, as the Christian Church took centre stage in later antiquity in the distributions to the poor in society, so it became enormously wealthy.[27]

Newcastle University

[25] McGuckin, 'The vine and the elm tree' (n.23, above) and A. van den Hoek, 'Widening the eye of the needle. Wealth and poverty in the works of Clement of Alexandria', in *Wealth and poverty in early Church and society*, ed. S. R. Holman (Grand Rapids 2008) 67-75.

[26] L. W. Countryman, *The rich Christian in the Church of the early Empire: contradictions and accommodations* (New York 1980); B. W. Winter, *Seek the welfare of the city: Christians as benefactors and citizens* (Grand Rapids 1994).

[27] See the ground-breaking studies of Peter Brown: *Poverty and leadership* (n.4, above); *id.*, 'Augustine and a crisis of wealth in Late Antiquity', *Augustinian Studies* 36 (2005) 5-30; *id.*, *Through the eye of a needle* (n.4, above); and R. Finn, *Almsgiving in the later Roman Empire: Christian promotion and practice (313-450)* (Oxford 2006).

INDEX LOCORUM

Literary Sources

1 ENOCH
94.8   100

AESCHYLUS
Pers. 231-45   20
237-38   8

AGAPETUS
4   76
16   76

ALEXIS
F16   23
F76   23
F78   23
F130   21, 22, 29
F131   2, 22
F204   23

AMMIANUS MARCELLINUS
14.7.1   55
23.6.23   88, 91
23.6.25   88

AMPELIUS
Lib. memor. 15.17.4   49

AMPHIS
F30   23

ANAXANDRIDES
F34   23

ANDOCIDES
2.11   37

ANTIPHANES
F157   23

F159   23, 27
F164   23
F188   23
F204   23
F217   23

APPIAN
BC 1.11   99
2.18   84

APULEIUS
Apol. 18.11   49
23.6   47
101.4-5   47
101.6   44

ARISTOPHANES
Eq. 1247   24
V. 788-91   23
F402   23, 28

ARISTOTLE
Fragmenta Varia 8.44.528   37
Pol. 1256a1-1258b4   31
1258a38-b4   31
1258b12-33   31
1258b23-25   31
1259a16-18   35
1259a18-23   34, 35
1259a23-31   35
1259a28-31   41
1259a30-31   35
1259a31-36   36
1295 a-b   77
Rhet. 1361a12-15   8

ARKHIPPOS
F23   23, 26

ARRIAN
FGrHist 156
  F9.13-14   30
  F47   91

ATHENAIOS
  3.118e   24
  6.224b-c   23
  6.224c-d   23
  6.224d-e   23
  6.224f-225a   23
  6.225a-b   23
  6.225c-d   23
  6.225e   23
  6.225f   23
  6.226a-c   21
  6.226a   23
  6.226d-e   23
  6.226e-f   23
  6.226f-227a   23
  6.227a   23, 26
  6.227b   23
  6.227b-d   23
  6.227d-e   23
  6.227e-228b   23
  6.228b-c   23
  6.228c   23
  7   23
  7.313-314   23
  7.325e   27
  8   23

AUGUSTINE
Ep. 41.2   71
  227   79
  244   79

AUSONIUS
Epiced.
  1-2   73
  7   73
  11-12   72

BASIL OF CAESAREA
Homilia in illud dictum Evangelii -
Destruam horrea mea (*Hom.* 6)   58
Homilia dicta tempore famis
et siccitatis   95

Homilia in divites   95
Regulae brevius tractatae 92
(= Migne *Patrologia Graeca*
31.1145C-1148A)   100

CARMINA PRIAPEA 15.2 51
  16.7   51
  82.1   51
  82.5   51

CASSIODORUS
Var. 4.24   73

CASSIUS DIO
  40.12.1   84
  54.17.3   63
  63.1.1-3   85
  63.7.2   91
  68.30   91

CICERO
Letters to Atticus (Ad Atticum)
  4.8.1   45
  9.9.4   45
  12.6.2   45
  13.11.1   45
  13.23.3   45
On Divination (De divinatione)
  1.111   35
To His Friends (Ad Familiares)
  2.16.2   45
  7.23.3   45
  9.16.7   45
On Moral Ends (De finibus)
  3.67   97
On the nature of the gods (De natura deorum)
  2.95   95
On duties (De officiis)
  1.21-25   97
  1.21   97
  1.43-45   97
  1.151   71
  2.73   97
  2.84   97
  2.87   97

CLEMENT OF ALEXANDRIA
Quis Dives Salvetur? 11-13   102

CODEX JUSTINIANUS
1.27.1.22-38	59
1.27.1.41	72
4.40.4	56
4.43.2	57
5.5.7	74
6.43.3.1	74, 75
7.7.1.5	74
8.10.12.5e	75
11.41.7	75

CODEX THEODOSIANUS
1.4.3	56
6.2.13	64
6.2.15	65
6.2.23	66
6.4.12-13	67
6.4.13	66
6.4.21	67
6.4.25	66
7.7.4	55
9.19.2	55
9.31.1	55
9.42.5	57
10.10.31	55
11.1.2	55
11.1.6	55
11.1.18	55
11.1.26	55
11.3.5	55
11.5.4	55
11.7.12	55
11.22.2	55
12.1.33	55
12.1.72	55
12.6.15	55
12.6.23	55
12.13.2	55
13.3.1	73, 74
13.3.2	72
13.3.3	73
13.3.4	73
13.3.8	71
13.3.8.pr.-1	72
13.3.9	72
13.1.1	73
13.3.1.2	72

13.3.8	72
13.3.10	73
13.3.12	73
13.3.13-19	73
13.3.1-4	73
13.5.5	54
15.9.2	55
16.2.15	55
16.2.31	55
16.5.52	67
16.5.54	67

COLUMELLA
Rust. 3.3.14	44, 51

CORNELIUS NEPOS
Phoc. 1.4	49

CTESIAS
FGrHist 688
F37-40	84

DEMOSTHENES
8.66	8, 19
20.15-6	16
20.29-87	17
20.76	16
20.105-111	16
21.48-50	16
22.69-78	17
24	12
24.5	14
24.17	15
24.37	15
24.59	16
24.68-90	14
24.68-9	15
24.69	15
24.91-5	14
24.91	14
24.92	14
24.95	14, 18
24.96-7	15
24.99	15
24.101	15
24.139-41	15
24.155-56	14
24.176-86	10, 17

24.176-77	17
24.177	17
24.181	17
24.182	18
24.183	18
24.184	19
24.185	19
24.192-93	15
24.192	15
24.210	13, 14, 16, 20
24.211	15
24.212-14	13
24.215	11, 16
24.216	16
35.32	24
35.34	24
56	37
56.7-9	41
57.34	26

DE REBUS BELLICIS

2.2	58

DIGEST

1.18.6.2	56
2.4.25	76
27.1.6.2	72
33.7.27.3	45
33.7.27.5	45
48.2.8-11	57
48.2.10	57
48.19.28.2	75
50.9.4.2	70
50.9.127.1	71

DIODOROS

16.8.6-7	37

DIONYSIUS OF HALICARNASSUS

Dein. 10.654	30

DIPHILOS

F31	23
F32	23, 24
F67	23, 27

ECLOGA ISAURICA

17	76

ENNODIUS

Ep. 7.7	73
8.8	73
9.14	73
9.21	73

EUPOLIS

F199	24

EURIPIDES

Suppl. 238-45	76-77

FLAVIUS JOSEPHUS

AJ 18.48-50	87

FLORUS

Epit. 2.13.10-12	84

FRONTINUS

Strat. 4.3.3	48

GAIUS

Inst. 1.9	53
4.18.4	76

GALEN

Meth. Med. 1.1	71

HARPOKRATION

s.v. μετοίκιον	26

HERMIPPOS

F63	24

HERODIAN

3.4.8	85
3.9.11	85
4.10.4	85
4.11.3	85
4.11.6	85
4.15.3	85

HERODOTUS

1.69	40
5.49	84
6.119	40
7.118-20	84
9.80-81	84

HESIOD
Works and Days 111   95

HESYCHIOS
s.v. Αἰξωνίδα τρίγλην   27

HOMER
H. Dem. 488   95
*Od.*14.56   95

HORACE
Ep. 1.7.44   46
    1.7.80-81   44
    1.7.81   46
    1.14   46
Sat. 2.6.8-9   48
    2.6.10-13   48

ISIDORUS (OF SEVILLE)
Etym. 4.13.1   70
    4.13.5   70

JEROME
Ep. 120.1   101

JOHN CHRYSOSTOM
Hom. Matth. 66.3   60
In paral. 4   72
In cap. V et VI Gen. Hom. XI   72

JULIAN
Caes. 335b   58
Contr. Heracl. 207 c-d   74
Ep. 75b   73

JUVENAL
Sat. 8.109   48

KHIONIDES
    F5   24

KRATINOS
    F44   24
    F236   23, 27

LEONTIUS
Vita S. Johannis Eleemosynarii 26   69

LEX VISIGOTHORUM
    11.1.5   72

LIBANIUS
Ep. 40.1-2   65
    723   73

LIVY
    2.9   98
    2.30   99
    2.34   99
    4.51   99
Per. 18.7   48

LUCIAN
Dem. Enc. 31   30

LUCRETIUS
    5.1269-80   58

LUNKEUS (OF SAMOS)
    F20 (Dalby)   23

LYSIAS
    22.5-6   36, 41
    22.12   41

MACROBIUS
Sat. 1.7.1   73

MARTIAL
    1.116.5   49
    2.32.3   49
    7.31.8   49
    7.91.1   49
    7.93.5   49
    10.61   49
    10.92   49
    12.16   49
    12.25   49
    12.72.1   49

MOVSES KHORENATZI
P.H. 2.35-36   91

NIKOSTRATOS
    F5   24

NOVELLA(E) IUSTINIANI 90.1	76

NOVUM TESTAMENTUM

Act.Ap. 2.44	100
4.32-35	100
Apoc. 18.3	102
2 Ep. Cor. 8-9	100
Ep. Gal. 2.9	101
Ep. Jac. 1.10	101
2.5	101
1 Ep. Ti. 6.17	102
Ev. Luc. 1.53	101
6.24	100
12.22	100
12.33	100
14.33	100
Ev. Marc. 10.21	100
4.19	100
10.21	100
Ev. Matt. 6.19	100
13.22	100
19.21	100

OLYMPIODORUS

F41.1	66
F41.2 (Blockley)	66

PAULI SENTENTIAE

5.4.10	53
5.22.3	74

PAULINUS
Vita Ambr. 25.1-2
66

PAUSANIAS

1.6.3	84

PETRONIUS

48.3	51

PHAEDRUS

4.5.23	46

PHILOSTORGIUS

Hist. Eccl. 3.15	72

PHILOSTRATOS

Vita Apoll. 1.25	85
1.30	85
1.33-34	85

PHOCYLIDES

F10 (Hiller-Crusius)	77

PLATO

Leg. 5.728e-729a	77

PLINY (THE ELDER)

NH 5.89-90	88
6.120	88
6.122-23	88
6.122	84
18.8.41	49
26.1.3	61
26.3	77
29.17	71

PLINY (THE YOUNGER)

Ep. 1.19	61
1.24.1	50
1.24.3	50
2.4.3	50, 51
5.14.8	50, 51
6.3.1	44, 49, 50
6.3.2	49
8.15.2	50

PLUTARCH

Crass. 16.1-3	84
21.6-9	84
23-32	87
32	84
32.4-5	84
Dem. 28.4	30
Mor. 836e	68
TG 8.3	99
9.5	99

POLLUX

6.48	24

POMPEIUS TROGUS

41.2.4	85

PROCHEIROS NOMOS 27.22   57, 76

PROCOPIUS
BG 1.1.38   73

PROVERBS
10.2   101
10.4   94
22.16   100

PSEUDO-ARISTOTLE
Oeconomica 1345b33-35   38
1346a6-9   38
1346a25-31   38
1346b14   39
1346b19-26   37
1347b3-15   37
1348b17-22   37
1348b33-36   37
1352b14-20   37
1353a15-18   37

PSEUDO-PAVSTOS BUZAND
3.1   91
4.14 e 24   91

SEBEOS   91

PTOLEMY
5.18.7   89
5.20.1-2   88
5.20.6   88

QUINTILIAN
Decl. Maior. 13   48

SALLUST
Cat. 33   98

SALVIANUS
Gub. Dei 1.10   78
3.10   78

SENECA
Ben. 2.28.3   51
2.9   98
5.24.3   51
Ep. 90.36   96

Vit. Beat. 24-25   102

SOPHILOS
F2   23

STEPHANUS BYZANTIUS
Ethn. s.v. Βολογεσσιάς   88

STRABO
16.2.5   84

SUETONIUS
Aug. 41.1   63
Jul. 42   71
Nero 13   85

SUIDA
s.v. Σανατρούκης   91

SYMMACHUS
Ep. 1.67   79
2.10   78
3.32   78
3.37   73
4.67   66
5.55   66
7.127   79
8.64   73
9.4   73
9.44   73
Or. 7.6   64
8   66
Rel. 21.6   80
23.3-4   79
26.3   79

TACITUS
Ann. 2.57   85
13.42.6   102
15.24   85

THE SHEPHERD OF HERMAS
Similitude 2   102

THEOPHRASTUS
Char. 6.9   4, 26
HP 5.8.1   37

THUCYDIDES
2.13   8, 20
2.36   7
2.40   16

VALERIUS MAXIMUS
4.4.6   48
4.4.7   49
7.1.2   49

VARRO
Rust. 3.12.1   44
3.16.10-11   44

VELLEIUS PATERCULUS
2.46.2   84

VETUS TESTAMENTUM
De. 15.4   95
Is. 29.19   96
Je. 22.13   96
Jo. 22.19   96
Pr. 10.2   101
10.4   95

VIRGIL
Georg. 1.125-28   95

VITA CAESARII
1.41   74

XENARCHOS
F7   23, 28

XENOPHON
Oec. 1.1.7-16   8
Cyr. 8.8.3   84

ZOSIMUS
2.38   66
3.23   88

Inscriptions

Année Épigraphique (AÉ)
1980, 504   79
1989, 137   79
1989, 165   79

Corpus Inscriptionum Latinarum (CIL)
5.715   43
5.4084   81
5.4489   45
5.7405   79
6.9162   81
6.26259   43
6.41336   79
8.759-60   80
8.969   80
8.1283   80
8.11025   79
8.12260   80
8.15880   79
9.1563   79
9.2074   79
9.3685   79
9.4129   43
10.407   45
10.478   80
10.5349   79
10.1354   79
10.6720   43
11.2835   79
11.4096-97   79

Corpus Inscriptionum Semiticarum (CIS)
2.3916   90
2.3917   90
2.3924   90
2.3933   90
2.3949   90
10.124   90

Inscriptiones Christianae Urbis Romae (ICUR) 5.13410   81

Inscriptiones Graecae (IG)
1^3.89   37
2^2.216-217   17

2².1128	37
2².1623.276-285	29
2².1631.169-70	30
2².1632.189-90	30
2³.447	29, 30

Inscriptions latines de l'Algérie (ILALG)
1.2100	79

Lex Irnitana
86	61

Monumenta Epigraphica Christiana
2.1	81
X.5	81

Recueil des inscriptions chrétiennes de la Gaule (RICG)
1.129	80

P. J. Rhodes and R. Osborne, *Greek Historical Inscriptions 404-323 BC (RO)*
22.7	29
22.76	29
22.91	29
88.9-11	9

Supplementum Epigraphicum Graecum (SEG)
15.836	91
50.188	25

Papyri

J. Maspero, *Catalogue général des antiquités égyptiennes du Musée du Caire. Papyrus grecs d'époque byzantine (PCairoMasp)*
67151	72

Ravenna Papyri (J. O. Tjäder, *Die nichtliterarischen lateinischen Papyri Italiens aus der Zeit 445-700 I. Papyri 1-28 (P.Lat.)*)
4-5 B IV 6-7	79
4-5 B VI 10	81
7.97-104	80
6	81
7.97-104	81
10-11 B IV 4	80
17.39	81
20.123	81
25.6-7	81
29.1	79
29.2	81
29.8	81
30.92	81
31.ii.10	81
31.iii	79
31.iii.3	81

INDEX

For ancient authors see also the Index Locorum

Abellinum 79
Achaea 100
Achaemenids 83, 84, 85, 88
Aegina (Aigina) 23, 27, 30, 33
Aeschylus 8, 20, 83
Africa – see North Africa
Agapetus 76
agriculture 2, 5, 44, 45, 46, 50, 59
Alexander (the Great) 83
Alexandria (Egypt) 6, 70, 102
Alexis 4, 21, 22, 23, 24, 28, 29, 30, 32
Ammianus Marcellinus 54, 55, 66
Ampelius, L. 49
Amphis 23
Anaxagoras 103
Anaxandrides 23, 24
Androtion 12, 17, 18, 19
Antinoopolis 72
Antiphanes 23, 24, 27
Antoninus Pius 73
Apollo (Pythian) 49
Apollonios of Tyana 85
Appian 99
Aquilius Regulus, M. 49
Aristonikos 4, 21, 22, 24, 28, 29, 30, 31
Aristophanes 21, 24
Aristoteles (of Marathon) 29
Aristotle 4, 8, 30, 31, 32, 34, 35, 36, 40,
    41, 76-77, 95
Arkhestratos (of Gela) 25
Arkhippos 23, 24, 25
Arles 73
Armenia 84, 87, 91
Arsacid Kingdom 5, 83-92
Arsacius 94
Arsanias River 91
Artabanus II 87, 88, 89
Artaxata (also Neroneia) 91

Assyria 40
ateleia (see tax, exemption from)
Athens 3, 4, 7-20, 21-32, 34, 36, 37,
    38, 39, 40, 41;
    acropolis of 17;
    agora of 12, 26, 27, 28;
    assembly in 15, 30, 39;
    boulē of (council) 12, 15;
    laws in (see Legislation, Athenian);
    – see also Second Athenian League
Atilius Regulus, M. 48, 52
Atossa 8, 20
Atropatenes 87
Augustine 71, 79, 103
Aurelius Symmachus, Q.: see Symmachus
Ausonius 72, 73

Babylonia 83, 85, 89, 90, 102
Barnabas 100
Basil of Caesarea 95, 100
Bazas 73
Black Sea 24, 38
Bolae 99
Bordeaux 73
Byzantion 36, 37, 38, 39, 41, 56, 76

Cadiz 24
Canaan 96
capital 1, 3, 8, 9, 10, 12, 19, 20, 24, 26, 28,
    31, 34, 54, 57, 59, 62, 63, 77
Capua 79
Caracalla 85
Caria 12 – see also Mausolus
Carrhae 83, 84, 87
Cassius Dio 83, 84
Catullus 45
Cervidius Scaevola, Q. 45
Chabrias 17

Characene 89

charity 16, 76, 94, 95, 100, 103 – see also
  euergetism

China 93

Chios 35

Christianity/Christians 1, 6, 58, 71, 72, 77,
  89, 94, 95, 97, 98, 99, 100, 101, 103

Chrysippus 97

Cicero 45, 71, 95, 97, 98, 102

Cimitile 79

Cincinnatus 49, 52

citizenship 71

Clement of Alexandria 6, 102, 103

Cluvius Martinus, S. 79, 81

coinage 13, 27, 33, 57, 59, 76;
  and counterfeiting 58;
  exchange ratio of 23, 37, 41, 59

Columella 44, 51

comedy 4, 21, 23, 24, 25, 30, 32
  – see also Aristophanes, Alexis

commerce – see trade

company (hetaireia) 34

Conon 17

Constantine 57, 58, 64, 71, 72

Constantinople 64, 67;
  senate of 66

Corinth (Korinthos) 24, 27, 100, 101

Cornelius Nepos 49

Cosmas (Saint) 72

Crassus 83, 84, 87

Crates 103

Crimea 24

Critobulus 8

Ctesias (of Cnidus) 83, 84

Ctesiphon (capital of Arsacid
  Kingdom) 91

curiales 54, 55, 62, 80

Cynicism/Cynics 96, 101, 103

Cyprus 37, 39, 40

Cyrene 37

Damasus (bishop of Rome) 80

Damian (Saint) 72

Democritus 103

Demosthenes 3, 4, 7, 8, 9, 11, 12, 13, 14,
  15, 16, 17, 18, 19, 20, 37

Diodorus (Athenian politician 4th C
  BCE) 12

Dionysios (I, of Syracuse) 35, 41

Diphilos 23, 27

doctors – see physicians

Donatism 67

Dorion 25

Draco 15

Dysarius 73

Egypt 23, 24, 26, 33, 37, 38, 39,
  41, 69, 81

Euctemon 12

euergetism 6, 17, 94, 96, 97, 98

Euphrates River 83, 84, 88, 91

Eupolis 24

Euripides 76-77

exchange 4, 8, 21, 22, 24, 27, 30,
  31, 37, 41, 59, 62

Falisci 46

fish and fish-mongers 4, 21, 22, 23, 24,
  25, 26, 27, 28, 29, 30, 31, 32, 36, 38

Flavius Phoebammon 72

freedmen 26, 57, 63

Frontinus 48

Furius Chresimus, C. 49

Galatia 94, 101

Garni 91

Gospels 77, 100, 101, 103

Greece 5, 10, 11, 12, 71

Greeks 20, 34, 35, 41, 84, 85;
  in Babylonia 89

Gregory of Nazianzus 73

Gyges 49

Harpalos 30

Hellespont 24

Herakleia Pontike 37, 38

Hermogenian 57, 69, 76

Herodian 85

honour (timē) 7, 8, 9, 11, 12, 13, 14, 16,
  17, 18, 54, 75, 76, 78, 79, 81, 97, 98

Horace 46, 47, 50, 52

Illyricum 73

India 62, 84, 87, 89

inequality 1, 3 – see also poverty

Interamna Lirenas 79
investment 1, 8, 42
Isidore (of Seville) 70
Isocrates 19, 68
Italy 50, 66, 73, 79, 80, 99

Jerusalem 100, 101
Jews 87, 94, 96, 97, 98, 101, 103
John Chrysostom 60, 68, 72, 77
Julian 73, 79, 94, 95
Justinian 59, 74, 75, 76
Juvenal 45, 48

Kara-su River 91
Keos 37, 39, 40, 41
Khairephilos (of Paiania) 24
Klazomenai 37, 38, 42
Kleomenes (of Egypt) 37, 38, 39, 41
Korea 93
Kratinos 23, 24, 27

Laconia – see Sparta
Lamian War 30
Laurion 8, 34,
law, see legislation
legislation 4, 8, 10, 11, 12, 13, 14, 15,
    16, 17, 19, 22, 23, 28, 29, 31, 32, 36,
    41, 53, 54, 55, 56, 57, 65, 67, 68, 71,
    72, 74, 75, 76, 97, 99;
    anti-cartel 36;
    Athenian 12, 14, 15, 16, 22, 23;
    Roman 53, 54;
    Spartan 16;
    Theban 16; – see also *nomos*
leisure 3, 32, 103
Libanius 64
liturgies (Athens) 8
Livy 98, 99
Locris 15
Lunkeus (of Samos) 23, 25
luxury 60, 83, 84, 85, 86, 92, 95, 96,
    102;
    of the East 6, 84
Lydia 40
Lysias 41

Macedon 37, 39, 40, 100

Macedonians (Byzantine Imperial
    dynasty) 76
Macrobius 73
Madauros 79
Manlius 98
Mantua 81
Marcius Philippus, L. 46
market(s) 1, 4, 22, 24, 25, 26, 27, 28,
    29, 30, 31, 33, 34, 35, 37, 40, 41,
    84 – see also fish
Marmara, sea of 24
Martial 49, 50, 52
Mausolus (of Caria) 12
Media/Medes 85, 87
Menander (see Menandros)
Menandros 21
Mesopotamia 83, 88, 89, 90, 91
middle class 3, 5, 53-82;
    definitions of 55, 57, 60-63
Milan 81
Miletos 35
miltos 37, 39, 41
Minturnae 79
Modestinus 76
money 3, 8, 13, 18, 19, 26, 27, 39, 57,
    58, 59, 60, 64, 66, 69, 72, 75, 76, 94,
    98, 100, 102 – see also coinage
monopoly 4, 5, 33-42, 89
Mthsurkh 91

Naucratis 12
Nero 84
Nippur 90
nomos 13, 14, 15, 16, 17, 18, 19, 20, 29
North Africa 2, 59, 79, 80

Ocriculum 79
Olympiodorus 65, 66, 69
Ostrogoths 73

Pacorus I 87
Pacorus II 88, 90, 91
Paestum 80
Palmyra 89, 90, 91
Pangaion 37, 40
Pantikapaion 24
Parthia/Parthians 5, 81-92

Peiraieus 25
Peloponnesian War 9
Perdikkas (of Macedon) 37, 39, 40
Pericles 4, 8, 9, 20
Persia 40, 83, 85, 86
Persian Gulf 89
Phaedrus 45, 46
Philip (II of Macedon) 37, 40, 49
Philostratos 85
Phocion 49
Phocylides 76, 77
Phrygia 95
physicians 5, 70, 71, 72, 73, 74, 79
Plato 77, 96, 100
Plautus 45
Pliny the Elder 61, 71, 84
Pliny the Younger 5
ploutos, see wealth
Plutarch 68, 83, 84, 99
Pollux 24
Pompeius Trogus, Cn. 85
Porcius Cato, M. 44, 45
Postumius, M. 99
poverty and poor 1, 2, 3, 5, 6, 29, 32,
    48, 54, 56, 57, 58, 59, 60, 63, 64, 66,
    72, 74, 75, 76, 77, 93, 94, 95, 96,
    97, 98, 99, 100, 101, 102, 103;
    threshold of 69
price(s) 4, 22, 23, 27, 28, 29, 30, 31,
    36, 37, 41, 57, 59, 72, 98, 99
profit 4, 8, 9, 14, 16, 26, 27, 28, 29, 31,
    32, 35, 41, 47, 89, 94, 101
property 5, 12, 46, 55, 56, 57, 58, 61,
    63, 64, 65, 69, 70, 76, 96, 97, 100, 102;
    moral value of 75
Pythocles 37, 38

Quinctius Cincinnatus, L. – see Cincinnatus
Quintilian 48

Ravenna 79, 80, 81
Reate 81
resources 7, 8, 9, 11, 16, 17, 19, 28,
    31, 33, 34, 35, 65, 87, 88, 91,
    100; exploitation of 86, 92
revenue 8, 16, 28, 35, 36, 38, 39, 40, 45
Roman, law 53, 54;

senators 46, 50, 55, 59, 61, 62,
    63-67, 69, 70, 71, 73, 78, 79, 80, 98,
    99; physicians – see Physicians
Rome 47, 65, 67, 71, 73, 80, 81, 84,
    85, 86, 91, 98, 99, 102; urban
    prefecture of 64

Sabine land 46
Salamis 8
salary 59, 69, 74; of physicians 72
Sanatruces 91
Saronic Gulf 27
Second Athenian League 7, 13, 29
Second World War 93
Seleucia on the Tigris 84, 89, 90, 91
Seleucid Empire 83, 86
Selymbria 37, 38, 42
Sempronius Gracchus, T. 99
Seneca 96, 98, 102, 103
Sentius Redemptus, M. 79
Sicily 35, 51
Silphium 37, 38
slavery/slave/slaves 8, 22, 23, 26, 32,
    43, 47, 53, 54, 57, 59, 63, 68, 74,
    75, 77, 84,
Social War (Greek) 17, 19
Socrates 8
Solon 13, 15, 16, 22
Sophilos 23
Sparta 16, 95 – see also Legislation and
    Spartan
Spoletium 73
State 2, 4, 5, 6, 7, 32, 33, 34, 35, 36,
    37, 38, 39, 40, 41, 42, 54, 71, 75, 77,
    83, 84, 86, 87, 88, 89, 91, 92, 97, 98,
    99
Stoicism 96, 97, 102
Surena 84, 85, 87
sustainability 1, 9, 41
Symmachus 64, 66, 73, 79, 80
Synesius 64
Syracuse 35

Tacitus 83, 85, 102
tax 1, 3, 14, 19, 42, 65, 66, 72, 87, 94,
    98; exemption from (*ateleia/immunitas*)
    16, 36, 71, 72, 73

Tell Abu Su'ud 90
Tell al-Khubari 90
Tell Babil 90
Tell Bandar (Kish) 90
Tell Irsheideh ibn Alwan (Hamrin) 90
Terence 45
textiles 85, 102
Thales of Miletos 35, 36
Thebes (Greek *polis*) 16, 29 – see also
   legislation, Theban
Themistius 64
Theoderic 73
Theodorus (of Erchia) 68
Theodosius 66
Theophrastos 4, 26, 31, 32, 39
Thessaly 95
Thucydides 4, 20
Tigris River 88
timber 25, 37, 38, 39, 40
Timocrates 12, 14, 15, 16, 17, 20
Tiridates 84, 85, 87, 91
topoi 72, 76; literary 23, 58, 78;
   ethnographic 85
trade 5, 6, 23, 26, 31, 36, 51, 55, 58, 86,
   88, 89, 91, 102; in fish 27, 29, 30
   – see also fish and fishmongers; in grain
   30, 36; routes 87, 88, 89, 90, 92
Trier 80
Tullius Cicero, M.: see Cicero
tyranny 35, 36, 39, 98

Valerius Fortunatus 66
Varro 44, 46
Veii 46
Vicetia 79
Vienne 73
virtue 4, 18, 19, 64, 77, 89
Visigoths 72
Vitruvius 45
Vologaeses I 5, 87, 88, 89, 90, 91
Vologaesias 89, 90
Volsinii 79
Volteius Mena 46

wealth 1, 2, 3, 4, 8, 13, 18, 19, 20, 33,
   36, 53, 54, 55, 56, 57, 58, 59, 64,
   65, 66, 67, 68, 69, 74, 77, 84, 85, 86,
   89, 92, 93, 95, 96, 98, 99, 100, 101,
   102, 103; consumption of 3, 60, 62,
   94;
   creation of 1, 2, 3, 5, 36, 42; distribution
   of 1, 3, 54, 97; non-material (immaterial)
   3, 4, 7-20; material 7-8, 12, 16-17, 19,
   20

Xenarchos 23, 28
Xerxes 8

Lightning Source UK Ltd.
Milton Keynes UK
UKHW030153240223
417572UK00008B/498

Gallery Books
Editor Peter Fallon

OF ALL PLACES

John McAuliffe

OF ALL PLACES

Gallery Books

Of All Places
is first published
simultaneously in paperback
and in a clothbound edition
on 1 July 2011.

The Gallery Press
Loughcrew
Oldcastle
County Meath
Ireland

www.gallerypress.com

ISBN 978 1 85235 514 2 *paperback*
      978 1 85235 515 9 *clothbound*

Contents

Old Style *page* 11
The Coming Times 12
Of All Places 13
Grave Goods 14
Bringing the Baby to Rossaveal 15
A Mountain Road 16
Badgers 17
The Listowel Arms 18
Crash 20
On 'The Road to Sintra' 23
Aerialist 24
Continuity 26
A Danger to Shipping 27
My Adolescence in New Zealand 28
Jane Eyre in Derry 29
North Korea 30
Capital 31
Night Manoeuvres 32
Week 2 33
Batman 34
Loose Ends 35
Arguing about Stars near Inch 36
Marriage, the Realist Tradition 38
Snow 40
New Year 41
Of All Places 42
Northwestern 43
A Likeness 44
House Fire 45
Influence 46
The Changing Room 47
Canvas 48
A Game of Li Bo 49
St Turvey at Lusk 50
A Deaf Ear 51

Sunrise 52
Recess 53
Interludes
   1 CALLING OUT 54
   2 MOWER 54
Black Box 55
The Oasis on Tuesdays 56
The Territorial Army 57
Odd Hours
   1 DAYLIGHT SAVING TIME, OUTSIDE BLACKBURN 58
   2 THE NEWS ON RITZ STREET 58
   3 READING ON TELEGRAPH 58
   4 DAYLIGHT SAVING TIME, ST LOUIS 59
Transfers 60
By the Sea, in England 62
A Name 64
The Whole Show 65
Address to Russ 66
The Hallway Mirror 67
A Midgie 68

Acknowledgements 70

for Nancy

Old Style

Not just the lay-by, or the motorway
        or its central reservation.
Not just the ring road, or the cul-de-sac
        with its pretty forsythia border.
Not just the house, or its extension,
        and its hundred windows shining away.
Instead the known world and the unseen,
        to which you'll come back:

that is, the point of departure, the destination,
        and all points in between.
A free drift to nowhere in particular.
        All that way, and back again.

The Coming Times

The towns are not so dark that no one enters;
in nearby docks the nights
advance on empty lots.
Fanatics gather in community centres.

A dry spell engenders nostalgia for rain.
The news will consider
the negligent doctor
and who is immune to the variant strain.

In cooler queues low-slung jeans
date the waspie;
the bright bars are smoke-free
as the ocean's photic zones.

The downturn floats the clearance sale:
staff migrate
and the market
anticipates no return; churches fill,

the ice cap melts, the deserts spread:
north and south
a dolphin's found in every port;
new forms of algae feather the tide.

The boats will travel day and night
and some make land.
For the time being, out of mind
is out of sight:

from the dawning dark
no one shouts, no walk-outs.
Someone organizes scouts,
someone patrols the park.

Of All Places

. . . limestone later, then gneiss and a little quartz,
corbelling later again; the antler-pin points
towards an open central place and an arable,
U-shaped valley, undulating and deciduous;
a shell midden, and a stone circle
realized with ramp and pulley, not built to be visible;
and later still, *material*, modern, a quarry
for walls, roads and, now, a history of guided tours,
making a guest appearance in videos of gap years
with earphones and smoke and ring roads and glossy
primary coloured photos of strangers
and, here we are, on the cairn of stones with a pebble,
or taking something for the windowsill, maybe a seashell.

Grave Goods

Before he abandoned it to go horse-riding in Cuba
my brother sent me from Silicon Valley a postcard of Ishi
swimming in a creek in what used to be Yahi country
between the mountains and the ocean. He looks like America,
smiling, his hair as black as the river he swims in.
When I look for it, visiting that west coast for the first time,
I find the museum built around his life has been pulled down.
He'd worked there, after he burnt his hair in grief, as a cleaner
    and warden.
Its anthropologists loaded his coffin with acorns, his bow, fire
    sticks, venison
and his songs: of coyote, of vulture, of grasshopper and of
    earthworm.

Bringing the Baby to Rossaveal

'If the real world is not altogether rejected'
— W B Yeats

The field is a limestone heat sink. A goat
and a pony stretch where stone walls meet.
The sea wind is head-high or, at the five-barred gate,
a passage we brave to the open pub. A wet May
and a dry June. The traffic. The roads. Not a cock of hay.
Goodbye to the first times, goodbye Galway.

Under adjoining, improvised trestles, folded into
her awkward car seat, the baby sleeps through
Germans to whom we speak French poorly,
the house red, a mug or two of coffee
and the sun making light of the menu.
Goodbye to the first times, goodbye Galway.

Pushing the squeaking buggy to the B&B
I overlook her quick enquiring glances at the moon
as I try to recall, going through security
with my shoes undone, what is stowed away
among recycled shopping bags in the undercarriage —
Goodbye to the first times, goodbye Galway —

a bottle, a banana, in this, the softest year and day
of living, anyway, our Lord, in the institution of marriage,
the sun at night, Galway under the volcano of dawn
we fly into, one time, with everything else at bay,
the baby squeaking, like the small wheel, the sun gone down.
Goodbye to the first times, goodbye Galway.

A Mountain Road

The visitor explained how to make 'A Mountain Road':
as in the original, a line of sea, the road and fields,
which some of us personalized. His had a black hill,

which those without black paint painted a very dark green.
You couldn't tell the difference when he tacked
all twenty-eight versions of 'A Mountain Road'

high around the draughty classroom which now recedes
stone by stone into its own mountain road,
the hill beside it black and visible, beyond its empty fields

and new forestry, the lighthouse on Loop Head
whose cone of light sweeps across the soft grey shore
and seems, minute after minute, to find and inspect it.

Badgers

During training, on the Cows Lawn, one of the smokers,
a boy from Ballylongford, coughed up blood, black clots of it.
We stood on the sidelines till he was taken away.
This was the time O'Hare, the Border Fox, was on the loose.
That day, arriving home from school, who didn't promise
he'd never ever take a pull again? Not in the school bog,
not in the back way, not in the fag-breaks at the petrol station.
But another rumour released us. It was the farm and badgers:

brock, feral, slow-clawed terror of the ditch and yard,
wind-pissing shit-spreader, emptier of field and house.
Its fellow travellers, then as now like garrulous crows,
swore the opposite, the blood-dregs nothing
to *their* stone-silent survivor, always in the right,
and us and the herd safer. Or so they put it about even as,
barely visible behind the numbers, old tales resurged
about loosened fence-posts and sloping, scraped-up footpaths.

O'Hare could not be found by the guards: that smokeless week
I stood in the porch (under a new, secure intercom)
rubbing a leaf between my thumb and index finger,
noticing a little movement in a Volkswagen
parked, as it had been all along, past the last gate,
as if this were a garage forecourt and not
a dead end, a river facing it, its animal sentries
unvisited as those on many another road.

The Listowel Arms

The silver, Georgian teapot he presented to her —
is it still in Chequers, or did she take it home to Finchley?
He meant civil conversation, talks,
but was not unhappy, says a biographer,
when the hacks construed it as the boss
putting the grocer's daughter in her woman's place,
the grocers' sons suiting the occasion to the usual offence.

I saw him twice. At a hotel opening,
with a woman who might have been his daughter,
and a school half-day when I'd skipped training
and was cycling home. I came on
an unexpected crowd, where I saw not a one
of my friends and classmates, investors in the future
of systems analysis and the virtual share

but, like a captain on the night of a match day,
this small, bustling, jostled colonel
of William and Market Streets, surrounded on Mart Day
by hundreds of men, a river of tweed.
I veered up the back way, though, and turned
for the Square where, after his scandal, the town saw Parnell
at a window in the *Arms* make his final biblical call,

'Thus far shalt thou go', before taking tea in that same bar
where the merchants still rendezvous for elevenses,
between the town's churches and the unrestored castle
which I skidded by, chancing a breather
near the racecourse bridge's damp concrete angle
which rubbed BRITS OUT and the Malvinas
up against *who* loved *who* and sex cartoons,

the river pouring under, a nightfall of rain on its back,
absorbing the west Limerick and Co-op surplus,
wheeling it all past the town's built-up backyards,

the Island's empty racetrack
and this tyre-spinners' gravel car park,
the town's learners practising turns and how to reverse,
the heat and 2FM turned up to the max.

Crash

1

Out of the water
they recover a cap,
a petrol tin, oranges,
cake wrapped in foil
and a notebook.
At a lit-up cottage,
the Irish teacher's,
they arrest
the stranger,
his hands bleeding,
who spins them a story
about driving bank clerks
around the Ring of Kerry.

In the morning
the tide uncovers
two bodies;
six months later,
a different story,
the third turns up
in the Laune:
'guests from the future'
driven from Dublin
in the old-style road-dark,
planning to divert
the Valentia transmitter
and radio the *Aud*,
Casement and Germany,
'"Mother" is on her way.'

2

But their *Briscoe*,
one of two stolen cars,
lags in Killorglin,
then accelerates
toward a light
that wavers,
it turns out,
across the bay.
They teeter to a halt
at that spot on Ballykissane Pier
where a memorial's
inscribed stone
compels us,
day trippers
on a detour
from the Ring
and liking
the water's glint,
to remember

3

an armed man
stepping out into
the lapping dark,
tipping the car
off the pier
into the river.
So he alone
scrambled out
towards a local,
the Irish teacher,

home on holiday,
carrying a lamp
and shouting
'Face the light,'

who carried him off,
then sat on the wet gun
like a laying hen
until at long last
the police finished
the report
that drew tears
from Casement,
in irons
on the Dublin train,
and broke
the night down
so it could not
except as a monument
be put together again.

April 1916

On 'The Road to Sintra'

Fernando Pessoa, in Lisbon, imagines the road to Sintra,
invents a borrowed, pimped-up Chevrolet,
then wonders who he will have drive it today.
Caeiro? Or Ricardo Reis? Or de Campos, child of America,

the obvious choice who, behind a tinted window,
will look to the estates on the left
and the moonlit fields on the right
like a benign celebrity or a returning hero

but who, now that he is propped behind the wheel
(which sends a shudder through his hand
to the shoulder he glances over),

mutters to us, to himself, about not losing control,
about replacing 'or' with 'and'
and keeping an eye on the rear-view mirror.

2/10/09

Aerialist

i.m. Vitaly Kharapavitski

I'd talked us all back to Ireland, a week in Killorglin and a plan
to take shovel, bucket, armbands and an inflatable fin,
a picnic basket and a tartan rug to a different beach
each mid-morning. It was quiet and all worked out, so much
we might have dreamed it and never gone — except
that one day we parked on Inch Strand and ploughed it up
as the tide around us did what it does.

Cooped up inside at night was a different prospect
in a rental no one could pretend was Bali or Venice.
For entertainment, ice-cream vans and posters for a circus,
not exactly an infrastructure. The 'Royal Russian Circus':
20 euro a head. I cursed the Celtic Tiger and paid, cash at the till,
wishing briefly I'd stayed, done an MBA and, some violence
to the language, lived it deal by deal.

Every artist looks after his own props. The balloon
'exploded into flames', the cage fell, then the heavy steel ball.
Becoming witnesses, one or two hundred people
thought it was part of the act, fire as magic, whoosh and clatter,
nothing irregular in the mid-air routine.
The reports say he was Belorussian, 26, a clown or
'an aerialist in a clown costume'. And that he threw his wife clear.

We'd seen, in Rosbeigh, pre-show and a week earlier,
hanging around, nerveless and going nowhere an elephant,
a giraffe and, between them, a zebra. Canvas and steel
were shaped into a marquee. And from behind Coomasaharn
glider after glider hung in the sky, coasting away clear to the north.
A new bungalow advertised art, another a scuba school
and night-kayaking in the phosphorescent ocean

by which that night, stars and stripes on each enormous brow,
the elephants balanced on buckets like shuttlecocks,
while the giraffe nodded, stately and gawky, and a shabby lion
made his unheard-of roar, still a memory on each nearby farm.
A crowd of method actors, the circus animals, though
instead of a tiger the MC, for the sake of form,
squirted water at us from a flower between acts.

The 'Sadovs' had performed for one year and had one stunt:
in it he couldn't find her, she fooled and hid,
the story so simple we gripped the wooden ringside,
grinding our heels into the matted grass and, would it ever end,
opened our mouths like parents as he kept
falling over and out of the hot-air balloon. Over
and over he went, *poor man*, who would throw his wife clear.

Weeks later, and back across the water, I saw online
the Dublin owner of the Royal Russians, or its spokesman,
speak of close-knit community, the harness, the hoist,
and the families of the deceased and bereaved flying over.
It seemed for a while, here, as if things might be as they were,
autumn closing in, a net that at the last moment would come apart
taking only the leaves from the trees and the name of the year.

Continuity

The wind sails leaves around the house like late notices
of the garden's deterioration. Turn a blind eye.
RTE longwave announces gigs in familiar venues.
I like the presenter's comfortable thoughts of tonight
and the day after, until, that is, he introduces
'The Holy Land' by the Bothy Band and then
advertises a poetry broadsheet and a silver plaque,
before attacking, quote, the crimson tides
and purple mountains, end quote, someone (who?)
might waste his money on instead in Woolworth's.
There's a snatch of a shipping forecast
and I'm unloading the dishwasher when I hear a new voice,
which strands me by announcing, 'This is *The Archive Hour*,
and that was *The Long Note* thirty years ago today,'
out of earshot as I am of the autumn sun and rain
which the radio forecasts, too, on this hour that's gone
south with its silver plaque, its piano and bodhrán,
where, in Woolworth's, a crimson tide progresses
beneath a purple mountain and someone hums a reel.
He knows the start of it but puts a question mark
against the title: it's 'The Holy Ground' but he doesn't join
    the dots.
He has places to go. There will be time again for names and
    dates,
for taking it all down, for credits, for footnotes.

A Danger to Shipping

On the beach, on Stephen's Day, out for a brisk walk,
away from the season's leftovers and tinsel,
we stop to look at a bulky, silky left-behind mass
which a coastguard explains to a crowd of us
is probably a wooden trunk or mast.
                                        Long as a shark,
shiny and peacock-eyed with goose barnacles,
black and silver, it looks alive, a frothing tongue,
which, a danger to shipping, is unreturnable
and, he says, must be burnt before the tide can turn.

My Adolescence in New Zealand

for Bill Manhire

I didn't want to go to bed and then
I didn't want to get up. The men,
my uncles and father, planned to watch
the international, a grudge match,
on the new remote-controlled TV.
I was beginning to get ideas about coffee.
I sniffled and coughed, my nose in a book.
The *Rainbow Warrior* turned into Helen Clark.
Those days we worried about serious things.
I was never into *The Lord of the Rings*.
I preferred biographies of polar explorers:
a long journey and evidence of errors
disappearing like a snowflake in Antarctica,
a dropped knife tuning up for the orchestra.

Jane Eyre in Derry

Seven hours with Charlotte Brontë
on the Galway-Sligo bus to Derry
and on arrival, reader, it would be hard not
to have a problem with the shut, shuttered pubs,
the early closing of unknown bookshops,
the picketed cinema not screening *Prêt-à-Porter*,
the black cab's same old uncongenial story . . .
But I'm happily lost in writing a list
at the loose end of your shift
when here you are, you and the bright air
of your short, boyish haircut
which you wear, in Altnagelvin,
like an amulet
to stop roughly half the staff knowing
what they believe in.

North Korea

Time is not wasted in your subtle temples.
Warm air from the south blows about
your rusting trees, a fine dust settles
on the new shop's lintel and on the local
of the regular and the fly by night.

The weather thins out, turns unseasonal
and makes a word of the ditches' rustling,
an expression that escapes us, a smattering
of another language. The road crumbles
at each new estate's stone-clad entrance.

No one drives anything out of there.
It plays the part of its life, just once,
to retired horses and standing stones.
At the junction no one will hear
a whisper about the coming year.

Capital

for Catherine McAuliffe and Patrick Barrett

At the river field's five-barred gate
a rust-brown spate
of Angus and Hereford
mullocked and shouldered
through our unplanned, half-lit meanders
across Fyanstown's seemingly trackless acres,
showing us what is always to hand,
the lay of the land,
its bullshit,
its cowshit,
and its cow roads that saunter
with the flow, natural
as Tara's ancient capital
and the flat, invisible Blackwater.

Night Manoeuvres

Dressed as jedi and druids they fought like Saxons on the
    date of the equinox;
the security detail handcuffed 'Maud, the Edwardian
    archaeologist',
then forced her into the lotus position. One of the jedis
    opened a suitcase
and started a songwriting class. We wore sheets and 49p
    glow-sticks.

Stonehenge, Woodhenge. We danced anticlockwise till the
    sun rose
on the fenced-off holes and rifts of the latest excavation.
Wardens, like builders checking gas pipes, wearing hats and
    brighter clothes,
fell over themselves: who will protect the circle of standing
    stones?

Week 2

Let the books outstay their return date.
Let it be said that we are sleeping late.
Let the garden continue to grow more like a dump.
Let the room go cold round this mid-season slump.
Let scientists be someone else's concern
as their particles accelerate slowly at CERN.
Let today's headlines give no one the hump.
Let the friendlies occur to some other chump.
Let the weather be forecast, the Dow deflate.
Let the sun go down and the moon circulate.
Let milk sour in the fridge, and the cream turn.
Let nothing happen, again, except you return.

Batman

At the same secure gate, after the interview,
I met you with your new retinue

who, over drinks in *The Rising Sun*,
explained things, then needled us about Irish abortion,

as private a matter as that lab
that no one would mention. But you took the job

and we phoned around,
praised medical science's miracle fund,

their pledge to back whatever your research examined.
The art deco reading area was like a deep end

in the library's converted pool.
There were poems and new paintings on every wall.

One unglamorous year later
the site, on the green belt, was under the hammer:

Christopher Nolan shut the place down
and spent two weekends shooting *Batman*,

his *Gotham* vans a nice change from the unmarked cars
used to film, each Wednesday, the protesters.

Who filmed them, of course, in return.
That was the Wednesday cat-and-mouse routine,

the necessary taxi, drummed on,
given dog's abuse by the committed and the vegan

till you forgot, once, and walked out the main gate,
'the last time,' you said at home, shaken and in no state.

Loose Ends

The sun deceives the open door.
Crystals form on the windowpane,
you know what someone else would say.
I had something else in mind.

Videos, a telex, little magazines
hang on under the TV
which looks as if it will survive
the weather which surrounds us.

There's a scratching in the roof.
Is that the bell? For what? The cabinet
is dust and chandeliers. Loose ends
press on like an argument.

Arguing about Stars near Inch

In a clay and wattle cabin I glimpse
what looks like an axle-tree
hung with candles and lamps
and draw, by firelight, a new geography.

On the hub of a burning wheel you read
a twinkling, sidereal calendar.
Each keyhole of light has decreed
we do not err or wander.

Even if I could square the telescope
and its multiplying suns
with the angel's sword and its flaming hope
there's more to this world than common sense.

You say, as we walk the raised beach at Inch,
the world is nine-tenths star.
But how do they begin, or finish?
What will it mean to see that far?

Which of us revels in the explosion of hydrogen,
the vault-crushing fact of origin?
The mediating rowan will drown;
dust and wind may well ruin,

shred *or* interlock each stellar ring, disc and jet,
pulsar, dwarf,
straggler, gas giant and knot.
The names exceed the photograph

you would develop in a twilight that turns civil,
then nautical, silver and bright
to orange on purple,
the distant campuses now so starry with electric light

that we hardly see the sky move,
in time with us, through space,
in dark rooms unimaginably above
this wooden halfway house.

Marriage, the Realist Tradition

There are introductions. A letter arrives. Already
we sympathize with the solitary reader, the interrupted study
in a house no one visits. Who would want to?
We are gripped by an idea, a pilgrimage turns into
a road trip. In the awful weather monsters shrink and, indoors,
assume human forms. We might grow into these foyers and
    porches.
Where were we? The twin no one ever knew returns.
A mysterious stranger's glance means a head turns.
It is a gaze we follow; now, an inheritance or marriage
is in the balance. New laws or wars throw a shadow, like
    knowledge,
on what used to happen, but won't ever happen again. Is this
the improbable lift-off into another world, like and unlike life?
Illness sudden as eclipse, or that famous intervention —
love — makes impossible a life of their own invention.
A misunderstanding, a wrong name taken to heart?
No place here for the bad student considering art
but the novelists, the last to specialize in everything, produce
with the frenzy of an enormous unselfconscious youth
a city like a farm, and characters with something to say or
something to hide and, later, a denouement, on the moor
or in the car park, foreshadowed with subtle hints, maybe this
the improbable lift-off into another world, like and unlike life?
Someone's paying attention to the weather, its big picture;
there is an etymological diversion, an old man (someone's
    father?)
who retells or invents (will they, won't they?) the monstrous
    past.
A letter arrives (stop describing the clock — her mother's) —
    open it!
We sit around a table, old and flat and round,
waiting for the girls and the boys to arrive, then head in hand,
no longer talking, we're discovered by the same old story.
    The plot

creaks into place around us, a picture frame gilded and ornate,
too neat and a little too close to whatever we call home,
which is where (we saw it coming) she takes his name,
stitching everyone into the same black and white pattern
and, somewhere off the page, an ending we believe in.

Snow

It's not, tonight, what we'd expected to see
through that couple reflected in the window,
the window that first reflects their having tea,
then empties as you point, get up and go
out through the kitchen's unlocked back door
to where at least a half an inch of snow
has taken on a shine, and creaks at your
going out to see and feel its weird spring show
and what it will take with its turn for the worst,
its touch of ice, the magnolia burning, the daffodil
and crocus lidded with its soft shift,
the room behind you bright as its inch of windowsill,
a voice, not mine, across the way saying it'll be OK,
as we skirt your footprints, steaming, tilted, at bay.

New Year

It might never happen;
this blue sheet of dawn,
this bright coldness, won't,
any more than
the receding sweep of night
or the ice-carrying wind
will, ever again,
foreclose a decade.

And so what if
the worst, the moon
in Aquarius, Capricorn ascending,
awaits: the year is a guide to itself,
the dawn, not of what might happen,
but what will, once,

frost crisping
the sodden underfoot, the residue
of last year's avalanche warping
the deck, trees loving
the deep freeze along each tip
of their forking either/or;

crows and a fat robin
observe squirrels scoot and dart
through the driveway's
high evergreen
wavering so-so,
its 'what are the chances',
its answering 'on balance'
and not budging an inch.

Of All Places

'Even in Kyoto / hearing the cuckoo's cry / I long for Kyoto.'
— Basho

It takes imagination, crossing the car park, to long for
the car park, to miss in its empty numbered spaces
the pluming suspensions of another day, to see
cracks in this sidewalk wrinkle into a cold, western night
bearing coke, Silk Cut and Hula Hoops to a waiting room,
checking on you as you check a bleep, talking through
the drunks, the snifflers and the relatives,
talking into existence the work-life balance,
our imagined oceanic air, streets we'd walk
and occasionally lift our heads to look around at,
the teeming air above our social heads,
a future as much a fact as the hills and villages
we left and never knew — you and I, now and then
(car parked in the unforgotten outskirts),
walking through the city dark, away and toward,
dreaming of moving, next to one another.

Northwestern

1

The sun has turned the redbrick chimney gold,
deepened it, as in an old window's flawed glass,
so it seems to waver when, framing it below,
the wind touches up the green last stand
of the tall magnolia and the rowan,
its reds a constellation the birds steer by,
a twittering along the boughs.

2

In pictures things look golden, grand.
Hard to credit they'll disappear
but the world of time is the world of sound.
The wind today I never heard before,
a sound within a sound, an oasis in the trees,
a whisper that co-existed, here and there,
with the usual cornered breeze.
August, that tree losing its lustre,
taller this year and a sweet noise I hear disappear.
If I could simplify it, beyond confusion,
the sound it would make would be the sound of a siren.

A Likeness

               The wind makes itself known
in the laurel, a soft buffeting of the washing on the line;
the ivy on the fence is veined with lime
and starts its terraced nodding at a lower breeze
which brings with it the cabbage white and the admiral.

Now the two winds come at once, the buffeting
and the ivy turned downside up, sea-green,
the fence a little visible and, overhanging it all,
the brambles, blackberries on their tongues pale green and pink
and black with tiny straw hooks. Picked ripe, they grow back.

House Fire

1

Called to the yard
('Look, look,' he shouts),
I see the fallen bird
and hold my son's hand
but what grips instead
are the goggle-eyed flies,
their broad foreheads
like miners' helmets
lighting up their feelers
on the slippery grey-purple
of the bird's exposed keel . . .

2

I couldn't take my eyes
off the scene (I see it still)
as rooted in it as,
over the road, the local
look-out boys
who circle, hour after hour,
the remains of the house,
giving it the once-over
and, nothing to answer for,
know what they prefer.

Influence

Let's stick, you say, to describing what *is*,
weather ridged like a dune, blown into angles
like whipped, whitened cream, then brown-on-grey
like frozen muddy fields animals trample.
The deck and the deck furniture a window display,
cake slices and muffins with overwhelming icing,
the sort kids like the look of but won't eat.
We chance town, an obstacle course,
for the banquet in *Ocean Harbor*,
our only company tanks of eels, crabs and lobsters.
Trees creak in the wind, lined and ermine,
as we raise a beer to the idea of influence,
the Year of the Tiger and learning acquiescence
to the weather, an icicle that grows and tapers,
a stiletto blur of blue and grey.

        But its solid forms, the day after,
tire like memory, depleted and depleting,
not the same thing at all now and in the way,
its scuffled pages another recognizable allusion
to what might be the case another day,
meltwater pooling in tyre tracks and footprints.

The Changing Room

She 'dances' between the double mirrors of the changing room,
one foot at a time, as if she's working the treadle —
up, down — on an old-fashioned loom
till, finding in her hand the curtain, she makes of it a parcel
into which she twists all but her feet and head of curls,
then hide-and-seek and count to, almost, 5,
and here she is, the one object of a thousand T-shirts and ten
    thousand shoes
which she will step in and out of:
the world, suddenly more of it than we think, whirls
this way and that round any point she cares to choose.

Canvas

The work is placed in a plastic bubble
into which the nitrogen is introduced. It is critical
that this takes place separate from
the public galleries, in a prepared room.
Ideally the treatment deprives
the infestation on the canvas,
and sometimes the oils, of oxygen.
In two weeks no living matter will remain.
The painting may be hung again.

A Game of Li Bo

Historically games of displacement are replaced by games of strategy.
— An Illustrated History of Board Games in China

This is before the disappearance of the figure.
The artist deliberately buys a good mirror,
the work is finished if it appears unmarked by its maker.
In one image, a game of Li Bo, the dice thrower
holds his opponent's future like a penny in his fist.

And it's too late for the other to ask, which fist.
Reward and punishment are a cosmic force:
shadows fall everywhere from the cold skies,
whole inches of canvas betray no common light source,
each moment a last thought saying its goodbyes.

St Turvey at Lusk

i.m. Xavier McGrath-Long

No shortening the road from the sea at Lusk,
a quiet road even when we'd the car stopped
and the book open at this strand's or that boreen's story.

Inside, on time, the clock-hands stuck at ten to two.
Most of our children doubled around the back
of the dusty community hall. You held Jethro in your arms

and Xavier, who won't ever be skirted,
led you to the lectern where you would speak forever,
the pair of you white as sheets but bearing in your arms

everything thrown at you and what no one would want back,
our holed bucket of love, our tears too,
what even Turvey, immortal of the local story,

couldn't stop though he'd once stopped,
with a hatchet, the Irish Sea at Lusk.

A Deaf Ear

The sun's a no-show,
the scrub winter-green,
dense and hard to shake

as a night, years past,
something in full swing,
smoke filling a room,

in a back corner
girls drinking bubbly
and, when I look up,

one's in the kitchen
throwing shapes, lovely,
the latch unlifted still

on traffic sounds,
the sparrow's chirrup,
the day I'll wake

to this bald block
under its blank sky,
not exactly a visitor,

more a latecomer
and, not miles away,
an absence it turns on.

Sunrise

There are nights I snag on a single morning —
lodged where it can't be got rid of —
a boy, the local poet's son, arrived so late
I threatened a visit to the Head
and got, in return, a sleepy reply:
'My father, sir, took me to Knockanure
to wait for the dawn — to see the sun.'

He drew me a picture later, a line
like a brim or a lid or a shade.
Mortal thoughts our mutual friends:
no sign of the sun, the frost a web of mist.
More than ever I like to see
what's in front of me and nothing else.

Recess

Overlooking farmland and waves of noise from a school
  canteen
the small cannon, called a *Parrott*, is green
from one-hundred-and-fifty years of weather, a landmark
for speed-walking locals and bus tours which disembark,
the guides saying something irresistible about wounds and
  cocaine.

I'm taking notes on this coppery summit when a bird flies
  out of it,
then a bell rings and I hear a slow flap approach and don't
  know
what to expect: cameras and muttering, war and time not
breaking down into anything more particular than a landscape now,
places bearing people's names that hint at logic,

attaching themselves to a boy like burrs or a nettle sting
when he'd walk the fields, ducking electric fencing,
making eye contact with bulls that looked fierce and thick,
then backing slowly along dykes, away from birdsong,
to where a river lines another town like the margin of a book.

Interludes

1 CALLING OUT

I can't say where I'm from, but here's a picture:
indoors, Sunday afternoon is MTUSA;
I'm outside, though, wrecking the back end of the garden
where the orchard wall is glass and tar, a border.
I call the stables dungeons, I call the trees my countries,
the paths I lead between them highways, my ways.
I call out to my brothers and here they come, on their bellies.
We crawl across the lawn and won't be seen.

2 MOWER

Flower beds and a slope to cut an angle across,
but your mind's elsewhere: the mark is
a thin line of uncut spears of grass,
clear as a signature. Later,
on new shades of green, you rake into the grass box
soft clouds of grass, buttercups, daisies, casual cowslips
    and clover.

Black Box

The stable I called a dungeon is the coal shed:
going there a 'big production', my mother sighs,
starts in the living room. By the cold fireplace
I slip the tin caddy out of a 'traditional' brass box,
its relief a bumpy picture I can feel and almost see,
a coach and horses from another century.

Soot gathers at the bottom like cornflakes
left over in the cereal box.
I pour it on the husks and ashes fallen through the grate,
then trail more soot — my name in my mother's mouth —
across the wet yard's muddy gravel
and start to scrape and clink the coal into the scuttle,

poking the coals into a black on black jigsaw puzzle,
practising how to whistle and piece things together,
fine dust freezing back into some fantastic, original shape,
as I heft the lot, blacken the carpet — I still hear my mother —
and build a pyramid from paper twists and *Zip*,
the hoover going, damp hissing off the wet coal.

The Oasis on Tuesdays

That year looks different now, a picture of the moon
from a stacked and crumby desk or, out a window,
noon pinning shadows to the brown and grey planes
of the rusting trees and the cooling breeze
of autumn's imminent descent on us all. You
had a mind of your own, in my thoughts,
particular as a border-dweller,
touchy about that cold sky and its auctioneer,
his promised walk down tree-lined interlinking
representations of the good and well-earned life.
But some nights it was night-time in the lifetime of waiting,
the glass half-full next to the shaking speaker,
in its thudding blare: a shape is cast (who could have told?),
abstract and familiar, into the smoking air.

The Territorial Army

The rain was nobody's business, a surprise.
In mud it's harder to feel like the law. Or order.
On the frontline one read *The Romance of the Rose*
and *Viz*, dreaming up a kind of Afghan reader.
An academic from Yorkshire saw stars and luck
in the rain and the scale of the disaster. He came back.
A librarian carried *The War Poets*, a set book,
and consulted it on the plane home, a sceptic.
First day back, in the mobile library as usual,
he carried thrillers, cookbooks and dictionaries
to the wretched of the north, his training bounty
a thought with a ladder in it: he'd climb it and see
two weeks in Oaxaca by an infinity pool,
hot, dry Mexican air and human voices.

Odd Hours

I DAYLIGHT SAVING TIME, OUTSIDE BLACKBURN

In the extra hour the sun's a circle we can look at.
The last leaves fill the cuttings. Bollards, a parked car,
no one disembarks. What we are steams up the air.
The mill, in the sunset's wash, is starry and backlit.
There's a sound, somewhere away down at the back,
like coughing, or someone having some kind of attack.

2 THE NEWS ON RITZ STREET

Between Ritz and Brunt, and Playfair and Lincoln,
a comfortable sofa soaks up a month of rain;
a boy swings a birch so its leaves touch, brush
the ground; an older woman
makes inroads, with her sweeping brush,
on the low tide of freesheets and take-away discards
that mount the footpath and approach her —
the wind picking up, the sun in her eyes —
and her brush, brush, sweep, keeping the path clear.

3 READING ON TELEGRAPH

In the basement of its second-last second-hand bookshop
two poets address themselves to
one another, rows of folding chairs and that plaster and damp
    combo,
the only thing on show not facing the chop.
Somewhere something must be happening. There's no till.
As I leave it follows me up to street-level.

4 DAYLIGHT SAVING TIME, ST LOUIS

Skinker and Delmar, University City, and the Thai Café
has chairs on its tables still. Likewise Tex Mex and Sushi All Day.
Another walker says, 'I'm from Kansas.' A beat. 'I don't know
 anything.'
A mile or a mile and a bit: the morning giving up in the Metro
till the penny drops. Retracing
my steps, each door is open, little bits of money moving to
 and fro.

Transfers

On the sale of works of art from the Bank of Ireland collection,
24 November 2010

Their backs to the crowded quay, a couple sails away from the
 regatta:
in lakes nearby mountains reverse into the distances
and stones line up, in order, at the brink. Seen from another
 shore
the bay steadily darkens with the prospect of herring
and no sign of another boat to spread its net like a tablecloth
into the long night and the water ahead of it.

The red tractor idles in the yard when it should be in the field,
children wait in hand-knits and short trousers with the animals
or bring home fish in a galvanized bucket or turf on a white
 donkey,
bearing with them an autumn day. An old man raises his hand
and lapwings crowd around the house, its black rich soil and
 eggy sun,
a world known for the first time as they reel through
Holyhead: why leave it all

for the creased benches of a vent-heated waiting room, a life
as at home with the cooling tower as the night ferry,
fixing devices unheard of in Borneo or Ballyconnell,
while the places they played in as children suddenly look
 skeletal and strange?
Years of birdsong are withdrawn into the folds of unusual
 drapery. Daffodils find
a vase on a sill, the city's trees are tangled capillaries, a memory

of a bank of thatch-coloured cloud separated from thatched
 cottages
by a winding hill-bound lane they will drive on holiday,
one building dwarfing its neighbour, the entrances indistinct.

Whitewashed walls support turf, a ladder, a barrel, and their
    shadows: he sees her,
now they arrive, standing between windows, a blue dress
    against a blue pillar,
her white throat binding one thing into another, a soft dune
    of light.

By the sea, again, brighter but empty, the rocks develop a
    prowling quality
and, obeying another law of perspective, the couple stands
    before a rick of turf
like it's the open bonnet of a touring vehicle, *circa* 1938:
hesitant bystanders at a fire sale, they stand apart
(she links her hands behind her back, he holds one lapel of his
    marsh-coloured mac)
and stay together, the water and hills their own eternal
insubstantial history, grand ruined illusions of colour and light.

On their wall the image of another wall, each tiny leaning
    stone almost free
of its companion. Under an expanding mountain the multiplying
    extensions,
disappearing yards and accreting kitchens foster unlikely foliage
as if each interior and side elevation were a facet of some
    murkily imagined freedom.
Domesticity burns itself into the rusty archive of coasts and
    edges,
trees disguise the horizon's bottom line, a scratched-out human
    figure, the field
a meadow of bluebells, a hare escaping a hound on the point of
    twisting it into the air.

By the Sea, in England

for Conor O'Callaghan

It's not like the lip or verge of anything.
There are no surfers here who paddle and balance
to where a reef splits the currents
into a wave's right-angle.
Instead beachcombers stockpile
driftwood, or sieve for fossils and a king's shilling;

and heavy machinery, for the links or the farmer,
ships inland
industrial loads of seaweed and sand;
seagulls gabble and scramble up,
into the gale, at the sight of a ship
from Santander;

residents walk the pier, kick the wall
and, about-face, puff and windmill
one day into another.
No cold, spraying wind blows off this shore
like a monomaniacal point of view.
Its slow tides might as well be hung with snow . . .

It is windbreakers draped with striped towels,
the brisk noise in a sand dune's endless morning,
the flask and the sandwich, the breakers breaking
netless courts, names drawn with shovels,
the fortified castle and elaborate moat,
the dull shine off the tide's cloudy aftermath . . .

It's not like standing
at the lip or verge of something,
not here, where the sea peters out,
the rumour of a distant pool. But if it's not

that lisping, withdrawing crash on a bronze beach
it is, halfway to silence, this hush

which is, too, not just anything
and carries across
the stony foreshore and the strand's fine grain
what could pass for a canal's stillness,
cyclists — familial, in single file — cresting
the sea-defence's low and wavy bank. Their inland tune.

A Name

The big window and beyond it again the flowering beanstalk
    and the climbing frame,
fountains of fern and a recovering buddleia. I'd like a *name*
for how these busy, so-called 'hard-pressed servants of my
    will', the years,
go by the by like forgotten days and half-remembered
    quarter hours.
Would naming it change anything? Evening, all shadow and
    charm, wanders by.
Among the wildflowers the beady strut and ratchet of a
    magpie.
Through the window come those go-betweens, the wasp and
    the fly.

The Whole Show

I don't learn. I should sit, elbow on knee,
among the creatures, observe the stupid fox contend
with a bin, the earthbound worm
co-operate with the micro-managing magpie,
the sky calling out, the earth replying
with its inevitable ear. In between and up to date
next door's garden leaks knotweed and bamboo.
The wheelie bins obsolesce in different colours.
Blackbirds and a robin compete for the shaking laurel.
Maybe I know where this is going. A four-faced god,
who supervises, sits at our feet. Maybe not.
By the time you stray here, the outcome, forget it,
the whole show could be over.

Address to Russ

True reasons for not making it into the office and doing a day's work on the hard copy of (then) variously titled manuscript, this book

Knee-high snow. Though I could have walked it.
Or stayed put. The kids were sick so I had to mind them.
I was sick and confined to bed. The car was stolen.
The front door blew in: I had to guard the house.
I'm waiting for a call from my bank, and my mother.
I'm expecting a delivery. I've been called in to teach.
I had work to catch up on, marking, admin.
I was stuck in the middle of a really good book.
I felt like buying some ice cream, a cone, instead.
I'd someone to collect at the airport.
My computer is broken and receives no email
so I've called a technician who's not arrived yet
and he has, as they do, a list of excuses
as long as your arm or a week of Sundays. To be honest
there's no need for the hard copy or an office
or an appointment, not for this,
but it might take something like an appointment
to get me out of this eternal kitchen,
where I relive the 1.1 earthquake
that made the walls shiver around
the domestic scene I've left behind,
things, truth be told, I could not really broach
even with Russ, barber, unlikely muse, as he applies
the steel, the little slow juts and nicks and trims
of the number 3, as we keep in our field of vision
the box in the corner with the transfer latest,
something continuing outside this deep freeze.

The Hallway Mirror

You walk by with an armful of school shirts.
The ironing. But where's he gone? He's
outside, a standing column in the air he breathes,
the snow general and the falling flakes his obedient recruits,
conscripting everything to the same white flag.
His sisters, wildcats, growl and laugh.
We unload the washing, kiss, relax into the indoor arts
till the open door admits him in a crinkled fog,
wearing the usual get-up, marrying a word to life.

A Midgie

I pick a midgie out of my red wine.
The garden goes greener in the lilac time.
This will go down on the permanent record.
A night is nothing if not its own reward.
The foxgloves corked with bees.
The snail outlining a life of ease.
The black things wait. Or may never show.
That's innocent. I know, I know.

Acknowledgements

Acknowledgements are due to the editors of the following magazines, periodicals and books where some of these poems, or versions of them, were published first: *An Afterglow: A Gallery of Connemara Poems* (edited by Des Lally and Peter Fallon), *Almost Island*, *Best of Irish Poetry 2008* and *2010*, *Cork Literary Review*, *Dark Matter: Space Poems*, *Gallous*, *Icarus*, *International Literary Quarterly*, *The Irish Times*, *The John McGahern Yearbook*, *Kaffeeklatsch*, *Makeout Creek*, *The Meath Anthology* (edited by Tom French), *The North*, *PN Review*, *Poetry Ireland Review*, *Poetry London*, *Poetry Review*, *The Rialto*, *The Spectator*, *The Stinging Fly* and *The Watchful Heart* (edited by Joan McBreen).

Versions of some of these poems also appeared in a pamphlet *A Midgie* published by Smith/Doorstop in 2010.

'Arguing about Stars near Inch' was commissioned by Maurice Riordan and resulted from collaboration with John Dyson. 'A Deaf Ear' was commissioned by Mary Griffiths of the Whitworth Gallery as a response to Willie Doherty's video, *The Visitor*.

The Basho epigraph on page 42 is translated by Robert Hass.